FROM THE REVIEWERS

"*Coached for Life* captures the essence of what it means to be a coach. It describes the philosophies that work in the arena of sport, and the philosophies that work in life. I recommend it to everyone who wants to succeed in either—or both."

BOBBY BOWDEN,
Head football coach, Florida State University,
National Champions 1993 & 1999

"*Coached for Life* tells us that coaches are, first and foremost, teachers, and that lessons on how to live are learned on the athletic field as well as in the classroom. Its deftly honed narrative shows how the values imbued on the practice fields and gridiron of a small Catholic high school in Montana carried over to the adult lives of football teammates. This is not a tale of gridiron glory or one of glamorous careers. It is instead a blend of stories capturing 'the greatness that is realized when ordinary people do ordinary things extraordinarily well.' It also serves to remind us why 'Coach' is a lifetime honorific."

REV. THEODORE M. HESBURGH
C.S.C., President Emeritus, University of Notre Dame

"This is a book that should be made into a movie! It's the story of faith and love in action, and illustrates how the world can be impacted when spiritual values infuse a football team."

DR. TONY CAMPOLO
Professor Emeritus, Eastern University; founder of the Evangelical Association for the Promotion of Education, and spiritual advisor to former President Bill Clinton

"As CEO of the largest residential real estate network in the world, I see firsthand the importance of the work our teachers and our coaches do, in shaping our youth into disciplined, motivated, and ethical adults. *Coached for Life* is an outstanding book that exemplifies how the lessons learned while in school, and on the athletic field, can last a lifetime."

MARGARET KELLY
CEO RE/MAX International

"I know intimately the good work teachers and coaches do in America. My father and brother were both teachers and coaches in Montana for over 50 years. *Coached for Life* reveals the extraordinarily positive impact teachers and coaches have on the lives of the young people they teach and coach, on the communities in which they live and work, and, importantly, on the way of life we share."

MARC RACICOT
Former Governor of Montana
and former Chairman of the Republican National Committee

"As a business owner and State Senate Leader, I have been a big supporter of education. *Coached for Life* gives wonderful accolades to the great work our teachers and coaches do in America every day."

GLEN TAYLOR
Entrepreneur and owner, Minnesota Timberwolves, NBA Team

"*Coached for Life* demonstrates that attention to the small details not only leads to success on the football field, it leads to success in life. It is also a wonderful reminder of the positive impact coaches—at every level of the game—can have on their players."

SONNY LUBICK
Former head football coach, Colorado State University

COACHED
FOR
LIFE

FOR
LIFE

Ed Flaherty | Jack Uldrich

ISBN 978-0-615-27882-7

Books may be ordered on the Internet at **www.coachedforlife.com**

Cover/interior design by Koechel Peterson & Associates, Inc.,
Minneapolis, Minnesota.

Manufactured in the United States of America

DEDICATION

To every coach and teacher.
For the countless lives you have touched
        and will continue to touch.

And to two life-changing coaches,
        Bill Mehrens and John "Poncho" McMahon,
        for your touch on our lives.

JACK ULDRICH

Jack Uldrich is a renowned global futurist, independent scholar, sought-after business speaker, and best-selling author. His books include the best-selling, *The Next Big Thing Is Really Small: How Nanotechnology Will Change the Future of Your Business,* and the award-winning, *Into the Unknown: Leadership Lessons from Lewis & Clark's Daring Westward Expedition.* His latest book is *Jump the Curve.*

Mr. Uldrich's other written works have appeared in *The Wall Street Journal, The Futurist, Future Quarterly Research, The Wall Street Reporter, Leader to Leader, Management Quarterly,* and hundreds of other newspapers and publications around the country. He also writes a regular column on emerging technologies for "The Motley Fool" and is a frequent guest of the media worldwide— having appeared on CNN, MSNBC, and National Public Radio on numerous occasions.

In addition to speaking on future trends, emerging technologies, innovation, change management, and leadership, Uldrich is a leading expert on assisting businesses to adapt. He has served as an advisor to Fortune 1000 companies and is noted for his ability to deliver provocative, new perspectives on competitive advantage, organizational change, and transformational leadership.

EDWARD F. FLAHERTY

Graduated from the University of Wyoming and received a Master Degree from George Washington University. The consummate entrepreneur, he has started or purchased approximately three-dozen companies in his career, whose combined annual sales approach one billion dollars. He's been an active member of the corporate and non-profit community in Minneapolis and St. Paul, Minnesota, serving on a numerous board of directors. This is his first book.

AUTHORS' NOTE

In the course of writing this book, scores of interviews were conducted over hundreds of hours with the story's participants. All events described in the book are true. At times, however, we had to piece together the narrative from a compilation of fragmented and faded memories. In those rare instances where participants' memories conflicted, we attempted to discern the facts as objectively as possible.

In many cases, conversations could not be remembered verbatim, nor could the precise physical or emotional setting of those conversations be recalled. In such situations, we took literary license and reconstructed the context and tone of the dialogue to the best of our ability. In so doing, however, we always strove to be true to the spirit of the people and characters involved.

Any errors, misinterpretations, or mistakes in the story are solely our responsibility.

Ed Flaherty & Jack Uldrich

CONTENTS

ACKNOWLEDGMENTS

The writing of this book has been a labor of love for both of us. We must begin by thanking our spouses, Julie Flaherty and Cindy Uldrich, for the patience they demonstrated in reviewing countless drafts of the manuscript as well as for their constructive criticism. The book is far better as a result of their efforts. Their encouragement, priceless.

Next, we would like to thank our mutual friend Stan Donnelly—not only for introducing the two of us, but for being the book's biggest fan and its most constructive critic. His many suggestions and comments made for a stronger and more readable book.

Next, we would like to acknowledge the many members of the 1962 Great Falls Central Mustangs who allowed us to interview them and offered many wonderful insights into how the coaches positively influenced their lives. The following were especially helpful: Byron Weber, Dick and Jerry Kuntz, Greg Steckler (Brian Elliot), Mike Walsh, Wally Berry, Gary Wolf, Billy Sprinkle, John O'Rourke, Dale Roos, George Leffler, Chuck Boyle, Mike Donovan, Dave Nash, Jim Neufeld, Barry Newmack, and Fred Zadick.

Other participants from Great Falls Central who were instrumental to gaining a deeper and richer context for the story were: Valerie (Dickerson) Coleman Morris, Fred Berry, Patty (O'Loughlin) Murphy, Harvey Livix, Sister Michelle Holland, Father Jack Krier, and Father Harold Arbanas.

We would also like to thank Angie Wenande for the thousands of little things that she did on a daily basis to help us pull together this book—everything from locating teammates to researching old newspaper clippings.

Along the way, a number of people also provided useful and

constructive comments that significantly strengthened the book. We begin by thanking Claire Uldrich and Myrna Klobuchar for their excellent work editing the final manuscript. Next, in no particular order, we would like to acknowledge all the people who reviewed various drafts of the book along its path to publication, including Catherine Glynn, Jeremy Van Meter, Bill Shikany, John Miller, Mike Snow, Dan Prins, Bruce Schadow, Dennis Flaherty, Neil Ugrin, Carroll Bishop, Bill Shikany, Jack Hughes, YPO Forum II Group, Joanna and Leni Wellington, Buzz Blakeslee, Peter Ritten, Bob Pryor, Dick Conklin, Chuck Dalich, and Jack Jackson.

Also, to my mom, Rose Flaherty, who saved all the memorabilia you see here in the book, and to my dad, Larry Flaherty, a Roundtable member, and my biggest fan.

To my children, Brad, Beth, Jill, Cody, and Caleigh Flaherty—you are the All-Star Light in my life. I love you!

Finally, this acknowledgment would not be complete without thanking Bill Mehrens and John "Poncho" McMahon—and their wives, Shirley and Francie. For without them, there would be no story.

INTRODUCTION

In the winter of 2002, a dear friend of mine, Ed Flaherty, whom I have known since our early days in the Young Presidents Organization (YPO), told me a story. It was, in its barest essence, the story you are about to read.

He didn't tell it well. He was energized enough to relate the gist of it, but far too private to initially relate the full range and depth of the story's most interesting—indeed, incredible—turns and circles. Because Ed was, and still is, such a large part of the story, I know that his genuine modesty worked as a hindrance, rather than a help, in its earliest recounting. In fact, if there is any real omission in the finished story, it is a lack of seeing the complete nature and results of Ed's personal leadership, both then and now. He excels in leading by example, and consequently, in the best sense, he is supremely ill-equipped to tell of its effects and his role in a team's or business's achievement.

Fortunately, the story itself demanded its own telling, and I simply kept asking the questions that it forced me to ask. As Ed uncovered more and more of the story, I was amazed.

When he finished, there was only one remaining question to ask: "Ed, of course you already know what you must do, don't you?" He nodded, paused, and said, "But I am not a good enough writer to trust myself with this—I need to find someone who is."

I happened to know Jack Uldrich. He is one of the most interesting people I've met, and if you've read the frontispiece that lists his other works, you can understand the spanning breadth of his interests and abilities. Naval officer, independent political candidate and leader, and a writer accomplished in fiction and the author of two best-selling business books, Jack is a man who combines acute observation with action.

I suggested that my two friends meet, and it has given me deep satisfaction and enormous pleasure to see the mixture of these two men—whose partnership was formed on a handshake—create such a compelling work. It has been years in the making. From cross-continent travel to do more in-depth interviews and research, to painstaking writing and rewriting without ever succumbing to embellishment, they have had to work hard to keep the written story manageable and digestible.

This is the story of a high school football team. There seems to be no shortage of them these days. But there is not one like this one. The Great Falls Central Mustangs were part of a small Catholic school that was, you will see, hugely successful in every way anyone would wish a school to be. At the same time, the team's 1962 season was surrounded by an international setting that was, by any accounts, uncertain, if not frightening. But mainly the team was deeply influenced by people. Some they knew. Others, who had set many strains in motion earlier, they did not.

This is the story of young men—and not so young. It is a story of dreams and goals and expectations. It is a story of fears and failures and successes and surprises, and it is the story of lives won and of lives lost. But running beneath it all is a current of human achievement: Of how to learn it, and of how to earn it; of how to teach it—and pass it on. Seen in that light, the story of the Mustangs is but a moment arrested. For it began long before the season of 1962, and it continues on...even now.

Stan D. Donnelly
Saint Paul, Minnesota

FOREWORD

Over the course of my career, I have had the pleasure of coaching thousands of young men. As any coach will tell you, they are all special. A few select individuals, however, inevitably end up occupying a unique place in their heart. For me, one of those players is Bill Mehrens.

Early in my coaching career—while I was still at Carroll College in Helena, Montana—Bill was my starting halfback. He was a talented, dedicated football player and a delight to coach. He was hard-working and always focused on improving himself and making his teammates better. No edge was too small to escape his notice.

It was no surprise then that he should have initially selected coaching as a career. Nor was it a surprise that he—along with John "Poncho" McMahon, his assistant coach—would apply the same tenacity to coaching that he displayed in earning an All-American honors as a football player.

If there was any surprise to his success, it was just how quickly he grasped the most important elements of being a successful coach. First, he became a superlative teacher; and, second, he adopted the philosophy that producing winning results on the playing field was only part of his job.

Most sports fans today are familiar with the quote, often attributed to Vince Lombardi, that says: *Winning isn't everything, it is the only thing.* Over the years, the quote has taken on a life of its own, and as a coach, I can understand its intuitive appeal to the competitive nature that resides in so many of us in the profession.

Unfortunately, far too many people have come to interpret the statement in a superficial, shallow, and, ultimately, counter-productive manner. Lombardi himself later acknowledged that he regretted the statement and said that what he meant to say was *Winning isn't everything, but making the effort to win is.*

The difference in phrasing is an important one, but it still doesn't accurately capture the true purpose of coaching—to get the most out of your players. That is because coaching is not simply about winning on the field; it is about preparing and teaching young men and women how to compete and win in the most important game of all—life. As such, the number of wins a coach compiles is secondary to the number of lives he or she positively influences. *Coached for Life* reminds us of this simple but often forgotten fact.

What this book also reminds us is that the work of any successful coach or teacher cannot—and should not—be viewed solely by whether, at season's end, his or her team has earned the label of champion. Rather, a coach's success can only be accurately measured years later—after the lessons, values, and principles they instilled in their players have had the chance to manifest themselves in the form of their players becoming better parents, spouses, community leaders, teachers, and, perhaps even, coaches.

Only then, in the dim hindsight of time, can we truly judge how successful a coach has been. Unfortunately, few coaches have the opportunity to view across the chasm of time and bear witness to the fruits of their labor as is so clearly presented in *Coached for Life.*

It is my hope that every teacher and coach—as well as any player who has been positively touched by a coach—finds time to read this book. That is because I know in my heart that this book could have literally been written about any of the thousands of deserving teachers and coaches who so often toil in anonymity but continue to pour their heart and soul into the vital job of instilling values in this country's youth. *Coached for Life* reminds us all of the important work of our professions and serves as a tangible reminder that in the game of life—where *Winning Really Is Everything*—America's coaches and teachers have compiled more "wins" than most of us will ever realize.

John Gagliardi
Head football coach, Saint John's University, Collegeville, MN

PROLOGUE

"Great things are not done by impulse,

but by a series of small things

brought together."

—VINCENT VAN GOGH

October 26, 2002

orrie's Supper Club, located in Black Eagle, Montana, sits perched on the western side of the Missouri River, just opposite the city of Great Falls. The western paintings adorning the wall behind the bar capture the cowboy spirit of its patrons, while the black-and-white photos of the old abandoned copper smelter plant give quiet testimony to the history of the area's deep association with the mining industry.

The large crowds that gather there—even during the middle of the week—are more a tribute to the high quality of its steak, ravioli, and famous thick, brown-broth minestrone soup and less a sign of the area's affluence. Great Falls has always been a middle-class town with solidly middle-class values.

In the basement of Borrie's sits a small, wood-paneled banquet room that bears the unmistakable

signs of having hosted too many grooms' dinners, company Christmas parties, and countless other business-related functions. Its low ceiling and dim lighting make the room seem even smaller and give off the air that nothing of any great import has ever happened here.

From outside appearances the group that convened in the room would have done little to dispel this notion. In fact, the participants of the meeting themselves—the members of the Great Falls Central Mustangs 1962 football team—would have attached little significance to their reunion. They were merely gathering to celebrate the 40th anniversary of their 1962 season.

Yet what transpired that evening is the stuff of greatness. It was not the transitory or artificial greatness that comes from reliving the long faded memories of high school gridiron glory. Instead, the reunion captured the greatness that is realized when ordinary people do ordinary things extraordinarily well.

In this case, the reunion was a manifestation of how the principles and values that two ordinary football coaches—in partnership with the school's faculty—instilled in a group of boys, turned them from average football players into extraordinary ones, and, more important, transformed them from boys into men.

At the beginning of the evening, it was evident that four-decades' worth of living had taken its customary toll on many of the players. Their hair was grayer, hairlines had receded, and waist-lines were expanded. Time had also extracted some of its more punishing effects: war, alcoholism, a car accident, and illness had taken the lives of five of their teammates—Glenn Fish, Bob Murray, Gene Ouellette, Voyd Richtscheid, and Clark Kochivar.

Still, the atmosphere in the banquet room was upbeat and celebratory. Beers and soft drinks were raised, good natured insults were swapped, and a hearty meal was had by all. Players did their best to catch up on the lives of their teammates. Photos of spouses, children, and grandchildren were passed around; war stories, business successes and failings were recounted; and life's other highlights were conveyed as best as they could be in the short amount of time available.

It was not until the end of the evening that Ed Flaherty, one of the team's old co-captains and the main organizer of the reunion, took the microphone and called upon each member of the team to get up and tell the group what "they had been up to for the last 40 years."

He began by handing the microphone to Dick Kuntz, a solid, barrel-chested man with a bald pate, whose tough exterior faded upon seeing his warm, vibrant eyes. It was an auspicious choice. Had Flaherty instead turned to his left and handed the microphone to Wally Berry, one of the team's other co-captains and a reticent man not particularly comfortable with sharing his inner emotions, the dynamics of what transpired next would have changed. It is quite possible that the true impact of the 1962 season would have forever remained a secret even to its participants.

"I am now the assistant superintendent of secondary schools in Great Falls," Kuntz began in a modest, soft tone. Only two of his teammates—his brother, Jerry, and his best friend, Billy Sprinkle—understood how far he had truly come. That is because they still remembered the shy kid with the thick black glasses who bore the stigma of not being allowed by a nun to take any advanced courses because she didn't think he had the "smarts."

"I am where I am today," began Kuntz, who was looking directly at his two old high school football coaches, Bill Mehrens and John McMahon, "because of you two." The intimate nature of his remark silenced the room.

"Everything I learned about life and leadership...I learned from the two of you. You taught me to set my goals high, to have pride in myself, my teammates, and my school. You preached fundamentals, practiced discipline, and demanded excellence in everything we did. You demanded that we be well-conditioned and that we know our positions inside and out. You even demanded excellence in the small things: from how we stood at attention with our helmets under our left arm and our right hand over our heart during the national anthem to how we huddled and then clapped our hands as a team after breaking from the huddle." Kuntz's comments elicited a few chuckles from his old teammates, but they also had the effect of cracking open a vault of long-sealed memories that resided in each of his teammates.

"They might seem like quaint memories," continued Kuntz, "but they really had an effect on me. You made me believe that we were capable of even more than we could imagine. You drove me—and all of us—to be the best that we could be; and, speaking for myself, I know it changed my life." He paused to look again at his two old coaches. "The phrase might sound like that old Army slogan: 'Be all you can be,'" said Kuntz, before stopping again, this time for a short editorial. "By the way, I can't stand the Army's new slogan, 'An Army of One.' What the heck is that?" he said derisively. "I want our Army to be a team—not an Army of One."

The aside drew some more laughter, not so much for the comment as for the fact that many of his teammates couldn't help but think that it was not Dick Kuntz they were hearing but rather their old coaches. "In the end, though, you taught us that as satisfying as it was to perform at our highest individual level, it was even more satisfying to do it as part of a team. I have never forgotten the experience of the '62 season. In fact, I have taken it with me everywhere I have gone in life.

"You may not remember this Coach Mehrens," said Kuntz, still unable after 40 years to call him anything except "Coach," "but I returned to Great Falls Central as a student coach in 1968—the year after you left to go into the FBI. I really regret not having had the opportunity to coach under you, but I am grateful for the lessons you instilled in me as a player.

"From the time I was in seventh grade, I knew I wanted to coach. And the reason I wanted to coach was because I learned from you the positive influence a coach could have on a kid's life. For the next 12 years, I coached at a variety of levels, and wherever I went, I always tried my best to emulate you and to create the sense of community that Great Falls Central possessed." The sincerity of Kuntz's comments caused a well of tears to form in Mehrens' eyes. The old coach swallowed the lump in his throat but did little to fight back the tears as they began to stream down his face.

"I also tried to emulate you too, Coach McMahon," continued Kuntz. The affection he still held for his old line coach was evident in his tone. "But I don't think anybody will ever be able to do that."

"Thank God!" came the well-timed and quick-witted response from Dave Nash, a former lineman who, like all the other 1962 Mustang linemen, had suffered under the relentless drilling and yelling of McMahon. "I don't think the country is ready for two 'Ponchos,'" continued Nash, referring to McMahon's old nickname.

After the laughter subsided, Kuntz continued, "From you, Coach McMahon, I learned the importance of hard work, discipline, and focusing on the basics. In 1988, a few years after I had retired from coaching to focus on teaching, I was given the chance to build my own school when I was asked to become principal of Paris Gibbons Middle School. As many of you know, our old high school was converted into Paris Gibbons Middle School. When I reentered the school for the first time that summer, I was flooded with memories from my time there—and especially our 1962 season—and I vowed at that moment to do my best to instill in my students the same values the two of you, along with the rest of the staff at GFC, instilled in us. But more than that, I also set out to make a team out of the teachers at the school. And following your examples, I think I was able to do that.

"As principal, the responsibility of remodeling the school also fell to me. The first thing I did was have the old chapel converted into my office. That had to have had the nuns turning in their graves," added Kuntz with a wry smile. "But besides that I made only one other request, and that was that the old Great Falls Central tile seal by the door of the gymnasium be retained. I did it for two reasons. First, I wanted the current students to know a little about the history of the school. Second, I wanted a personal daily reminder of the excellence that you demanded of your players. It was over that very seal that all of us in this room," said Kuntz, gesturing to the players seated before him, "would walk every day as we went out to practice. And it was on that practice field, under your direction and guidance, that I learned the most valuable lessons of my life. So to this day, every time I see that seal or walk over it, I am reminded of those lessons. From the bottom of my heart: Thank you."

He then looked both of his old coaches in the eye and repeated his thanks. "Thank you, Coach Mehrens. Thank you, Coach McMahon. I wouldn't be where I am today without you." The room was silent as Kuntz handed the microphone back to the player seated next to him.

What followed was not a standard litany of life's successes—though the group was clearly accomplished. Instead, one player after another gave moving and inspirational testimonials as to how the two coaches helped mold them into a high performance team, and how the lessons they learned that season not only shaped their lives but how the lessons continue to influence their lives and the lives of others to this day.

These are their stories ...

CHAPTER I

"Leaders are made, they are not born.

They are made by hard effort,

which is the price all of us pay

to achieve any goal

that is worthwhile."

—VINCE LOMBARDI

LIGHTING THE FIRE

Bill Mehrens' and John McMahon's Stories

May 2, 1955

Armed with nothing more than two letters of recommendation from his current and former college football coaches, Bill Mehrens, a soon-to-be graduate of Carroll College, a small liberal arts college in Helena, Montana, arrived in the office of Father Harold Arbanas, the principal of Great Falls Central Catholic High School. He was there to interview for the head football coaching position.

Located on the corner of Central Avenue and 24th Street in a neighborhood surrounded by modest middle-class homes, the school had opened its doors only five years earlier. In the

27

aftermath of World War II, the influx of people moving into the area strained the city's existing Catholic high school, St. Mary's, and it was decided that a new, bigger school was needed. With the support of the Catholic diocese of Great Falls, the city's numerous parishes and feeder elementary schools, as well as the assistance of the region's three distinct congregations of religious women—the Ursulines, the Sisters of Humility of Mary, and the Sisters of Charity of Providence—Central strove to provide its students with a superior education grounded in its Catholic tradition. As Father Arbanas ran through this history—including a brief tutorial in which he elaborated on how the nuns at Central were still as tough and hardened as their predecessors who helped settle Montana in the late nineteenth and early part of the twentieth century—Bill Mehrens, with his clear brown eyes and broad shoulders, sat erect in his chair and absorbed every word. He wanted this job.

Arbanas, a former championship figure skater with a solid, athletic build and a jovial air about him, then outlined his vision for the school and its mission. "My goal is to give our students the best high school education in the nation—bar none." The way he said "bar none" told Mehrens that behind the priest's friendly façade lay a man of great determination. "Most of our students come from hard-working families. Many parents are farmers, ranchers, or smelter workers. Most own only one car, and more often than not our students wear hand-me-downs because their parents are scraping by to just pay the tuition. They define prosperity not by whether they have a TV antenna on the top of their roof, but by whether their children go on to college— something that most of them could never even dream of.

"Regardless of where they come from, the priests, nuns, and lay faculty of Central see every student as equal, and we *expect* them to do their best." Arbanas stopped and reiterated his last point by adding, "We *expect* every student at Central to succeed.

Every child has a wealth of untapped or underdeveloped talent, and it is our job as their teachers and mentors to tap into those talents and nurture them to their fullest extent—be those talents in the sciences, arts, languages, or athletics.

"But it is not enough just to provide them with the intellectual tools they need to succeed in this world; we must also develop their moral character in such a way that they can then apply their gifts to their surrounding community.

"As a former student at Butte Central and having attended a Catholic college yourself," continued Arbanas, "I have no doubt that you are the beneficiary of a similar philosophy."

"Yes, Father, I am," replied Mehrens. "I'm also a product of—and a believer in—discipline. My parents were not of the 'spare the rod' school of thought, and neither am I."

Arbanas smiled. "As are we, Mr. Mehrens. There is no doubt that our students need structure in their lives—and benefit from the same—but we are even more resolute in our belief in the Golden Rule: *Do unto others as you would have them do unto you.*" Arbanas went on to discuss a little more of his philosophy before he turned to the purpose of the interview: to find a new football coach. "Tell me, why do you want to coach?"

It was the perfect opening for Mehrens, who, as always, was meticulously well-prepared. He had done his homework on Great Falls Central and took Arbanas's question and ran with it.

"To begin, let me say that everything you have told me about Central fits perfectly with my own view of both education and athletics. As a coach, I see my job as more than just guiding the Mustangs to victory. Foremost, I expect—and will demand—that every kid do his best. I will demand excellence, and I will do my best to give my students and players the tools they need to succeed both on and off the field.

"The reason I want to coach is because I view sports as an excellent way to develop character. Kids need to have goals, and

they need to understand that they are more than members of a team, as they are representatives of this community. And, as such, they have responsibilities to their community. They need to understand that there is no such thing as a free lunch, and that the core component of success is hard work. They need to learn to give 100 percent in everything they do and then take pride in a job well done. Win or lose, if my kids work hard and give it their all, I will consider the game to have been a success."

"I am glad you mentioned this notion of community," replied Arbanas, "because it is vital to what we are trying to achieve here at Central. For the past few years, I have sensed students at Central have had this notion of being the poor stepchild to the town's public high school. I want to rid ourselves of this feeling. In fact, we *will* rid ourselves of it." Arbanas's conviction was resolute. "People are who they are, not because of where they come *from,* but rather because of *where* they are going. There is a big difference. We here at Central care nothing about the former—and everything about the latter. We are what we make ourselves, and I intend to make every student a winner.

"Central is moving up from Class B to Class A in athletics this year, and I believe it will help our school's image, but I want everyone, including the students who don't play sports—either because they don't have the talent or because they need to work after school to help support their families—to take pride in our programs and our school. As a coach, you can help send this message—often in a way that other teachers cannot."

Arbanas wrapped up the interview by saying, "This is what I want to happen after our teams have defeated an opponent. I want the opposing team's players, coaches, fans, and teachers to say, 'Wow, we just got whipped by the better team...but aren't they just the most respectful and classiest bunch of kids you've ever seen?'"

He concluded the meeting by taking Mehrens on a tour of the school and telling him that he would be in touch. The 22-year-old Mehrens thanked the priest for the opportunity to interview and, as he shook his hand, said, "I agree with your goals, and I know I can help you achieve them."

Two days later, Mehrens received a call from Arbanas and was asked if he would like to be the school's new football coach. Mehrens agreed on the spot. A one-year probationary contract was forwarded via the mail the next day. The contract was extended in 1956.

After notching two winning seasons in his first two years of coaching Class A football, Mehrens then led the Mustangs to its first-ever state championship in 1957. He repeated the achievement the following year, tying with Miles City for the championship. That same year he negotiated a five-year contract to stay at Central.

August 25, 1945

Anaconda, Montana, was a tough place to grow up in the 1930s and '40s. The Anaconda Mining Company was the town's big employer, and if the workers in the smelter went on strike—as they often did—most of the town suffered.

Early in his life, John McMahon and his family were spared the tougher hardships of strikes because his father worked at the Rocky Mountain Brewery—one of the few industries immune from the vagaries of a strike-inflicted economy, because beer was consumed in equal quantities in both good times and bad times in Anaconda.

In 1942, when he was just four, the family's fortunes changed when McMahon's father died a needless, although not uncommon, death. He succumbed to an ear infection that grew progressively worse due to a lack of penicillin.

With a world war raging and three young children to support, McMahon's mother was forced to take a modest paying job as the Anaconda city treasurer. Times were tough, and later, after the war, whenever the miners went on strike and the town's coffers

dried up, the McMahons, like everyone else, were forced to buy their groceries through the local union hall.

The loss of his father had one positive outcome, however. It caused McMahon to seek refuge in sports at an early age. Sports, in turn, gave him an outlet and an identity. He began playing baseball at the age of seven and had a nickname slapped on him before he ever swung at his first pitch.

Back in the war years, Anaconda was the kind of town where almost everyone had a nickname—be it Bull, Red, Paddy, Moose, or Ox. And its kids played baseball the way it was meant to be played—on Saturday mornings without any parental supervision. Often, the only adult around was a college-aged kid named Ed Kalafat, who acted as umpire.

When McMahon stepped up to the plate for his first at bat, Kalafat, who later went on to play professional basketball for the Minneapolis Lakers, asked him who he was. "John McMahon," he replied. Unsatisfied with his uninspirational response, Kalafat studied McMahon's small, stocky stature for a moment and, on the spot, decided he bore an uncanny resemblance to the Cisco Kid's faithful sidekick, Poncho. As nicknames so often have a way of doing, it stuck. Sixty years later, McMahon is still called Poncho by his closest friends and associates.

As the summer weather faded and fall arrived, Poncho switched sporting allegiances to football. Due to his young age and small size, his mother was opposed to him playing football, but because she was preoccupied with putting food on her young family's table, and because football was such a strong part of Anaconda's identity, she soon gave in to her son's repeated pleas.

And so it came to be that in a small park, not far from Anaconda's main mine pit, that Poncho McMahon received his first introduction to coaching. It was an experience that has stayed with him, and one that he counts among the most formative coaching lessons he ever received.

Poncho arrived for his first football practice full of boyish enthusiasm. His expectations were even higher because Hank Laughlin—one of the town's best athletes and the kind of guy a young kid in a town such as Anaconda could idolize—had agreed to be the coach.

Laughlin began practice by calling for McMahon and the other boys to huddle around him. McMahon and his other wide-eyed peers rushed over and stood ready to absorb every nugget of Laughlin's worldly football wisdom.

In a deep baritone voice, Laughlin said, "When I tell you to do something, I expect you to do it." He repeated the statement with great force and added, "Do you understand?" The young players were still nodding their heads appreciatively when Laughlin barked, "Hit the ground!" The sudden and unexpected directive stunned the kids, and they remained frozen in their upright positions. "I said, hit the ground!" This time every player heeded Laughlin's directive and dropped to the cold ground.

As they lay there, Laughlin told them they were to get up only when he said they could get up. The boys were still in a semi-state of shock when Laughlin walked to his car and drove away. No one knew what to make of the situation—least of all seven-year-old John McMahon. A conversation soon commenced among the older boys. "Is he coming back?" one asked. "Yeah, he's coming back...he's just testing us," replied another. McMahon listened intently as the minutes passed, and the older boys contemplated their next step. After a few more minutes, a consensus emerged that Laughlin wasn't returning. Like prairie dogs cautiously popping their heads out of their holes after a close call with a predator, the boys began to stand up one by one. Just as the last boy had gotten up and was finishing wiping the dirt from his pants, Laughlin's car came screaming around the corner of the park. The coach jumped out of it and yelled, "Who said you could get up!"

No one dared respond, and Laughlin ordered the kids to hit

the ground again. Everyone did as they were instructed. Laughlin then jumped back into his car and drove away a second time. For 15 minutes, the boys lay prostrate on the cold, hard ground until a similar conversation to the earlier one began. "He's not coming back this time," said one. "This is stupid," replied another. Still, no one ventured to get up—Laughlin's ferocity on the football field was legendary among the residents of Anaconda, and it didn't seem beyond the realm of possibility that he was the kind of coach who wouldn't hesitate to put a good lick on any kid who refused to follow his orders.

After waiting a few more minutes and scanning the environment to see if there were any signs of Laughlin, one of the older boys mustered the courage to get up. Soon the others followed. After a few disparaging remarks about Laughlin having taken a few too many hits to his head on the gridiron, the boys concluded that it was foolish to waste a perfectly good Saturday morning waiting for a coach who apparently had no desire to coach. They decided to split into teams and play a pickup game of football.

Just as they were lining up for the opening kickoff, Laughlin came barreling around the corner. This time his car jumped a small embankment and screeched to a halt a few feet from the boys. The skid kicked up a fine layer of black soot—residue from the town's mines—and covered the players.

"Who said you could get up?" yelled Laughlin. "Didn't any of you hear a single word I said? When I tell you to do something, I expect you to do it! And I expect you to do it until I say you can stop. If you can't follow this simple rule, take up a different sport." Laughlin was not smiling. He was dead serious and glowered at the ragtag collection of boys standing before him. He could care less that they were all less than 10 years of age. "See that backstop," he then asked, pointing to a fence on the far horizon and about a mile away. "Run to it." The boys took off like jackrabbits.

When the last player returned, Laughlin—for the third time—commanded them to hit the ground. Again, he departed. This time, though, no one dared move. No one said a word. A half hour later Laughlin returned and directed his players to get up.

"Now remember this," he said, "when I tell you to do something—do it! If I tell you to block someone, do it until the whistle blows. Same thing goes on defense—you are to keep tackling until the whistle blows. I don't care how many of your teammates are already piling on who has the ball. If the whistle hasn't blown, stick your nose in there." Looking around at the wide-eyed faces, he asked, "Does everyone understand?" Everyone nodded their heads. "Good. You've just learned the two most important lessons in football—listen to your coach and never quit." Laughlin allowed his words a minute to sink in and then said, "That concludes our first practice."

It was a valuable education, and over the ensuing months, Laughlin instilled in McMahon a number of other lessons, including a deep appreciation of the importance of fundamentals. He taught the young McMahon how to get into a proper stance, how to keep his head up, and how to anticipate things on the football field. Laughlin also convinced McMahon that even smaller and slower players could often outhustle and outplay larger and stronger opponents, provided they had the right attitude and were willing to work hard. They were all lessons that McMahon took to heart and later became core to his own coaching style and philosophy.

September 28, 1951

In his first four weeks of college football, Bill Mehrens had learned more about the game than he had in the previous four years. This was less a criticism of his high school football coach at Butte Central, who had honed his techniques and improved his skills enough to garner Mehrens all-state honors at the halfback

position, and more of a tribute to his college coach, John Gagliardi, who, in spite of being only 24 years old at the time, already had five years of high school and two years of college football coaching experience under his belt. In 1943, after his high school team's coach was drafted into the army, Gagliardi lobbied the school's principal to take over coaching responsibilities. He was so successful that he was asked to stay on after he graduated.

Mehrens' decision to enroll at Carroll College in Helena, Montana, had been predicated upon two separate and independent factors. The first was that he really wanted to work for the FBI and was under the false impression that a law degree was a prerequisite for a career with the agency. Since Carroll had the strongest pre-law program in the state of Montana, Mehrens felt the college provided him the best chance of achieving his goal.

The second reason he selected Carroll was because he knew that Gagliardi, in just two seasons, had taken the school's football team—which school officials were seriously considering dropping because of a losing record and a lack of interest in 1949—and turned it into a winner. In 1950, the Fighting Saints won their first-ever conference title. Always competitive, Mehrens had toiled gallantly on mediocre teams in high school but was now eager to play for a winner.

When he arrived at the small liberal arts school in mid-August for the start of football practice, his introduction into what constituted a successful football program began immediately. "Practices start at 7 a.m. and 4 p.m. promptly," snapped Gagliardi before Mehrens had even suited up for the first time. "If you're late, you don't start. No excuses." It was a lesson Mehrens watched Gagliardi enforce the first game of the season when he benched the team's starting quarterback for arriving five-minutes late for a chalk talk the day before the game.

Mehrens' next lesson came when he sneaked a peek at his coach's clipboard before practice one day. Every minute of the two-hour practice was broken down into compartmentalized sections. Not a single minute was left unaccounted. It was a trait Gagliardi had himself picked up from Notre Dame coach Frank Leahy during a summer coaching clinic. Leahy, who was just coming off a perfect 10–0 season and a national championship in 1949, was also instrumental in helping Gagliardi land the job at Carroll by providing him a letter of reference. Gagliardi taught Mehrens the importance of wringing out every ounce of productivity from a practice. He even insisted that every player work on their specialties before practice began. If a player was a center, he was expected to be working on his snaps. Guards worked on their pulling techniques, and running backs practiced their footwork and handoffs. Anyone caught idle could expect to find himself either running laps or on the receiving end of a stern lecture—often both.

Mehrens soon learned that his coach had the first two weeks of practice precisely sequenced. Gagliardi knew he only had so much time to prepare for his first game, and he knew exactly what he wanted all of his players to know before their first game.

The next lessons followed in quick succession. First came the fundamentals. Gagliardi went over everything from how to get into a proper stance to how to make a proper tackle. These techniques were then repeated continuously until the players could do them in their sleep. It was Gagliardi's policy that he didn't want his players thinking about the basics during a game. He just wanted them done.

It would have been sufficient for Mehrens to have learned these lessons on the practice field under Gagliardi's tutelage, but he had the added benefit of having them reinforced in the classroom. For his lone elective during his freshmen year, Mehrens selected a newly added coaching course offered by John Gagliardi. It was a fateful decision because it represented a slight detour from his well thought out plan to become an agent for the FBI.

The detour widened through a series of one-on-one discussions with Gagliardi over the next two years. In the early 1950s, Carroll College had a very modest budget for football. It was so modest that the team couldn't afford a team bus to travel to away games. Instead, Gagliardi and the few upperclassmen who owned cars assembled a caravan and drove themselves.

In addition to hitching an old wooden trailer to his car for carrying equipment and supplies, Gagliardi usually got stuck ferrying the few underclassmen who were on the team as well as his assistant coach, Father Ray Hunthausen.

On Friday, September 27, 1951, the Carroll College Fighting Saints caravan set off for Vancouver to play the University of British Columbia. Mehrens made the most of the situation and plunked himself down in the backseat. Although Gagliardi was only six years older than himself, Mehrens knew enough to recognize that he was not only a winner but also a special and unique coach. He spent the better part of the trip picking Gagliardi's brain. The themes of discipline, hard work, and repetition were constantly stressed, but Mehrens was surprised when his coach threw in a little psychology. Gagliardi told Mehrens that it was important to treat each player on an individual basis. "Some responded better to a kick in the butt and others to a pat on the back," he said. Still others had unique life experiences that a coach had to consider. Gagliardi knew from experience what he was talking about. For the first few years of his college coaching career, it was not uncommon for him to be instructing war veterans who were attending college on the GI Bill and were older than himself. Regardless, Gagliardi told Mehrens, "You have to treat everyone fairly. No exceptions." Often, the conversations were made more memorable by the philosophical and spiritual ruminations of Father Hunthausen, who, later in life, would go on to become the Archbishop of Seattle.

As memorable as those discussions were, what ultimately had

the greatest impact on Mehrens was seeing Gagliardi's coaching philosophy in action on Saturday afternoons—and sometimes before.

After the team arrived in Vancouver for its game against the University of British Columbia, Gagliardi caught the team's starting tackle, a 26-year-old college senior who had spent two years with the Marine Corps fighting in the Pacific, smoking in his hotel room. Gagliardi didn't allow smoking during the season and promptly benched the player, who also happened to be the team's best and strongest lineman. Even late in the game with the score knotted at 13 and Carroll driving for what would have been the go-ahead score, Gagliardi refused to allow the player in the game. "The rules are the rules," he said when the man pleaded to be forgiven and begged his permission to go into the game. Gagliardi didn't budge, and it likely cost his team a victory. The drive stalled, and the game ended in a tie. The message, however, was received loud and clear by everyone on the team. *No one is above the rules.*

It was a lesson Mehrens learned himself the following Monday. The previous week in class, Gagliardi had assigned a paper. Due to the extraordinary length of the trip to and from Vancouver, Mehrens didn't have a chance to complete the assignment. Because Gagliardi had been with him the entire trip, Mehrens expected his coach to grant him an extension and was shocked when he received an "F" for his failure to turn in his paper on time. Adding insult to injury, Mehrens was told that if he didn't improve his grades he would not be allowed to continue playing football. "You've come to college to get an education, Mr. Mehrens," Gagliardi said. "Football is a game. An education lasts forever. Never forget that." Mehrens heeded his coach's advice, hit the books, and stayed on the team.

Following the tie to British Columbia, the Fighting Saints went undefeated the remainder of the season and won their second conference title. The following year, as a sophomore, Mehrens, who was a four-year starter, helped guide Carroll to its third consecutive conference title.

The next year—1953—Gagliardi accepted the head coaching job at St. John's University in Collegeville, Minnesota, where he has remained the last half century. Over his career, Gagliardi has compiled the most victories in NCAA football history. As of the 2008 season, he had 461 victories and a winning percentage of .781.

In his senior year, employing many of the techniques Gagliardi had ingrained in him, Bill Mehrens had an outstanding year and was named to the 1954 Catholic Colleges All-American Football Team. However, it wasn't on the gridiron where Gagliardi had his greatest impact on Mehrens. The lesson that most resonated with Mehrens was a simple one. Gagliardi always told him that *"Ordinary players doing ordinary things extraordinarily well will win games."* He then added it was the coach's responsibility for seeing that those ordinary players were taught this lesson and given the tools to do extraordinary things.

The advice led Mehrens to a new calling. J. Edgar Hoover and the FBI would have to wait. In large part due to Gagliardi's influence, Mehrens put his pre-law and FBI career aspirations on hold and decided to pursue a different, but no less promising, career. He became a high school football coach.

Armed only with a letter of recommendation from his current coach, Father Hunthausen, and his old coach, John Gagliardi, Mehrens received his first opportunity when Great Falls Central took a chance on him and offered him his first head coaching job in the spring of 1955.

August 21, 1961

Lieutenant Colonel William O. "Bill" Dickerson arrived at Father Arbanas's office at 8 a.m. The tall officer cut an imposing figure. His Air Force uniform was immaculately pressed, his shoes spit-shine polished, and his bearing undeniably military. The two men shook hands, and the priest invited Dickerson to have a seat.

It was not unusual for many of the officers stationed at Malmstrom Air Force Base to send their children to Central. Since Arbanas had taken over as the principal, he had practically willed the school to new heights by virtue of his forceful personality. In 1959, *Life* magazine had rated it among the 25 best high schools in America.

What separated Dickerson from the other officers who visited the school was the color of his skin. Lieutenant Colonel Dickerson was black. "I'm here because my family and I have just been transferred from Tokyo," began Dickerson, "and I'm looking for a school for my daughter. I visited the public school the other day, and I didn't like what I saw." Arbanas said nothing, but it didn't take a rocket scientist to figure out that the less than enthusiastic response Dickerson and his daughter received was likely related to their race. Great Falls had very few black families, and racism, while not prevalent, was not uncommon either. "I have every intention of seeing to it that my daughter receives the education she needs to attend college."

Arbanas looked Dickerson in the eye and replied, "I—and the rest of the staff here at Central—have the same expectation." Never one to dance around sensitive topics, the priest cut to the chase. "Great Falls Central is a Catholic high school. That means we are grounded in the teachings of our faith. My staff and I treat everyone the same. Let me be honest with you though. At the present time, we have no other black students." Dickerson absorbed the news without reacting to it. "What's your daughter's name?" continued Arbanas.

"Valerie."

"And what grade will she be in?"

"She'll be starting her sophomore year."

"Does she have any special interests?"

41

Dickerson contemplated the question a moment and then replied, "She's a gifted speaker."

Arbanas smiled. "It just so happens that we have an excellent speech and drama teacher here at Central. I'll arrange for you to meet with Father Harvey Livix right after we're through. He's just down the hall. I can also guarantee you that for the next three years your daughter will be afforded the same opportunities as every other student at Central."

"How do I know that?" replied the colonel.

"You don't. I am asking that you take my word on it." Dickerson eyed the priest skeptically. "Let me just tell you a short story that I think captures our attitude here at Central," continued Arbanas. "Last year, we had a wonderful boy named Joe Lloyd. He was a senior, and he also happened to be black. Lloyd was a good student and a good athlete. He was a particularly talented sprinter. This past spring he was preparing to compete for the state championship in the 100, 200, and 440 sprints when our coach, Bill Mehrens, noticed that his spikes were worn out. On his own initiative and with no prompting from Lloyd or his family, Mehrens bought the boy a new pair. He didn't do it because he felt obligated or sorry for Lloyd. He did it because he knew the Lloyds had sacrificed to send their son to Central, and he did it because he wanted to give Joe Lloyd the same chance his competitors had." Arbanas paused and then added, "Coach Mehrens would have done the same thing for any other kid because—like all of us here at Central—he believes in giving our students the tools they need to compete...on the track field, in the classroom, and in life."

Arbanas then walked Dickerson down to meet Livix. The following week Valerie Dickerson enrolled at Central.

March 16, 1962

Bill Mehrens had met John McMahon once before in Choteau, Montana. The meeting occurred the previous fall when both men were scouting an upcoming opponent. Mehrens was the head coach at Great Falls Central, and McMahon was a first-year assistant football coach at Billings Central, where he served as the coach of the junior varsity team and the varsity line coach.

The two were formally introduced by "Swede" Bushly, the assistant football coach under Mehrens, who happened to come from McMahon's hometown. Things deteriorated swiftly after formal introductions were complete. McMahon gave Mehrens the cold shoulder, figuring he was there to do a scouting job. He didn't have time for idle chitchat. Moreover, he wasn't the least bit interested in comparing notes with a coach from another school, especially the head coach of a rival school.

McMahon grunted something indecipherable about having work to do and arose from his bleacher seat and stalked away. "Poncho has always been an intense kid," offered Bushly, trying to explain away his rude behavior.

"Is this his first year of coaching?" inquired Mehrens. Bushly replied that it was. Mehrens laughed and said, "He'll learn the ropes soon enough and come to find out that we're not out to steal his reports. Heck, he might even find that we can help him a little. How'd he get the scar? It's huge," said Mehrens, referring to the large slash across McMahon's face.

"Car accident. Apparently, he and some buddies were driving home from Carroll for the Christmas holiday a few years ago and got into a severe accident. I forget the details, but I think the driver of the other car was killed. McMahon ended up getting something like a thousand stitches to his face."

"Really?" said Mehrens before adding, "He's a graduate of Carroll, huh?"

"Yeah, he played football through his senior year, but I don't think he saw much playing time that year, because, after the accident, his head kept swelling whenever he put on his helmet."

For the remainder of the game, Mehrens sat in the stands and

did his own scouting. As he was filling his notebook with reams of notes, sketches, and diagrams of various offensive and defensive alignments, occasionally he would spot McMahon on the far sideline or in the end zone. He was impressed with what he saw. McMahon was studying the teams from a variety of angles and perspectives. Mehrens could tell he was the kind of coach who wanted to uncover every advantage to help his team.

The following month Mehrens encountered McMahon again. This time he was lined up on the sideline opposite him as his Great Falls Central Mustangs faced off against their Catholic school rival, Billings Central. Mehrens' front line was the more physically talented of the two, but his Mustangs were worn down by Billings Central's smaller, nimbler, and more aggressive line. Great Falls gave up two late touchdowns and lost by a single point. In reviewing the film afterward, it was clear to Mehrens that Billings Central's line exploited the Mustang's Split-6 defense and had benefited from superior scouting and some excellent coaching.

The third time the two encountered each other was in the spring of 1962 at the divisional high school basketball tournament in Billings. Both Mehrens and McMahon were assistant basketball coaches for their respective schools and were biding their time until their teams played in the evening's later rounds.

Mehrens reintroduced himself to McMahon, who was easy to remember because of the large hockey puck-shaped scar that covered his face. Mehrens was pleasantly surprised to find him in a much more agreeable mood than the first time they met. McMahon even invited Mehrens to have a seat next to him.

He soon discovered why. Although John McMahon also coached basketball, it was clear that football was his true love. He would talk about it with anyone who would listen—any time of the year. Mehrens was no different.

"I like your team's chance to win the divisional championship," said McMahon, referring to the basketball tournament.

"Me, too," replied Mehrens. "They call themselves the Running Runts."

"I like it. You can tell your players are in excellent shape," said McMahon, who although he didn't really care for the sport, refused to take his eyes off the action on the court. His intensity and competitiveness was evident in the way he twisted the tournament program into a rod and smacked it against his left hand whenever something displeased him on the court. "Height in basketball, like size in football, is overrated. I'll take a well-conditioned team any day of the week. I noticed that most of the guys on your team are juniors and sophomores. Think you'll have a good football team this fall?"

"I honestly don't know," replied Mehrens. "I'm only returning two starters. My line is going to be pretty green."

"You can overcome that. Just make sure they're in top shape when they arrive for the first day of practice and then pound the fundamentals into their heads. Next teach 'em how to get into a proper stance and how to fire off the ball. Just keep working on those things until they can do 'em in their sleep. Even if they're small, if they can get into the neutral zone first and put the defense on the defensive, they can control the line of scrimmage." McMahon was now engaged in football, and there was no stopping him. "That was your team's problem this year. You had some really big guys—they just weren't quick enough. They thought their size would be enough to control their opponents. It's not. They needed to work on their quickness. They needed to learn how to anticipate things and make adjustments."

Mehrens didn't like hearing this critique from the younger coach, but he had to admit that McMahon was right. The offensive line on his 1961 team was almost as big as the starting line for the University of Montana, but he couldn't maximize their potential. Part of the problem was that his current assistant coach, Bushly—who also happened to be the head basketball coach—was more interested in and more knowledgeable about basketball than football. He simply wasn't grounded in the finer techniques of football.

Mehrens, however, was never one to lay blame elsewhere. "I agree," he replied. "We had some other problems as well. Our seniors just didn't assume leadership...and that was my responsibility. You said earlier that you'd take a better conditioned team over a more talented team. Well, I'd take a team that has some leaders who know how to get their teammates to work together over one filled with talented, individual stars." McMahon concurred, and for the remainder of the weekend whenever their teams weren't playing on the court, the two football fanatics found each other in the bleachers and talked shop. They didn't know it at the time, but each had found a gridiron soul mate.

June 1962

Swede Bushly's decision to retire from coaching was not unexpected. He was getting older, and his seniority earned him the right to focus on his true love—teaching science. When his 1962 "Running Runts" captured the Montana Western Divisional basketball championship, he decided it was time to call it quits on all of his coaching responsibilities. Mehrens wasted little time lobbying Father Harvey Livix for his help in hiring a new assistant football coach.

Mehrens was confident that he would find a receptive audience in Livix, who in addition to his responsibilities teaching speech and drama had also been asked by Father Arbanas to focus some of his attention toward improving Central's extracurricular and athletic programs. Livix jumped at the opportunity, and in his first year he and Mehrens had struck up a solid friendship that was based in equal parts on their shared faith, love of football, and commitment to excellence. Livix, with Mehrens' assistance, reinvigorated the Mustangs' football booster club, the Roundtable, by hosting an end of the year event in which he used his impressive networking skills to land some of the games top keynote speakers. In 1960, he brought in Frank Leahy, the former Notre Dame coach.

Mehrens had told Livix: "Harvey, I need a football man for my assistant coach. I have a great deal of admiration for Swede, but if we want to compete for a championship, I need a guy who knows football inside and out."

"I take it you have someone in mind," replied Livix, who appreciated not only Mehrens' passion for football but his competitive drive. He was also impressed with how Mehrens used sports to reinforce the school's mission of preparing Central's students for life beyond high school.

"I do. There's a young coach at Billings Central. He's got an economics degree from Carroll College, so he can teach, but he also—"

"Knows football," said Livix, completing the sentence for Mehrens.

"The guy *really* knows football." The enthusiasm in Mehrens' voice was like that of a small child describing to his parents the gift he most hoped to receive from Santa. Livix promised to speak with Arbanas about the matter. Arbanas, who had only recently been informed by the Archbishop that he was being sent to Billings Central to turn around that school, allowed Livix to conduct the interview.

Mehrens called McMahon and sounded him out about the job. Because Mehrens was only offering him a comparable position, McMahon said he would consider it only if the pay was better. On the spot, Mehrens offered him the possibility of living with him for the entire year. "It'll save you close to $500 a year in rent...you'll have your own room in the basement and the run of my house." It was a gutsy move, especially since Mehrens hadn't yet cleared it with his wife, Shirley. McMahon remained noncommittal, but at Mehrens' insistence he agreed to don his best suit and drive to Great Falls for the interview.

Father Livix had been thoroughly briefed by Mehrens on McMahon's football prowess, and based on his own inquiries into his teaching performance at Billings Central, he knew he would probably offer him a job. Livix was confident enough in his skill as a negotiator that he could convince McMahon to accept the job. But before he made McMahon such an offer, he wanted to get a sense of who his newest teacher and coach was as a person.

"So why do you want to teach at Great Falls Central, Mr. McMahon?" asked Livix to start the interview.

McMahon took a moment to size up the solid, crew-cutted priest before responding. "Let me be honest, Father. I want to coach football. I understand my primary mission is to teach. I have a degree in economics and am happy to teach that course or any other subject for which you think I'm qualified, but my career goal is to become a head football coach." McMahon was unsure of how the priest would react to his honesty, and in the ensuing silence he tugged at the thin black tie that was uncomfortably laced around his large, thick neck. It was clear McMahon was not a guy who either enjoyed wearing a suit or would ever look entirely natural in one.

Livix was instantly taken with his forthrightness, but he still wanted to know what made McMahon tick. "And why is that?" he asked.

McMahon pondered the question for a moment. By his nature, he wasn't a reflective man. He was more emotional, and football was his passion. It just made sense to him to follow his passion, which was evident in his response. "I love football. I love everything about it. I love the contact. I love the hard work, the discipline, and how players have to work together as a team." He then stopped, but it was clear he wasn't done answering—he was thinking.

"You know," he said, continuing, "my dad died when I was four. Sports—especially football—was all I had. I wasn't a big guy. I wasn't a particularly fast guy, but I had a coach who convinced me I was a football player...and because of that I think I'm a better man. The discipline I learned on the football field helped me make it to college—and I'm the first person in my family to have done that. And the toughness he instilled helped me survive my accident. There wasn't a day I didn't think I'd make it through that ordeal, and I'm convinced it was my experience as a football player that helped me persevere.

"So I guess I'd say I want to become a football coach because I think that's where I can do my best teaching, and because it is where guys like me—guys who don't have all the tools or who aren't necessarily book smart—do their best learning. I believe I can reach kids on the football field...kids who might not be able to be reached anywhere else."

"I see," replied the priest. He did not let on that he was deeply impressed by what he had just heard. Nor did he share with McMahon that his own father had died when he was young and that he had benefited from a teacher much like McMahon. "If I were to offer you the position, you will need to conduct yourself within the spirit of the Great Falls Central. Our primary mission is to provide our students with the academic and spiritual tools they'll need to achieve future success." McMahon nodded his head in agreement. Continuing, Livix said, "I agree with what you said about the values that football can instill in young men. But I also think some coaches these days go too far. Young men need models, not critics. Too many coaches lose focus on what's truly important. Don't get me wrong, I'm just as competitive as you, and I want to win. In fact, I expect Great Falls Central teams to win. But as I told Coach Mehrens when I came here a few years ago, I will not sacrifice either the values or principles of this school to win a football game. I want the students of Great Falls Central to win at the game of life.

"Let me put this another way, John. The Bible says that *'There is no fear in love. But perfect love drives out fear.'* Does that make sense?" McMahon had prepared himself to answer questions about

his coaching skills and his teaching experience, but biblical and philosophical questions were beyond his scope. He began tugging at his tight collar when, much to his relief, Livix let him off the hook by speaking again. "What I'm saying is that it's fine to be tough on our players, but I want you to remember at all times that you aren't just here to make them better football players— you are here to transform boys into young men."

"I understand."

Livix knew that McMahon did understand, and he knew that his understanding came from the best source—personal experience.

Now that Livix knew he had the right coach and teacher, he wasn't about to let him out of his office until McMahon had accepted the position. Aware that Mehrens had already invited McMahon to board at his house, Livix felt he still needed to sweeten the $2,500-a-year job offer a little. "If you commit to the job today, I'll give you a onetime bonus of $500." Livix didn't have the money yet, but he always subscribed to the "Where there's a will, there's a way" philosophy.

McMahon's eyes lit up at the prospect. He had been ready to accept the position before Livix even made the extra offer because he wanted the opportunity to coach under Bill Mehrens, who had already won two state titles. He quickly extended his meaty, calloused hand to the priest. "It's a deal," he said.

"Welcome aboard, John," replied Livix. "You've made a great decision. I know that you already know that Bill is an excellent football coach, but I want you to know that he is an even better person. And, to my mind, the two go together.

"I want to tell you a story about Bill Mehrens because I think it captures this point. A few years ago, we had a freshman by the name of Frank Kohanek. He was a big, strong kid. Probably weighed 240 pounds and was 6'3" in ninth grade. I mean the kid was *huge*. But he also had some real problems at home. His mother died when he was seven or eight, and his father took to the bottle too much. Sometimes when he came home late at night, he'd take it out on the kid." Livix's voice tapered off. If there was one thing he despised it was bullies, and when confronted with such people, the force of his otherwise warm and magnetic personality could grow stern. "Well, to make a long story short, Kohanek dropped out of school his sophomore year and enlisted in the army. He was only 16, but because he looked like he was 21, he had no trouble getting in. He served two years, and then last summer he returned to Great Falls. The first person he called was Coach Mehrens. He told him he wanted to return to school. Kohanek also wanted to know if he could still play football. Since he wasn't yet 19, Mehrens told him that he could.

"On the second day of practice, Mehrens arrived for practice at 6 a.m.—he's always the first to arrive and the last to leave—and he was surprised to see Kohanek's old, beat-up car on the street outside the school. He went over to investigate and found the kid asleep in it. Turns out Kohanek had no home or family to go to when he got out of the army. That day after practice, Mehrens took him aside and invited him to live with his family. At first Kohanek declined, but Mehrens told him it was not an invitation—it was an order. He told Kohanek that the only way he'd let him play was if he agreed to the arrangement.

"I'm telling you the story because I want you to know the kind of man you'll have the pleasure of working with. Coach Mehrens didn't have to do that. He just did it. *The great coaches don't just see their players for their athletic skills and talents, they see them as people.*"

August 16, 1962

Father Livix made good on his promise to find an additional $500 to lure McMahon from Billings to Great Falls by finagling it out of a more well-to-do member of the Roundtable. With the money, McMahon could have easily afforded a small apartment in town, but he still chose to take Mehrens up on his offer to live in the basement of his house because he wanted to save up enough for a down payment on a home of his own some day.

McMahon moved in with Bill and Shirley and their two daughters on the evening of August 15, 1962. The next day, Amos Alonzo Stagg, football's most famous coach and the "grand old man of football," turned 100 years old. Mehrens saw a mention of the milestone in the *Great Falls Tribune* while reading the morning paper and used it as an occasion to talk with his new assistant coach about the upcoming season. The pair would soon find that they didn't need any such artificial prompts to talk about football. It would soon be all they would talk about at meals—much to the consternation of Mehrens' wife.

"Look at this," said Mehrens, pointing to the article. "Coach Stagg is turning 100 today."

"No kidding? I'm just lucky that I've made it to 23," replied McMahon with a laugh. His infectious smile reached up toward the massive curved scar in his forehead and appeared to make a full circle on his face.

"I'll be lucky if I can survive this season," added Mehrens. "I've already told you our line is going to be pretty green. What I haven't told is that we've lost our starting quarterback for the first two or three games of the season. Gary Wolf broke his left arm last month. Our backfield still has a lot of potential, but now our line will have to work that much harder."

Mehrens then did a little coaching of his own on his new assistant coach. "I don't know if it was Stagg or my old coach at Carroll College, John Gagliardi, who said: *'If you accept a boy as he is, you'll make him worse. If you treat him as though he is capable of becoming something more, you'll help him reach that higher capability.'*" Mehrens paused and then added, "But that's what we're going to have to do this season. We're going to have to convince our boys that they are capable of becoming champions."

"That's why I'm here," replied McMahon.

August 17, 1962

The bluish-purple mimeographed letter, produced with the help of Bill Mehrens' wife, had arrived in the mail of all prospective Mustang football players two days earlier. It directed the players to report to the school gymnasium on the evening of August 17. The recipients of the letter were reminded to bring $2 for a mouth guard—a relatively new safety device mandated by the Montana High School Athletic League for the first time in 1962—and a jock strap. Scholarships were available for those who could not afford the fee. The letter concluded with a reminder that each player was also required to donate two white towels to the locker-room kitty.

By 4:55 p.m., 70 boys were seated in the bleachers. Each was aware of Mehrens' legendary penchant for punctuality, and none wanted to risk being even a second late, especially for the first meeting of the year.

At precisely 5 o'clock, Bill Mehrens and the new assistant football coach, John "Poncho" McMahon, entered the gym and walked to the front of the seated congregation. Looking like an older version of James Dean, except with a flattop haircut, Bill Mehrens began with a few welcoming remarks. His firm, authoritative voice then dropped a note as he turned to the business at hand.

"Football is more than just a game," he intoned, scanning the eager, anxious faces before him. "It is about life. It is about life because football teaches us that even people of limited talent and ability can play. It teaches us that if ordinary players do ordinary things extraordinarily well they can become champions. More important, it teaches us that because we're a part of a team, we have an obligation to play to our highest ability—not just for ourselves, but for our teammates.

"It's my job as head coach to get all of you to play to your highest potential. Once Coach McMahon and I have done that, it's our responsibility to get you to come together as a team—a team whose sum is greater than its individual parts. And when we have accomplished that, it is our job to give you the confidence to succeed on your own." Standing ramrod straight, with his solid gray T-shirt, clipboard, coaching shorts, and Converse sneakers, Mehrens looked every bit the high school football coach that he was. "But it starts with a decision: Do you *want* to contribute? If you do, you *will* contribute." Mehrens stopped to let his words sink in. "Let me make this as clear as I can. It's not complicated. If you want to contribute, I *will* find a spot for you on this team." Mehrens again stopped to survey the faces in the bleachers. He held his gaze on the long, angular face of Greg Steckler for a second longer than everyone else. He was surprised to see that the quirky and somewhat rebellious senior had decided to go out for football.

"You might be slow, you might have limited skills...but if you stick your nose in there, I promise you, you will get better, you will play, and you will help this team." Mehrens repeated the last phrase. "And you *will* help this team."

His gaze moved. It came to rest upon the wide-eyed, thin-shouldered, 135-pound frame of John O'Rourke. Due to Gary Wolf's injury, Mehrens had only recently informed him that he would be his starting quarterback for the first game of the year. "As coaches, it's not just our job to make you better football players. It's our job to make you better people. And that is precisely what Coach McMahon and I intend to do. The next two weeks are not going to be easy. In fact, this entire season isn't going to be easy. But few things in life worth pursuing ever are." Mehrens' eyes moved on. They settled on Glenn Fish, whom Mehrens expected to challenge for a starting position at guard. "But you will find over the course of this season, if you work hard, persist, and keep your nose to the grindstone, good things can—and will—happen.

"But the first trick to having good things happen is knowing *what* good things you *want* to happen. And the first step in that process is to set clear, firm goals. Before the beginning of our first practice this Monday, I want everyone to write down their goals for this team as well as your own personal goals on the 3x5 card that is being handed out." He nodded to John McMahon, who efficiently divided up the cards and handed a stack to each player seated in the first row.

"Pass 'em to the person behind you," McMahon grumbled. It was the first time any of the players had heard the new assistant coach speak, and his deep, raspy voice seemed to fit perfectly with his scarred face. His vocal cords sounded as though they were bruised.

"My only request," added Mehrens, "is that you set the bar high. I want your goals to be realistic, but they should also challenge you."

Next, the 1962 Mustang football playbook was handed out. Over 60-pages thick, Mehrens stated that he expected every player to know every play for his position. For those who had grown up in the Great Falls Central feeder system and played grade school football at the likes of Ursuline Academy, St. Thomas, St. Gerard's, Our Lady of Lourdes, or the handful of other Catholic schools, it wasn't as daunting as it looked. Mehrens had successfully woven his offense and defense into the grade school system, so that by the time they reached high school most of them came with a solid base of standardized knowledge. Still, the addition of a number of new plays together with Mehrens' admonishment that there was to be a graded quiz—with punishments meted out in the form of laps and sprints for every incorrect answer—caused even the seniors to thumb through the contents of the fat playbook with a look of dread.

For the remainder of the meeting, Mehrens ran through his expectations for every player on the team. He began by reminding them that football was like life in another important way. "There are boundaries on the football field, just as there are

boundaries in life. And I expect every Great Falls Central player to abide by the rules of this school and by my rules. Any player late for practice or a game will not start and will not play until the second quarter. No exceptions," said Mehrens, looking at Wally Berry, the team's star fullback.

Mehrens then informed the players that the Friday before every game he would conduct a comprehensive quiz to assess their knowledge of specific blocking and running assignments. The only acceptable score was 100 percent. Any player scoring less than that would not start. Again, there would be no exceptions. "Everyone is expected to know his job!" said Mehrens.

He concluded with a warning that his players were to accord themselves to the highest standards at all times. "Remember, you are representing this school. Any action on or off the school grounds not in keeping with those standards will be grounds for disciplinary action and, possibly, suspension or removal from the team. This includes maintaining at least a 'C' average in every class." And unlike the inflated grading systems prevalent at so many schools today, a "C" average at Great Falls Central in 1962 required real effort.

Only at the very end of the session did Mehrens take a moment to introduce McMahon. The new assistant coach remained silent. All he did was tilt his head to acknowledge that it was he about whom Mehrens was talking. For most players, an introduction no longer seemed necessary. They felt they had learned everything they needed to know about their new assistant coach from hearing his gravelly voice and feeling the glare of his intimidating stare. For the last hour, McMahon had simply glowered at them with a look that seemed to say, "I can't wait to get you on the football field."

Upon the conclusion of that first session, there was a general consensus among the players as they quietly talked among themselves after the session—well out of the earshot of either coach—that the new assistant coach seemed to represent a new and decidedly tougher era in Great Falls Central High School football. They further agreed that Coach Mehrens was setting a higher standard for this year's team. They had little idea how right they were. Both coaches were preparing to light a fire in their players that would not be extinguished.

WEEK ONE GAME PLAN:
Lighting the Fire

COACHING FOR LIFE TIP #1:
Focus first on the fundamentals.

QUOTE TO REMEMBER:
"Leaders are made, they are not born."
—VINCE LOMBARDI

KEY QUESTIONS TO ANSWER:
Have you established a firm foundation upon which to build a successful organization? Are your ground rules consistently applied to everyone in the organization, regardless of status or seniority?

Learning to Light the Fire

1. What was the first coaching lesson Bill Mehrens received from Coach Gagliardi?

2. Was this different from the first coaching lesson John McMahon received?

3. What did John Gagliardi believe was the key to success?

4. Discuss the role of setting high expectations?

5. Did Mehrens and McMahon view themselves as teachers or coaches?

6. What was the one thing that the coaches asked of all their players?

7. By the end of the season, what did the coaches hope to have accomplished?

CHAPTER 2

"You don't have to be a fantastic hero to do certain things—to compete. You can be just an ordinary chap, sufficiently motivated to reach challenging goals."

—SIR EDMUND HILLARY

SET THE BAR HIGH

Ed Flaherty's Story

November 9, 1961

Havre is a small farming and railroad community located amidst the golden wheat fields of north central Montana. It lies along the banks of the Milk River in the shadows of the Bear Paw Mountains. One of the town's more distinguishable features is its unique football stadium, which is carved out of a hill on the outskirts of town. This uncommon feature permits fans to park their cars along the edges of the stadium and watch the game from the comfort of their automobiles.

The venue is an unlikely place for a dream to be conceived. Yet that is precisely what happened on a crisp fall afternoon in early November 1961. "The Pony," as the stadium is nicknamed, was the site of the Montana Class A state championship game, featuring the Havre Blue Ponies and the Bozeman Hawks.

In attendance was a small contingent of players from the 1961 Great Falls Central Mustangs, an average team of modest accomplishment. The group arrived along with Coach Mehrens too late to snag one of the prime car spots perched along the outer ring. Even if they had, however, Mehrens wouldn't have allowed his boys to watch the game from such an impersonal position of privilege. He wanted his players to absorb the sights, sounds, and smells of a championship game, and he knew they couldn't do that from inside a car.

Mehrens, instead, directed his six clean-cut lettermen to take a seat in the middle of the visitors section of the bleachers. All were juniors on the Mustang football team, and he had invited them to the game because he wanted to plant a seed. Mehrens wanted his boys to witness the reaction that a hometown experiences when its team wins a championship.

Mehrens was confident, based on his own meticulous scouting of the two opponents, that Havre was the superior team. This was in spite of predictions in the newspaper to the contrary. The game proved him right.

As the last seconds ticked off the clock, the scoreboard showed Havre with a two-touchdown lead. A few isolated cars on the rim of the stadium began tooting their horns. Soon more cars joined in, and the rim of the stadium suddenly looked like a busy city intersection. As time expired, the horn from every car was honked continually and headlights flickered on and off, and a spontaneous celebration of raw emotion erupted. Girls were screaming, boys were jumping up and down, and grown men—indistinguishable from the giddy teenagers—waved banners from their car windows and careened around the stadium.

Down below, the Havre student body flooded the field. From the stands, it appeared like one gigantic, collective group hug. To the citizens of Havre, they could imagine nothing better at that moment than being the 1961 Montana Class A football champions. Mehrens made his players endure the entire celebration.

It had the desired effect. As the players piled back into Mehrens' 1958 mint-green and white Ford ranch wagon for the long drive back to Great Falls, one of the players commented on how he wanted to be part of a celebration like that.

Mehrens seized the opportunity and used it to steer the boys' energy into a conversation about what needed to be done for the 1962 Great Falls Central Mustangs to hoist the championship trophy in a year's time.

"The first thing," he said, "is to commit yourselves to that goal." In what then seemed to be a stream of consciousness but was, in reality, a calculated and well-rehearsed talk, the coach rattled off what each and every player—most of whom did not even start on the 1961 team—would have to do if the Mustangs were to become 1962 Class A state champions.

The reality was that quite a bit needed to be done. First, Great Falls would need to unseat the reigning champions, and based on what they had just witnessed, everyone knew that wouldn't be easy. The Havre Blue Ponies would be returning a slate of starters, including Lowell Gorseth and Glenn Havskjold, their two best players and the undisputed leaders of the 1961 state championship team. The two were known as "The Gold Dust Twins," because they were both running backs.

Sensing that the torrent of assignments, responsibilities, expectations, and goals he was heaping on them was beginning to dampen their enthusiasm, Mehrens shifted gears by saying, "We just have to plan our work and then...work our plan." He then went to work on their confidence. "We can win the state championship," he said matter-of-factly. "I have no doubt about

that. But you guys have to be willing to pay the price. It's steep, but it's not unbearable." He then added, "If you do, your time and effort will be repaid many times over—and not just on the field." The boys listened intently. His words were like gospel to them—although the latter phrase *and not just on the field* held little meaning to them.

During a short break for gas, as the other boys rushed to the restroom, Mehrens and Ed Flaherty—one of only two starters who would be returning in the fall—sat alone in the car as an attendant pumped the tank full. Mehrens initiated the conversation. "If we're going to win the state championship, and I believe we can, you're going to have to take a leadership role. You saw how Havre controlled Bozeman tonight. They're a good team, and they're returning their best two players. But you and Berry," said Mehrens, referring to Wally Berry, who would be the Mustangs' other returning starter, "are just as good. And next year isn't about the two of you getting better. It's about everyone else on the team getting better. More important, it's about everyone on the team working and playing together as a team.

"What I'm saying, Ed, is that next November is going to be here before you know it, and if you want to win the state championship, you've got to 'grab the bull by the horns,' get this team organized. There is no time to waste. The journey begins now."

September 1966

Ed Flaherty graduated from the University of Wyoming in May 1966. As was true of most young men of his generation, he was drafted into the Army. The choice before him was not whether he would serve. Great Falls, Montana, home to the Malmstrom Air Force Base, was fiercely patriotic, and the only question its sons pondered in the early 1960s was what branch of the military they would join.

Flaherty, however, pondered one other matter: How could he

fulfill his obligation as quickly as possible and get on with the rest of his life? As a college graduate, he contemplated serving as an officer and actually went to Officer Candidate School for a short time, but the thought of serving in a regimented military existence for the next four years was too much for Flaherty's cowboy spirit to handle. He opted instead to serve as an enlisted man in exchange for having his length of service cut in half.

Having received a bachelor of science in mathematics, the last thing he wanted to do was "grunt" work on some obscure backwater Army outpost in the deep south or Vietnam. It wasn't that the latter prospect bothered him so much. If he were called to fight, he intended to fight, but serving his country by cleaning toilets or engaging in some other mindless task was more than he could stomach.

Remembering Mehrens' advice to "grab the bull by the horns" and not waste time, Flaherty asked the Army for an assignment where he could put his freshly minted degree in mathematics to work. His request was well-timed, and he ended up working as a systems analyst. As luck would have it, Secretary of Defense Robert McNamara was in the midst of bringing the "best and brightest" young graduates to Washington, and the Pentagon was eager to hire sharp college graduates and pay them an enlisted man's salary. These "Whiz Kids," many of whom were from the elite Ivy League schools, ended up staffing offices in the Pentagon.

Not content with just doing intellectually stimulating work for the next two years, Flaherty, having learned the benefit of going the extra mile in high school, was accepted into graduate school at George Washington University. By the time his stint was complete, he was just three-months' short of receiving his MBA.

November 9, 1961, 10:10 p.m.

The remainder of the drive home from Havre, Mehrens subtly directed the conversation in much the same way his former coach, John Gagliardi, used to do with him. He kept coming back to the importance of goal setting.

After dropping off the rest of the players, Mehrens pulled his hulking station wagon in front of the Flaherty's small, post-World War II starter house. He looked his starting center in the eye and said, "It's up to you, Ed. I know you've got the competitive spirit, but you've got an important decision to make. You can either focus on your personal goal—becoming an all-state player and perhaps even winning a college scholarship—or you can devote yourself to a big goal and make those around you better and, in the process, make the team better. It boils down to this: Do you want to make something bigger than yourself?"

After Flaherty got out of the car and started to walk to his front door, Mehrens rolled down the window. "One last thing, Ed. If you focus on making the team better, that doesn't mean you have to abandon your individual goals. In fact, you'll find that it's just the opposite. By focusing on something bigger than yourself, you'll find the personal rewards are even bigger."

The hour was late, and Flaherty was tired. He had absorbed his coach's words without attaching much meaning to them. But certain insights have remarkable resilience and staying power. They can come from many places: a passage in a book, a preacher in a pulpit, or from witnessing an act of profound kindness. They can even come from the mouth of a coach talking through the rolled down window of a 1958 mint-green station wagon in the early evening darkness of a frosty November night.

January 8, 1962

Ed Flaherty had just returned from Christmas vacation and was seated in the second row of Mother Mary James' Religious Studies III class. He was figediting with his pencil as the Ursuline nun's soft but authoritative voice cut through the buzzing sound that emanated from the fluorescent light overhead.

"We are going to be studying the Beatitudes this semester," began Mother Mary James. She ignored an audible moan that came from the mouth of Wally Berry. "The Beatitudes form one portrait, and we must therefore examine them as a whole. When an artist draws a line or a musician strikes a note, each line or note may be graceful and masterful in and of itself, but it is the union of the lines and the completeness of the notes that reveals their mutual relation and their true beauty. And so it is with the Beatitudes."

As an Ursuline nun, Mother Mary, although she also taught algebra, had a strong grounding in the fine arts, especially music, and often used musical and artistic analogies to emphasize the points she was trying to make. The school's two other religious orders—the Sisters of Humility of Mary and the Sisters of the Charity of Providence—also had their own areas of expertise. The former specialized in teaching, and the latter were particularly well regarded for their knowledge of the sciences. The combination of the three orders' respective disciplines provided the students at Central with a classical Renaissance education. This unique characteristic was, however, lost on most students at the time.

"The first Beatitude is fundamental," continued Mother Mary, looking around the room. She spotted Flaherty. "And what is the first Beatitude, Mr. Flaherty?" Her question snapped him out of his stupor.

"Blessed are the poor in spirit, for theirs is the kingdom of heaven," he replied after a moment of thought. For once he was grateful for having the verses pounded into his head throughout the years.

"That's correct. And why is it fundamental?"

Flaherty's satisfied expression quickly faded. With an air of resignation, he shrugged his shoulders and replied, "I don't know."

A warm smile radiated out from the small nun's round face. "Don't feel bad, Mr. Flaherty. It's a rather hard concept to grasp at first, but once you understand it, it'll make perfect sense. Think of it like this: The heart must be empty before Christ's love can fill it. Therefore, a person who is in possession of this poverty of spirit is pronounced blessed. He or she is blessed because the spirit causes him to look outside himself for true enrichment." It was just the first of many such lessons Mother Mary James imparted on Flaherty and the rest of her class that semester.

December 24, 1976

For three years in the early 1970s, Ed Flaherty lived and worked out of a warehouse in Billings, Montana, where he was struggling to start a computer business. Things were so tight that for a time he was forced to share a tiny, dingy bathroom with the owner of the warehouse. By 1974, his situation had improved to the point that he was able to move to Minnesota and upgrade his business to a modestly priced basement office in the western suburbs of Minneapolis. Still, there were periods when money was so scarce he was forced to survive on a diet consisting largely of popcorn.

Over the next two years, he began to accumulate some savings, and for the first time in his career he could see a path to success—which for him was defined as being able to work for himself at a meaningful job while providing for his family. Longer term, he hoped to be able to give something back to his church and his community. But with just over $1,000 in the bank, he figured that goal was still a few years away.

On a cold Christmas Eve in 1976, he received a call from Sister Roseanne Fox, a friend of Father Harvey Livix and the sister of Father Bob Fox, who had also taught Flaherty at Great Falls Central. She was serving as a nun at a Catholic church in downtown Minneapolis.

Direct to the point of bluntness, Fox informed Flaherty that with the price of fuel skyrocketing, "Some people are being forced to choose between heating their homes and buying food." In December in Minnesota, Flaherty knew the choice was not an easy one.

"Ed," she said with the firm conviction of someone confident she was doing the Lord's work, "I need $1,000." The sum represented 10 percent of his annual salary and all of his personal savings. Flaherty balked. He now had a one-year-old son to consider. But before he could say anything, Sister Roseanne interjected a question. "How many players were there on your football team your senior year?"

Taken aback by the incongruity of the question, Flaherty thought about it for a moment and responded, "Thirty-seven."

"Thirty-seven," repeated the nun as though she were providing a dull student with an obvious answer. "Well, $1,000 will go a long way toward helping thirty-seven people have to make the difficult choice of deciding between going hungry or staying warm."

Whether it was divine inspiration or sheer luck, Sister Fox's reference to the 1962 team triggered something in Flaherty. He recalled his days at Great Falls Central, and he remembered Mother Mary James' constant admonishments to try and live the Beatitudes. He remembered his old coach's words: *Focus on something bigger than yourself.* Flaherty took a deep breath, let it out, and said, "I'll bring the check down right now, Sister."

March 26, 1962

The harsh Montana winter had given way to a *chinook*, a warm westerly Pacific wind that occasionally sweeps in from the west over the Rocky Mountains and has the ability to raise the temperature by as much as 40°F in a matter of hours. It made the season's first track practice an enjoyable excuse for being outside.

At the urging of Mehrens—who was also the school's track coach—Flaherty had encouraged a number of other football players to go out for track. Flaherty merely endured the sport as an inevitable seasonal hurdle that had to be cleared before the fall football season could commence. He was less concerned about the contributions they might make to the track team and more interested in ensuring that they improve their speed and strength for the upcoming football season.

After the requisite warm-up laps and calisthenics, Mehrens assigned each athlete to a quadrant of the field to work on his specialty. Flaherty, a javelin thrower, and Gary Wolf, a pole-vaulter, who was slated to be the team's starting quarterback, found themselves at the western edge of the field, across from the brick residence of the Bishop of Great Falls Archdiocese. The two conferred and agreed that their track skills, while above average, were unlikely to place them in the top echelons of their respective fields. They resolved that their time would be better spent honing their football skills. Together, the two beckoned over a couple other football players, also of limited or less than enthusiastic track skill, and began running through some basic plays out of the previous season's playbook.

Mehrens, who was coaching the sprinters, caught what they were doing out of the corner of his eye. While pleased with his players' commitment to improve as football players, he was not about to let it stand. He jogged toward the Bishop's residence.

"What do you guys think you're doing?" No one said anything. They could tell from his tone he wasn't happy. "I understand your first commitment is football...so is mine. But you guys are members of the track team now, and you have a responsibility to *this* team.

"I know there are other things most of you would rather be doing...either because they're more enjoyable or because you're better at them. But, unfortunately, that's not how life works. You'll often find that you have to do things that you don't like. You've got to start looking at things from a different perspective. It's easy to complain about and avoid the things you don't like in life, but the key to success is to recognize that there is an opportunity for growth and improvement in almost everything you do. It's just a matter of perspective. For instance," said Mehrens as he looked at Wolf, "the

68

pole vault can help increase your arm strength. And, Flaherty, if you follow through on the weight-lifting regimen I gave you for the javelin, it can translate into increased strength on the football field." Player by player, Mehrens walked through the benefits of being on the track and field team.

After practice, out of earshot of the other players, Mehrens pulled Wolf and Flaherty aside. "Look, I didn't want to say this around the other guys today, but I expect more from the two of you—a lot more. There is an excellent chance the two of you will be captains on next year's team. But being a leader doesn't just mean leading on the football field. It means being a leader in school, in town, and, yes, even on the track field."

He concluded his short lecture on a softer note. "Now, when you finish your track workouts in the future, if you still want to practice football—and I trust that you will—you're free, on your own initiative, to take the other boys into the gym and work on plays. You just can't do it during track practice—it's against high school league rules."

June 11, 1962

Under the Montana state high school athletic guidelines, coaches were not to have any contact with the players in an official capacity until late August—two weeks before the first game of the year. Mehrens always adhered to this rule. It did not, however, stop him from dropping subtle suggestions to his players about how they might use their time more constructively over the summer. His first suggestion to Ed Flaherty was that he gather up as many players as possible and start working on conditioning. "I don't want to have to spend any more time than is necessary getting you guys in shape when we begin practice in August. That's your responsibility," he said, looking at Flaherty.

Mehrens considered himself lucky to have Flaherty, who was affectionately known as "Big Ed," returning at center. Mehrens always maintained that the center position, along with that of quarterback, were the two most important positions on the field. As such, he strove to fill both slots with players who were as smart as they were physically talented.

Mehrens knew that he had in Flaherty a tough kid who possessed talent, intelligence, and dedication in equal amounts. He was mature beyond his years, both physically and mentally. Big Ed was the type of kid who had hair on his legs in seventh grade and was shaving by his freshman year.

In many ways, Flaherty was a man among boys. This trait though was less a matter of testosterone and more a result of having to grow up too fast. His mother suffered from depression, and during her more debilitating bouts, he was often called upon to provide for his two younger brothers for prolonged periods of time. His father, who often had to juggle bills just to meet tuition for his boys to go to Catholic school, had little choice but to place upon his oldest son's broad shoulders the extra responsibilities of cooking, cleaning, and doing laundry for the family.

By custom, Mehrens only designated the quarterback a captain of the team, but he was confident that Flaherty's peers would also select him as a captain. With this in mind, he focused a good deal of attention on him.

The three months between the end of school in early June and its resumption after Labor Day were filled with the usual assortment of summer jobs for the members of the 1962 Mustangs: ranch hand, smelter worker, grocery clerk, body shop assistant, lawn maintenance worker, janitor, and gas station attendant. The work was varied, but the jobs all shared the common characteristics of long hours, tedious labor, and low pay.

As the children of struggling middle-class parents who had chosen to spend what little discretionary income they had on a Catholic education, the kids had no choice but to contribute financially. Typically, their days started well before sunrise and ended only as the summer sun began its slow downward descent over the western horizon. Mehrens himself was no exception to the rule. To supplement his modest teaching and coaching salary, he delivered milk during the summer.

The late evenings, after first finishing whatever chores were expected of them at home, were the only free time the players had to themselves. With Mehrens' gentle guidance, Flaherty organized a series of nightly practices. While the other boys of Great Falls were cruising Central Avenue—the city's main drag—flirting with girls, hanging out at the Burger Master, listening to Chubby Checker and Pat Boone, or attending the latest *Three Stooges* movie at the 10th Avenue Drive-in Theater, the nucleus of the 1962 Mustangs was beginning to come together on the well-worn practice field behind the high school.

Had it occurred 30 years later, it would have been called a "bonding" experience—which was precisely what Mehrens had hoped would occur. Superior conditioning was a core component of Mehrens' coaching philosophy, but he was even more adamant that if his 1962 Mustangs were going to have any chance of wresting the state championship away from Havre, the players would first need to come together as a team. And Mehrens knew that he could not wait until August for that process to start.

So it was that on almost any given evening during the summer of 1962, a dedicated contingent of Mustang football players would go down to the school practice field or, on occasion, jump the wrought iron fence at Memorial Stadium and gather together for calisthenics, conditioning, running plays, and scrimmaging until it was dark.

Some evenings after he had finished making his milk rounds, Mehrens would swing by the field and watch his boys from a distance. If he noted a player was absent for more than a session, he would be sure to make an extra stop at Flaherty's house the next day to inquire into the matter. He didn't want anyone cutting corners, and he expected his captains to take care of such issues.

August 20, 1962

The sun was already high over the Highwood Mountains, which lie to the east of Great Falls, and its heat had dispersed with the thick coating of dew that only hours earlier blanketed the practice field. The time was 9 a.m., and the season's first practice had just ended. In spite of the fact that many of the players had spent a good deal of time conditioning themselves over the summer, the 100-yard wind sprints at the end of the practice had left even the best-conditioned players wondering how they were going to survive the day's second practice—let alone two more weeks of two-a-day practices.

As the players pulled off their soiled jerseys and sweat-soaked T-shirts and hung them in their lockers in the hopes that they would somehow miraculously dry in the interceding hours before the start of the second practice, Mehrens poked his head into the locker room and said, "I want to see Wolf now, Flaherty in 10 minutes, and Berry in 20."

Forced to abandon the idea of a long shower, Flaherty rinsed off and hustled up to Mehrens' second floor classroom, which also doubled as his office. Gary Wolf, the team's quarterback, came out of Mehrens' small office with a smile on his face and said, "You're next, Eddie."

"How's the arm?" asked Flaherty, looking at the plastered cast that surrounded Wolf's left arm. He had broken it a few weeks earlier while lifting sand-filled weights in his garage.

"Getting better, but Doc MacGregor says there's no way I'll be ready for Butte Central." Flaherty sighed. Butte Central was the Mustangs' first game of the season. They were a much larger Double A school, and Great Falls Central, a Class A team, had never beaten them in three opportunities under Mehrens.

"I guess O'Rourke will have to get the job done," said Flaherty, referring to John O'Rourke, the team's less skilled second-string quarterback.

"Guess so," replied Wolf, with an air of resignation.

In spite of being directed into Mehrens' office by Wolf, Flaherty still rapped on the door as a sign of respect. Students at Great Falls Central did not present themselves unannounced in the offices of teachers, priests, nuns, and, especially, the head football coach.

"Come in. Have a seat," said Mehrens, not bothering to look up. He was studying the 3x5 note card on which Flaherty had written his team and personal goals. When he did look up, he stared directly at Flaherty. Mehrens seemed to be taking the boy's measure. Still over-heated from the morning practice, the broad-shouldered Flaherty could feel the beads of sweat forming on his forehead. Finally, Mehrens spoke. "I'm pleased to inform you that you have achieved your first personal goal. Your teammates elected you captain—along with Wolf and Berry. Congratulations." The news was not unexpected, but Flaherty was still gratified upon hearing it was official.

Mehrens wasted no time dousing Flaherty's satisfaction by explaining the many responsibilities the title conferred upon him. "As captain, you're now officially one of the three confirmed leaders of this team, and that means you are responsible for both its development and its performance. With that in mind, I want to set aside your two remaining personal goals and focus on your goals for the team. After all, football is—above all else—a team sport." It was a statement Flaherty had heard countless times in his first three years at Great Falls Central, and one he would continue to hear the remainder of the season.

"Yes, sir," replied Flaherty solemnly.

"Do you think your goals for the team are realistic?" Mehrens asked.

"Yes, sir. I do."

Mehrens looked up at him and sat silently for what seemed an eternity. Flaherty felt more beads of sweat on his forehead. Finally, Coach Mehrens replied, "So do I." The new co-captain breathed a sigh of relief. "But they aren't going to be easy to achieve. I agree that we can win every game," continued Mehrens, referring to Flaherty's first goal, "but we can't afford to look past Butte Central. We have never beaten the Maroons, and we're going to be playing them on their home turf. Plus, Wolf just confirmed that he's not going to be ready in time." Mehrens showed no emotion, but the prospect still concerned him greatly. "I'm from Butte, and I can tell you Naranche Stadium is the toughest, nastiest place to play football in all of Montana. If the all-dirt field isn't daunting enough, the rocks and glass shards that cover the field are. But the most intimidating thing is the fans.

"Together with Wolf, I'll make certain O'Rourke is ready to fill in at quarterback. But as captain and the most senior lineman, you're going to have to convince the rest of your teammates that they can compete against—and beat—Butte Central. Do you think you can do that?"

"Yes, sir."

"I don't have to tell you our line is pretty inexperienced. You're the only returning starter. That means you're going to have to become an extension of Coach McMahon and myself on and off the field. We can't be there all the time. If you want to achieve the goal of winning every game and then achieving your second team goal—and the more important goal—of winning the state championship, you're going to have to help your teammates get better. It means you're going to have to push them hard. It's a crappy job. You're their friend, and I know you have known most of these guys since grade school. But if you want to be playing for a state championship in November, there are going to be times when you have to kick 'em hard."

"I understand, sir."

"I don't think you do...but you'll soon find out what it means to be a leader. And if we're going to challenge for the championship, you're going to have to do exactly that—lead. Wolf and

Berry are your co-captains, but they're different kinds of leaders. Wolf leads with his head. The guy is as sharp as a tack—the smartest kid I've yet coached—and I'm going to ask a lot of him. Berry is also a great player—probably one of the most talented I've ever coached—but he leads by example. He lets his play on the field do his talking. Neither of them, though, has the personality to really push the guys. That heavy responsibility falls to you."

"Yes, sir."

Mehrens again looked at Flaherty. He doubted whether the full magnitude of what he was asking of his new captain had sunk in, but he also knew enough about Flaherty to know that he had the raw material to do the job.

"Now, let's talk about your personal goals. I'm less concerned about your first goal," said Mehrens. "That's not because I don't think you can make the all-state team. I do. It's just that it's your second goal that's more important. Getting a college scholarship is your ticket to a better life." Flaherty nodded. "Has anyone in your family ever been to college?"

"No, sir."

"Well, you have the chance to change that, but like leading this inexperienced football team, it isn't going to be easy. Berry is going to be able to catch the attention of the media and the big college recruiters by virtue of his position and his ability to break runs for 60, 70, and 80 yards.

"You aren't so lucky. The key to an offensive lineman winning a scholarship is to do the small things—the ordinary things— extraordinarily well and do them well on every single play. If you do that, I guarantee you'll get noticed," said Mehrens. "But it starts with you leading by example, and it starts out there." Mehrens motioned with his head to the practice field, which was visible through his office windows. "You'll play like you prac- tice." Mehrens repeated the phrase, "You'll play like you practice. That means you have to run hard on every sprint. It means you have to be the first to fire off the line. It means blowing your guy back the farthest, and it means holding your block until the whistle blows. If necessary, it might even mean playing hurt."

"I understand, sir."

"I'm still not sure you do yet, Mr. Flaherty," replied Mehrens, who rarely conferred upon his players the title term "Mr." and only did it this time to impress upon him the significance of what he was saying. "Just remember what I said at the opening session the other evening. Football can teach you a lot about life. Set your goals high, practice hard, hit your opponents fast and forcefully, and make the necessary sacrifices. If you do those thing, this season—and this team—will be a success."

October 1986

Since Flaherty had donated $1,000 to Sister Roseanne Fox, his business had been more profitable than even he could have expected. He easily achieved his first goal of being able to provide for himself and his family, and he was convinced that his second goal—that of working for himself—was as secure as anything could be during an era when soaring energy prices, rising inflation, and interest rates threatened even the best managed businesses. Still, a question lingered in his head. Could he successfully achieve his third goal—that of growing and sustaining a large business?

Unwilling to abandon this goal and settle into the comfortable lifestyle that his modest computer business afforded him, Flaherty started an automobile oil change business with the little free time he had. He was convinced the business could be a success. It was a field that filled an unmet need in people's lives. Fewer people now had the time or desire to change their own oil. He knew he needed to act fast because he was certain that others would pick up on this trend.

He opened his first store, and by focusing on the small things, such as location, prompt service, cleanliness, and fair pricing, he was able to net close to a $1,000 dollars a month. It was a sizeable addition to his computer business income but not enough to sustain his growing family. He now had his second child on the way.

Flaherty recognized he had a choice to make. If he were going to achieve his third goal, he needed to change paths. He did the math and figured that if he could stay focused on the basics, he could open 10 stores in the next year. Along the way, he would earn a very healthy salary for the times and a downright princely sum for a kid from Great Falls, Montana.

Seeing the additional side benefit of investing in real estate, which buying the land under his stores provided, Flaherty sold his computer business and poured all of his capital—and then some—into the new oil changing business. Two years and many long hours later—hours in which he sacrificed time away from his family and pushed himself and his coworkers to the brink of exhaustion—Flaherty opened 10 stores and achieved his goal of earning $120,000 a year.

Never motivated by money for money's sake, Flaherty was aware that his long-term goal of growing a large business was finally within reach and, like that of winning a state championship, had a good chance of succeeding as long as he continued to do the small things well. As he always told his store managers, "Just keep doing the ordinary things extraordinarily well and the customers will keep coming back—and the profits will keep flowing."

Flaherty reminded his employees that the concepts of a successful business were simple. Just like getting to your opponent "faster and harder" gave a player a decided advantage on the field, the ability to reach new markets faster than your competitors provides a huge competitive advantage in the commercial marketplace.

After securing the Minnesota market, Flaherty expanded east into Wisconsin by opening stores in Madison and Milwaukee. In rapid succession, he moved into Ohio, and eventually his busi-

ness reached all the way to New York, where he had 30 stores upstate and an additional 15 in the metropolitan area.

By 1986, just 10 years after opening his first store, Flaherty owned 83 Rapid Oil Change locations. As the industry consolidated, Valvoline, Rapid Oil Change's largest supplier, was looking to get into the business after its competitor, Pennzoil, had purchased the Jiffy Lube franchisor. It opted to acquire Flaherty's companies in a very lucrative deal that assured him he would never again have to share a bathroom or subsist on popcorn.

August 20, 1962, 5:30 p.m.

Although one of the bigger players on the team, Flaherty consistently finished among the top runners in wind sprints—more commonly referred to as "gassers." As he completed the tenth gasser and with sweat stinging his eyes, he was hoping he had just finished the last of the day's grueling 100-yard sprints. As he turned around, however, he saw Greg Mills, a leading candidate to start at right tackle, sauntering across the finish line next to Mike Donovan, the team's heaviest and slowest player.

He glanced over at the coaches, but it was too late. McMahon had witnessed the same thing: Mills was loafing. The new assistant coach slammed his clipboard down to the ground. "No one gives less than 100 percent! No one!" he screamed. "If one of you is cutting a corner, you're all cutting a corner. Now, give me five!" The phrase "give me five" was code for running five laps around the track, and it translated into a run of just over one mile.

An audible moan emanated from worn down players. The run was difficult under normal circumstances, but at the tail end of an already brutal practice and with heat waves shimmering out of the finely crushed gray gravel of the track, it felt like a forced march over a mile of warm embers.

"You idiot, Cat Man!" spat Flaherty, referring to Mills by his nickname. "We are running because of you!"

"So what," responded Mills in a dull, exhausted tone. He had never cared for Flaherty, who in addition to being the president of the Key Club and a regular member of the Dean's List was also the kind of kid who always received top marks for deportment on his report card. In short, he was easy for Mills to dislike because their personalities were so different.

Flaherty continued to glare at Mills as he jogged. He then remembered Mehrens' words about the job of captain not being an easy one. He also knew the rest of the team had heard Mills' response. He knew he had to act.

Flaherty slowed down and waited for Mills to catch up with him. When he did, Flaherty swung his right foot into Mills' rear end and said in a tone loud enough for everyone to hear, "Move your butt!"

Mills recoiled at the public rebuke and whirled around to face Flaherty. He was about to throw a punch, but thought better of it when he saw the fury burning in Flaherty's eyes. He could tell Flaherty welcomed a confrontation.

"I'll meet you outside of the locker room after practice," said Mills tentatively.

"I'll be there," replied Flaherty, refusing to break Mills' stare.

On the sidelines, McMahon made a move to stop the conflict before it grew any more heated, but Mehrens placed a hand on his shoulder. "Hold it, John. I want to see what happens."

McMahon smiled. He also wanted to see what would happen but figured it was his job as assistant coach to break up such incidents. A moment later, Mills broke away from Flaherty's stare and began jogging again.

"Looks like Flaherty just earned his first stripe," said McMahon. Now it was Mehrens' chance to smile. "But there are still a few other guys he needs to get on."

As the faster runners completed their fifth and final lap, Mike Donovan, the only player on the team who weighed more than

230 pounds, was just finishing his fourth lap. Flaherty joined Donovan and ran the extra lap with him. Wolf and Berry, the team's other two captains, also joined the pair—as did Mills. It was Mills' way of signaling that he had rethought his decision to challenge Flaherty to a post-practice confrontation.

The coaches looked on. Their emotionless expressions gave no hint of their satisfaction. McMahon then turned to Mehrens and said, "Looks like Flaherty just earned his second stripe."

"And Wolf and Berry their first," said Mehrens. He then added, "We just might have something in this team."

As Donovan and the others finished, Mehrens, never one to subscribe to the philosophy of keeping water from players on hot days, directed his players to the hose attached to the exterior of the school and ordered them to drink plenty of water. He concluded the practice by reminding them that the next day's practice would start at 6:30 a.m. due to the hot weather. He also advised his players to soak their feet in brine for a minimum of 20 minutes—preferably while studying their playbooks.

McMahon, who disagreed with Mehrens' water policy and instead subscribed to the "water is for babies" theory, had other ideas. "Not so fast, lineman," he bellowed. "Get some water and then get your butts back here—we still have a little work to do."

When they returned, they found their new assistant coach standing atop a massive seven-man angle-iron blocking sled that stretched 15 feet in length. It would soon come to be viewed by every lineman as some sort of medieval torture device.

"All right, girls," he said, slapping one of the thin canvas pads that covered the sled, "let's line up. You can join the running backs for cookie and cakes as soon as you prove to me that you know how to hit!" He hit the padding again for emphasis and ordered the first contingent of linemen into position. Each player lined up in his three-point stance. Flaherty took up his position over the center position, and six others quickly followed suit.

"Flaherty, get your big butt down," roared McMahon. "You should look like you're takin' a crap in the woods. Now, on the count of three, hit the sled!" McMahon barked out the count, and Flaherty exploded out of his stance. He was followed by the other six hitting it at different times.

"No!" screamed McMahon. The veins in his neck protruded and appeared to be on the verge of bursting. He desperately wanted to swear at his new charges but had been warned by Mehrens and Father Livix that profanity was unacceptable at Great Falls Central for both students *and* teachers. Clenching his teeth, he said, "No machine-gunning it! I want all of you to hit the sled together...like you're a team."

Again, McMahon barked out the count. This time he varied the cadence and put the emphasis on the second "hut." The old trick caused Flaherty to jump offside and earned him an extra lap after practice. It also produced an admonishment from McMahon. "The one thing I won't tolerate is stupid mistakes, and that, Flaherty, was a stupid mistake. You know the count!

"The reason I won't tolerate such mistakes is because I know from experience that the team that makes the most mistakes in a game usually loses—and I hate losing. I especially hate it when my team beats themselves." Looking directly at Flaherty, he said, "So let's not beat ourselves."

Disappointed in himself, Flaherty dropped his head. "Get your head up, Flaherty!" yelled McMahon. This time his eyes seemed to roll into the back of his head, which together with his protruding veins gave him the look of a man possessed. "I don't ever want to see you or any other player on this team drop his head. You made a mistake. Don't feel sorry for yourself, don't kick yourself—just learn from it and don't do it again."

"Yes, sir."

"One more thing, Flaherty," said McMahon, spitting out his name. "If you—or anyone else is going to be offside—I at least expect you to put a lick on the defender. If we're going to lose some yards, the least you can do is let the opposing team know we mean business. Do I make myself clear?"

"Yes, sir!"

"Good. The next person who is offside and doesn't follow through with his block is going to be running until I tell him to stop. Do I make myself clear?"

In unison, the exhausted lineman responded, "Yes, sir!"

"Now get your heads up. I always want my linemen to look our opponents in the eyes. It's the only way you can let 'em know you're coming after 'em."

The players got into their stances, and, again, McMahon barked out the count. This time the team hit the sled in unison but didn't sustain their block. "Who said you could quit?" yelled McMahon. "You don't stop until I tell you to stop," he spat, "and you're not to stop until I blow the whistle! Do I make myself clear?" When they didn't respond loudly enough, he added, "What did you say?"

"Yes, sir!"

"If you think you're tired now, just imagine what you're going to feel like in the fourth quarter of the Butte Central game after breathing in that dust from Butte's mines the whole game. Now line up, and let's hit the sled again. Keep your heads up! Let the cowards knowing you're coming! I'm telling you guys, I'm doing you a favor! In two weeks, when we go to Butte, I want our opponents to pray for the game to be over by the fourth quarter because of the whupping we're putting on 'em!

"Hut! Hut, hut!" The lineman hit the sled in unison, and this time they didn't stop until McMahon blew his whistle. The exercise continued all the way down the length of the practice field and back up. Moving in 10-yard increments with the afternoon sun still beating down on them, each iteration became progressively more difficult, but McMahon did not let up.

"I want each of you to reach the neutral zone before your

defender," he hollered as he pushed the boys beyond their threshold. His voice was beginning to become hoarse. "I want you to put the defensive players on defense." Looking directly at Glenn Fish, he said, "Either you win or you lose. If you don't stay focused, you'll end up on the losing side." Worn-out, the linemen, with their heads up, backs flat, and feet shoulder-width apart, slammed into the sled in unison. Their guttural moans were drowned out by the sound of the heavy iron sled scraping across the field. Somehow each player summoned the remaining strength in their rubbery legs to drive the sled back well past the next 10-yard marker.

"You still haven't bucked me off, but at least you're starting to look like a football team," said McMahon, who always made it a point to finish his practices on a positive note. "I'll see you girls tomorrow. Now hit the showers—except for you, Flaherty. You still owe me a lap."

Flaherty completed his demerit lap and, exhausted, walked toward the locker room. He was surprised to see McMahon waiting for him outside. "You probably think I was picking on you today," began McMahon, "but I'm not. I don't care that you're the captain, the only returning starter on the line, or that you might even be all-state material. I am here to make you and this team better," he said pausing, "and the only way to do that is to ride you. You see, if you don't perform, it's as much a reflection on me, as a coach, as it is on you. I love to win, but for me to win, I have to get the best out of you, and that is exactly what I intend to do." He then moved closer and peered into Flaherty's eyes. "Do you like to win?"

"Yes," he replied defiantly. Flaherty thought McMahon was questioning his attitude and his commitment.

"I know you do. But if you want to win you have get more out of your linemen. You have to help improve their skills. You also have to give them confidence that they can compete and win— you have to make them winners."

Flaherty saw the passion in McMahon's eyes and nodded. As tired as he was, he actually felt energized by McMahon's admonishment as he walked back to the locker room. Flaherty wanted a line coach who cared as much as Mehrens, and now he knew he had one.

2005

After selling his Rapid Oil franchise, Flaherty went on to acquire over 100 hotels, shopping centers, and Applebee's restaurants, and then branched into the signage and display businesses. By early 1996, it was clear that one of his manufacturing facilities wasn't producing well, and he had serious reservations about both the facility's president and its production manager. After working closely with the president for months, he concluded that the man wasn't up to the job and let him go. That same afternoon he called the production manager into his office. Fully expecting to be fired after learning of the president's fate, the manager had already cleared out his desk.

"Jim," Flaherty said, "I'm not sure I have you in the right job. You do some things well, but there are other areas where you are weak." The production manager hung his head and braced himself for the ax.

"Keep your head up, Jim." The manager lifted his head. What he saw was not the look of a man poised to drop the guillotine. "I have failed you," continued Flaherty. "I haven't given you the tools to do the job. Nor have I had the time to focus much time or attention on you. The profitability of this facility is as much a reflection on me as it is on you.

"Together, I think we can do the job, but, first, the plant has to be reorganized, and you have to be given a new position with responsibilities more in keeping with your skill set." Flaherty went on to outline how he intended to make the production manager a division president with authority over a more clearly delineated area. He also promised to work with the man to strengthen those leadership skills.

Leaving the meeting, the manager returned to the plant with a huge smile on his face. Far from being fired, he was now energized about his future. A year later, the profits from the facility had grown 300 percent.

Over the course of his business career, Ed Flaherty, by mentoring hundreds of his employees in similar ways, has grown his net worth considerably. In fact, in 1997, in partnership with another successful businessman in the Twin Cities, he attempted the purchase of the Minnesota Vikings' professional football franchise. Although their group got outbid, he'd come a long way from a young man in a blue-collar Montana town.

Outside of his considerable business interests, which include among other things a number of food-related businesses, several restaurants and hotels, a signage business, and a vast array of real estate holdings, Flaherty has also focused his attention on creating things bigger and longer lasting than himself. In the late 1980s, after his first business success, he initiated a scholarship program to help at-risk students attend various Catholic high schools.

The stories of the kids who have benefited from the scholarships would fill a book, but a small sample provides a glimpse into the positive impact they have had on the recipients and their families. Matthew Lee, whose mother was sentenced to prison when he was just a young boy, was able to finish high school and was accepted to Harvard but choose instead to attend Bradley University on a basketball scholarship. Javier Collins, who never knew his father and whose mother died when he was a teenager, attended St. Thomas Academy in St. Paul, Minnesota, and then earned a college football scholarship to Northwestern University. He later spent five years with both the Dallas Cowboys—where he played in the game in which Emmitt Smith broke the NFL rushing record—and the Cleveland Browns. In

2005, he was one of a handful of NFL players selected to attend an executive education program at the Wharton School at the University of Pennsylvania.

John Doan, a Vietnamese-American son of a single mother, who was working two jobs to support her two sons, was also given the chance to attend St. Thomas Academy. Doan later received an undergraduate degree from Carnegie Mellon University in chemical engineering and went on to earn his masters degree from Harvard University's Kennedy School of Government. And two Liberian girls, whose parents were killed in a political coup in their home country, are now attending high school in a suburb of Minneapolis, headed for a future that only a few years earlier would have seemed all but impossible thanks to a scholarship from Flaherty.

Flaherty is also a strong financial supporter of Common Hope, a social service facility located in Guatemala that provides medical and job training assistance to over 5,000 families. In addition to underwriting a portion of the program, he helped build a school for 600 students and, to ensure that the students had an outlet for athletics during the area's long rainy season, he footed the entire bill to construct a new year-round gymnasium.

The program, however, that best captures Flaherty's spirit of providing for others is the housing program he helped to initiate. In exchange for member families donating 300 hours of community service, the program provides families with a new house.

The housing program, the school, the gym, and the scholarships all share one common element. They all strive to provide young people with a solid foundation. And while it may not be evident to the beneficiaries of his generosity, they can all trace the roots of their good fortune to the values two coaches helped instill in an impressionable teenager on the football fields of Great Falls, Montana, over 40 years ago.

Set the Bar High

QUOTE TO REMEMBER:
"You don't have to be a fantastic hero to do certain things—to compete. You can be just an ordinary chap, sufficiently motivated to reach challenging goals."
—SIR EDMUND HILLARY

KEY QUESTIONS TO ANSWER:
Does everyone in your organization have both a team-oriented and a personal goal? Do you, as a leader/manager, know what those goals are?

Learning to Set the Bar High

1. How did Mehrens and McMahon help their players set goals?

2. When did the coaches first begin establishing goals?

3. What specific techniques did they use?

4. Were the goals individual in nature, team-oriented, or future-oriented?

5. How did they reinforce goals?

6. How can you better help your protégés set, stretch, and, ultimately, achieve their goals?

CHAPTER 3

"It is a fine thing to have ability, but the ability to discover ability in others is the true test."

—ELBERT HUBBARD

YOU CAN DO THIS

John O'Rourke's Story

July 24, 1962

Bill Mehrens had just finished cutting his lawn with his push mower and had gone inside to get a refreshment when his phone rang. He picked it up and was surprised to hear the voice on the other end. "Hi, Bill, it's Bob MacGregor. I'm afraid I've got some bad news for you." The comment caused Mehrens' heart to jump a beat. MacGregor was one of Great Falls' leading physicians and better known by everyone in town as "Doc." Mehrens' first thought was that his wife and two young daughters, who had been shopping, had been in an accident. "What is it?" he asked pensively.

"Gary Wolf broke his arm today." In the relief that he felt over his own family's safety, Mehrens didn't immediately grasp the impact of the news—and what it meant to the Great Falls Central Mustangs' hopes for the 1962 season. After a moment's reflection, he became Bill Mehrens the football coach again, and all he could do was mutter a deep, guttural "ugh."

"It was a clean break," MacGregor replied, trying to ease the disappointment. "If he doesn't do anything stupid, lets it heal, and works at his rehabilitation, he might be back by late September."

"Really?" Mehrens replied hopefully. His mind was now fully engaged in assessing the situation. "Does 'late' mean September 21 or September 28?"

MacGregor understood the reference completely. The twenty-first was the day the Mustangs were to meet the Havre Blue Ponies—the defending state champions. "It'll be close, Bill, but I think with a little luck and a few prayers he'll be ready."

"I'll get the priests and the nuns working on the second part," replied Mehrens. "Well, if it had to happen, I guess I'm glad it happened now. It'll at least give me a chance to prepare O'Rourke."

"You're going with O'Rourke?" replied MacGregor. The surprise was evident in his voice. John O'Rourke was an enthusiastic, albeit modestly talented, athlete. His small frame—he was only 5'11" and 135 pounds—didn't instill fear in opposing teams, and his unassuming, reflective personality didn't naturally radiate the type of confidence Mehrens usually liked to see in his starting quarterback.

"I would go with Mike Walsh," replied Mehrens, "but you said I had to limit his play." Walsh, a superior athlete, couldn't engage in strenuous activity due to a serious heart condition.

"You do," replied MacGregor, switching back into doctor-mode. "A heart murmur is nothing to play around with." After a pause, he said, "I was thinking about Strizich. Don't you think he's got a little more physical ability than O'Rourke?" MacGregor, in addition to being the team doctor, was, like most residents of Great Falls, also a knowledgeable football fan and a fair judge of gridiron talent.

"That's probably true, Doc, but Strizich is only a sophomore. O'Rourke is more mature. What he lacks in speed and strength, he'll make up in smarts and preparation. Plus, if we're going to beat Butte Central in the season opener, we aren't going to do it on straight talent. We'll have to outthink 'em," said Mehrens with more confidence than he actually felt.

"Well, you're the coach. You're probably right. O'Rourke's a good kid. You better keep him safe though. The list of kids who can handle the quarterback responsibilities is pretty thin."

Mehrens knew MacGregor was right, but he had another, more immediate, worry on his mind. He knew word of Wolf's injury would travel fast, and he wanted to make sure O'Rourke heard the news from him first. He also wanted to let O'Rourke know that he had his complete confidence from the start. Mehrens understood that if the Mustangs were going to have a chance of competing for a state championship, it was vital his team get off to a good start—and that meant winning their first game against Butte Central.

If Great Falls were going to do that, O'Rourke had to play above his capabilities, and the first step in that process was to get him to believe in himself.

The O'Rourke family didn't live far from Mehrens, so after calling to check in on Gary Wolf, Mehrens walked over to their house to deliver the news. He arrived just before dinner. O'Rourke's father, Jim Sr., welcomed him into his living room. Mehrens explained the purpose of his visit, and the father then called his son into the room.

"Good evening, Coach," said O'Rourke, throwing a curious glance at his father, attempting to discern if he was in some type of trouble.

"Good evening," replied Mehrens. He then cut right to the chase. "I have some bad news. Gary Wolf broke his left arm today." Before O'Rourke could even register what that meant to him,

Mehrens told him. "You're going to be my starting quarterback for the season opener at Butte Central." He stopped to let O'Rourke absorb the news. "Doc MacGregor doesn't know when Wolf will be back, but, at a minimum, you'll be playing against Butte Central and Glasgow and, quite possibly, Havre."

O'Rourke's mind raced to the Butte Central game. He had been a resident of Butte until he was 13 and the economic recession of 1958 required his father to uproot his family and move to Great Falls in order to keep his job with the Great Northern Railroad. O'Rourke knew that Butte was a huge football town, and the thought of playing so many of his old friends in the hostile confines of Naranche stadium—Butte's infamous all-dirt football field—at first thrilled and then unnerved him.

Mehrens could sense O'Rourke's mixed emotions and was determined to build on the former while minimizing, or at least downplaying, the latter. "I know you've been practicing with the other guys almost every night," said Mehrens, addressing him more like a father than a coach, "and I don't know if you've been taking any snaps at quarterback, but you should start." He then smiled and added the word "immediately" to emphasize his point. "Are you going to be practicing tonight?"

"Yes, sir," replied O'Rourke.

"Good. Then why don't you deliver the news about Wolf to the rest of the team—if they haven't already heard—and then start going through the basic plays. I want you to spend all of your time at the QB position." Mehrens contemplated reviewing what those "basic" plays were, but he knew that Montana High School rules prohibited a coach from doing anything official before the first day of practice, so he refrained. "You might also want to work on the 'Belly Series' and mix in a few of the standard pass plays." O'Rourke nodded his head.

After dispatching with the basics, Mehrens got down to the real purpose of his visit—preparing O'Rourke to lead his team.

"This is a great opportunity for you, John. You've paid your dues the past few years. I know you haven't played much, but you know this offense as well as anyone, and by the time we get to Butte, you'll know it like the back of your hand.

"I also know you've been working hard this summer. I've got a great deal of confidence in you. You're smart, and you're a senior. I expect my quarterbacks—especially my senior quarterbacks—to assume a leadership position on the team. When you're out there on the field, I expect you to be an extension of me on the field. You're going to have to know what every player is supposed to do on every single play. And if they forget or don't execute, I expect you to rectify the matter." O'Rourke again nodded as Mehrens draped the cloak of leadership upon his thin shoulders. "Now, we've got almost six weeks before the Butte game. I'll need you to kick things up a notch during your nightly workouts, and when we start two-a-day practices next month, we'll take it to the next level." Mehrens wrapped up his visit by clearly laying out his expectations for O'Rourke. "Come September eight, I expect you to be the best prepared player on that field, and that means I expect you to follow my 'Standards and Principles of Preparation.'"

August 17, 1962

The 1962 Great Falls Central Mustangs' playbook was as imposing as it looked. It contained 60 mimeographed pages with a minimum of two plays per page. One play was diagramed against a 5-4 defense, the other a 6-3 defense. In the early 1960s, most high schools either played a standard 5-4—meaning five players were on the line in the down position and there were four linebackers—or the 6-3.

Every diagram was an orchestrated series of Xs, Os, and inverted Vs, with meticulously straight lines slashing across the page to designate whom every offensive player was to block and in which direction.

Mehrens had distributed the playbook at the first team meeting and told his players it was their responsibility to commit the "dive" series to memory by the start of the first practice. They were to have the whole playbook memorized by the following Friday, which was the end of the first week of two-a-day practices and the day before the first intersquad scrimmage.

It was a chore that taxed even the smartest of players. The quarterback's responsibility was increased tenfold because Mehrens insisted that they—as the on-field coach—know what every player was supposed to do on every play. Having suited up the previous seasons on varsity, O'Rourke had a solid understanding of the offense, but with only two weeks before the first game, he was feeling the pressure. His situation was compounded by the fact that he could only study at night after the two practices when he was physically exhausted.

Undaunted, O'Rourke studied the playbook with monk-like devotion. He even squeezed in time to study between the two-a-day practices. Unlike the other players who would go to the local A&W Root Beer stand for a quart of root beer and a catnap in the local park between the morning and afternoon practices, O'Rourke instead went straight home and cracked the playbook as if he were preparing for a college entrance exam.

He did so because he took his coach's "Standards and Principles of Preparation" to heart. As Mehrens constantly reminded his charges, "Nine out of 10 times it is the better prepared team, not the more talented one, that will win." And the first "standard" of preparation was having a solid understanding of the basics.

True to his word, Mehrens began practicing the core of his offense—the dive series—on the second full day of practice. For a full hour, as he also worked with his players on proper stance, spacing, and timing, Mehrens had his quarterbacks and running backs run the same play over and over again. He made them do it so many times that their physical movements became less a conscious act and more a rote muscle-memory response—which was exactly what Mehrens wanted.

O'Rourke soon learned to handle the basic dives with a grace that belied his slow speed. The Belly Series, however, was another matter. The play required the quarterback to read the defense and then, depending on the alignment, either make or fake a hand-off to the fullback. If the quarterback checked to the fullback, he would then move down the line and repeat the read to the half-back with the option of handing off, keeping the ball, or pitching it out to the wingback.

The play required quick thinking and reflexes, and the combination was not well suited to O'Rourke's strengths. Though he was a smart kid, he was the kind of student who achieved his success through sheer application rather than natural smarts. And with regard to his reflexes, he just had the poor luck to be born with slow-twitch muscles.

The relative speed of the running backs, especially compared to O'Rourke—whose teammates sometimes teasingly said was only fast at "running in one place"—exacerbated the difficulty of executing the play.

These factors often resulted in a missed opportunity or, worse, a fumble. Mehrens didn't spare O'Rourke from running laps if he fumbled or made an egregious mistake, but Mehrens also had the unique skill of distinguishing between a mental mistake—for which he had little patience—and a mistake caused from trying too hard. Most of O'Rourke's errors were the latter, and Mehrens knew it was his responsibility to get O'Rourke in the right mental state of mind before the Butte Central game.

"We're going to keep running this until we get it right," he said nonchalantly after yet another O'Rourke miscue. Repetition was Mehrens' second standard of preparation. He motioned the quarterback over to him. "You know what you're supposed to do," he said as he draped one arm over O'Rourke's shoulder pad. "You're just thinking about it too much. Just let the play unfold. If you do, you'll make the right read." The comment and the low-key manner in which Mehrens delivered it allowed O'Rourke to relax. Soon thereafter, like a person first learning to juggle, things eventually came together for the young quarterback. It took a lot of practice, but what had seemed difficult, if not impossible, only days earlier suddenly became feasible.

O'Rourke still wasn't proficient with the Belly Series, but Mehrens knew he had transitioned from the proverbial stage of crawling to walking. The boy still wasn't close to the running stage, but he knew it would come with time. The key, Mehrens told his quarterback, was anticipation. "Quickness in football is as much about anticipation as it is about speed. The more you understand the opponent's defensive alignments and how they might react, the quicker you'll be able to anticipate where *you* have to move."

Having at least established the basic runs to the point where his first team could execute them without a good possibility of a turnover, Mehrens turned his attention to the passing game. He wasn't a strong proponent of the passing game—few coaches in the early 1960s were—but he believed that any well-balanced offense had to mix in enough passes to keep the opposing defense from focusing too much on the run.

Mehrens knew O'Rourke had the few pass plays in the handbook down pat, but he also knew O'Rourke's lack of arm strength prevented any deep passes. He therefore decided to concentrate his quarterback's efforts on just two pass plays.

Much as he did with the running game, Mehrens followed the same strategy of gradually building up his quarterback's confidence by running the pass plays over and over again. For almost the entire practice on Friday afternoon, O'Rourke dropped back and fired a variety of short passes to his ends and his running backs coming out of the backfield. He did it all without an opposing defense in front of him—because Mehrens understood that he needed his quarterback to crawl before he could walk.

Saturday, August 25, 1962

Both Mehrens and McMahon arrived for the Saturday scrimmage as excited as two teenagers itching to test drive their first car after a week of tinkering with it in the garage. And like teenagers, they were both ready to push "their baby" to the hilt, except for one thing—John O'Rourke.

Inside their small locker-room office, which was scarcely larger than the steel whirlpool bath that sat right outside of it and smelled of Ben-Gay, Mehrens sat down with McMahon and said, "We can't afford to have O'Rourke hurt in today's scrimmage. I'm going to put him in a green jersey." The colored cotton pullover signified that its wearer was off-limits and not to be hit. More often than not, it also subjected the wearer of the jersey to a litany of snide comments by teammates questioning the wearer's masculinity. To compound the unfortunate situation, John O'Rourke was given the dubious distinction of being the only player on the field that day to wear such a jersey.

The very idea of allowing any football player to avoid contact went against the core of who John McMahon was as a coach. He shot Mehrens a look that bordered on incredulous. "You gotta be kidding me! We haven't even tested him in practice. If we don't do it now, he won't know how to react to the pressure that Butte Central's defense is sure to put on him. Skip Penny—Central's best and toughest player—will eat him alive. Plus, it's just not right."

"That may be," replied Mehrens calmly, "but we can't afford to have him hurt." McMahon just shook his head. "Now, that doesn't mean I want the defense to go easy on him," continued Mehrens. "Tell your guys to bring as much pressure to bear on him as they can—they just don't have permission to slaughter him."

"I'll do my best," said McMahon in a tone that bordered on exasperation, "but I don't know how you tell someone to be aggressive on the field and then, in the next breath, tell 'em to stop just when they're about to get to the good part. It's like putting a juicy steak in front of a hungry man and telling him he can cut it but not eat it. These guys have been waiting all week for a game-like scrimmage."

"Just do it," replied the head coach.

The annual intersquad scrimmage had all the trimmings of a regular season game with the exception of clean uniforms. One side wore its regular white practice jerseys, while the other wore red, light-cotton pullover vests. The event even attracted some fans, including most of the members of the Roundtable, who were as eager as the coaches to catch their first glimpse of the 1962 Mustangs. The scrimmage was even accorded game-like status by the local high school sports stringer at the *Great Falls Tribune*, who dutifully recorded the outcome in the paper the next day.

The opening offensive series could not have gone any better from Bill Mehrens' perspective. O'Rourke, running only dives and sweeps, efficiently marched the white team down the field on an 80-yard scoring drive that culminated with a seven-yard sweep by Voyd Richtscheid, the starting wingback, who was the only son of first-generation Polish immigrants.

Mehrens had specifically used only the easiest-to-run plays as a way of easing O'Rourke into the game. It was all part of a well designed program to slowly but progressively build his confidence.

On the second drive, Mehrens sneaked in the first Belly Series play. O'Rourke's lack of speed hampered the play's effectiveness, and it didn't gain any yards. But that didn't concern Mehrens. At this point, he was content the play could be run with no mistakes. That meant the defense would at least have to respect the fact they could execute the play.

By the third quarter, after running the easier aspects of the

Belly Series a few more times, it was clear that O'Rourke had gained at least a semblance of comfort with the play in a game-like situation. Mehrens knew it was time for him to take the next step in his confidence-building program. He called for the first pass play of the scrimmage—the 90 Belly Pass. It was a fake run followed by a short, simple pass to the halfback out in the flat.

O'Rourke took the snap and dropped back to pass. He caught sight of Bruce Campbell, one of the team's starting defensive ends, rushing in from his left and hastily fired the ball. The errant pass skipped a good yard in front of the intended receiver. Mehrens called the play a second time. Again, defensive pressure resulted in a similar outcome. It was clear that O'Rourke wasn't comfortable throwing the ball.

McMahon cast a glance at Mehrens as if to say, *He's acting this way even when he knows he isn't going to get hit.* Mehrens ignored the look and made a note on his clipboard to work on the play more the following week. He then sent in another pass play from the sidelines. This time Jerry Kuntz, the halfback, was to delay for a few seconds—as if he were staying in to block—then release up the middle and get behind the linebackers.

Kuntz executed the route perfectly and was wide open in the middle of the field, but O'Rourke, sensing pressure from the defense, released a high wobbly pass that sailed over Kuntz's head and was nearly intercepted.

Needing to punt, O'Rourke came off the field with his head low. "You got a little antsy on that one," said Mehrens, patting him on the helmet. "It's natural to want to get rid of the ball, but you have more time than you think. Also, if you ever see the linebacker moving up to stop the run, don't be afraid to audible at the line of scrimmage and call the play." After watching the punt, Mehrens returned his attention to his quarterback. He knew that the mild mannered kid was the kind of person who responded better to soft guidance than yelling. "The job of QB is more mental than physical—and you've got the mental skills. On that last play, for instance, you need to remember that even if you were being rushed, it's better to take the sack in that situation than turn over the ball. We can overcome the loss of a few yards. A turnover though, especially against a team like Butte Central, is going to be more difficult to recover from. You have the physical tools to get the ball there. You've got enough speed to at least temporarily evade the defender, and your arm is strong enough for the short pass. But it's the muscle up here," said Mehrens, pointing to his head, "that's the one you really need to use. Now, just keep your composure and go out there and play like I know you can."

On the next drive, Mehrens continued to emphasize the passing game. And in spite of being rushed, this time O'Rourke did exactly as he was instructed. He looked off the primary receiver and hit his halfback running across the middle. The play went for a long gain. It went an even longer way in building O'Rourke's confidence.

The White Team went on to win the intersquad scrimmage by a score of 20–14, and afterward Mehrens pulled his quarterback aside. "You had a good scrimmage today. There are still some things you have to work at, but you earned the team's confidence today. If you perform next Saturday as you did today, we have an excellent shot at beating Butte Central. We aren't going to do anything fancy. We're going to stay with the dives and sweeps primarily—because that's where our strength is. But I need you to keep working on the Belly Series and your passes. I suspect Central, after they learn Wolf isn't our starting QB, will attempt to stack up against our inside running game. When they do, we'll burn them for a couple of touchdowns."

The next day at church, Mehrens ran into O'Rourke's older brother, Jim Jr., and seized the opportunity to continue his confidence-building scheme. He told Jim how impressed he was with his little brother's performance and lavished praise on how much progress he had made in the last week. Mehrens knew the older brother would pass on his encouraging words to his younger brother.

Saturday, September 8, 1962

In 1962, prior to the building of the interstate highway system in Montana, the 150-mile drive to Butte took nearly four-and-a-half hours. The season's first snow the day before served to add an additional hour to the length of the trip. As the team bus navigated the twists and turns of the narrow two-lane highway that hugged the rugged Missouri River, the affirming words Mehrens spoke at the afternoon pep rally echoed in O'Rourke's head. Mehrens had told the enthusiastic student body that he was confident of the team's prospects going into Butte because of the team's senior leadership. He mentioned O'Rourke and said how fortunate the team was to have a leader of his caliber directing the offense. He said O'Rourke was going to make Butte sorry that it had ever allowed him to move to Great Falls.

Mehrens also reminded his audience that for the past few years O'Rourke had been waiting in the wings for this moment. He knew every play—and what every player was supposed to do—backward and forward. He had practiced all summer and was in the best physical condition of his life. Mehrens then concluded with a statement that was directed less at the student body and more at O'Rourke, "But John O'Rourke knows he's not going to be alone out on the field. He has an excellent team behind him, and this year's group of seniors knows that they are capable of beating Butte Central."

As the team bus churned up the eastern side of the Continental Divide, the large steel frames that lifted the miners of Butte down into the dark bowels of the copper mines came into view. Mehrens slid into the seat next to O'Rourke. He asked him if he had any questions about the game plan.

"I don't think so, Coach. I think I'm ready." His voice was tentative.

"You are," replied Mehrens confidently. He could sense

O'Rourke wasn't quite there, but his coaching instincts told him that any further coaching at this point would be counterproductive. "Still," said Mehrens getting up from his seat, "don't worry if you get a little nervous out there; it's only natural. After that first hit, your stomach will settle down, and you'll know just what to do."

"I hope so," said O'Rourke, desperately wanting to believe his coach.

"Trust me, you will."

The little psychological ruse worked. O'Rourke was nervous about playing in his old hometown, and his nerves would have continued to have grown worse if not for Mehrens' comments.

The same could not be said for the coach himself. Mehrens' stomach was beginning to roil at the thought of playing against his old school. By nature, he was hypercompetitive, and in his first three games against Butte Central, he had yet to come out on top. The most galling of the losses occurred the previous year when his squad was defeated on a blocked punt that was returned for a touchdown late in the fourth quarter.

After the team stopped at a local restaurant for an early dinner, which consisted of a steak, a baked potato, vegetables, and a glass of tea, Mehrens had the team retire to a separate room in the back of the restaurant. For the next hour, he and McMahon ran through the key plays the offense was expected to run. He then outlined what he expected the Maroons would do on offense. The entire time he kept digesting Tums. The notion of playing before his parents and old friends continued to turn his stomach.

At precisely 5:30, and according to the mimeographed schedule that Mehrens had handed out to every player the day before, which outlined everything from the exact minute they were to get on the bus to how many pairs of socks they were to pack, the team bus departed the restaurant for the Butte Central High School to get suited up in the visitors' locker room.

At 6:15, the team attempted to get back on the bus, but they were delayed by the mentally handicapped son of one of the Butte Central coaches. The boy had been instructed by his father, who was worried that some of the town's more aggressive fans might try to damage the visitors' bus, not to allow anyone on it. The son dutifully fulfilled his charge to the word. After a few tense minutes of Mehrens trying to reason with the boy, the situation was cleared up when the boy's father was called to the scene. The Mustangs were free to make their way to the infamous Naranche Stadium, the home field of the Butte Central Maroons.

As they approached the stadium, Mehrens ordered his players to close the windows on the bus and instructed everyone to put on their helmets. The reason for the precautionary actions was because four years earlier the window of an opposing team's bus had been struck by rocks in the stadium parking lot, and a small piece of flying glass had scratched a player's eye. Mehrens didn't bother to tell his players this was why he was taking the precaution. He figured that Butte's already intimidating image and the rumors of Naranche Stadium's all-dirt field being littered with shards of glass had already created enough mental stress for his team. He saw no reason to add more. He just wanted them to arrive unharmed.

On the short ride to the stadium, Mehrens perched himself next to O'Rourke and informed him he was being made a captain for the game. He did so because he felt the team's quarterback, by the nature of the position's assumed leadership, should be a captain. He also did it as a way to instill more confidence in the boy.

"How do you feel?" he then asked.

"Ready as I'll ever be, I guess," O'Rourke responded.

"Trust me, you're ready. This is your time, Mr. O'Rourke. You've got a great group of guys playing with you. Just keep 'em pointed downfield, and we'll leave here with a victory. Now, let's go over your goals for the game."

O'Rourke rattled them off as though he were reciting his ABCs. "Two hundred yards rushing for the team, fifteen first downs, no turnovers, and a victory," he said.

Satisfied, and not wishing to over coach, Mehrens moved on. John O'Rourke was ready.

By the time the Mustangs entered the stadium grounds, the stands were nearly filled. The remaining seats would be occupied by game time as the patrons of the local watering holes arrived just in time to catch the opening kickoff. But Mehrens and his team hadn't even reached the sidelines before the heckling began. A few Butte Central fans, knowing that Mehrens was a former Butte Central star, hurled unkind words his way. Some called him a traitor; most, though, mocked Mehrens with the fact that he had never yet beaten the home team in three attempts.

Mehrens tried to ignore the insults, but he still had to sneak a few more Tums. After putting his squad through its pregame paces, he called everyone down into the small locker room on the east side of the field for a last minute motivational talk and a prayer.

"This is it," he began. "This is what we have been waiting for since the end of last season. Our season officially begins in five minutes, but you guys have been working toward this moment since last November when you saw Havre win the state championship. Many of you have been working together all summer, and all of us have been practicing together as a team the last three weeks. We are ready. We are better conditioned, and we are better prepared. But what is going to get us the victory is our ability to work together as a team. We are strong individually, but we are stronger as a team." He looked at O'Rourke and then turned to Father Livix, who had accompanied the team to Butte. Normally, Mehrens didn't allow priests in the locker room except for really big games, and he considered beating Butte Central—a Catholic school rival, a larger Double AA school, and his former school—to be pretty important. "Father?"

Livix stepped forward. "Let us pray," he said. The coaches and the players bowed their heads. "To You, O Lord, we lift up our souls; in You we trust, O God; do not let us be put to shame, nor let our enemies triumph over us; no one whose hope is in You will ever be put to shame."

Just as Livix was finishing, a referee stuck his head into the room and asked for the captains. Mehrens told O'Rourke to make the coin toss. As the three captains jogged toward midfield, the public announcer introduced the first two Mustangs, Wally Berry and Ed Flaherty. He then paused a moment before introducing O'Rourke and said, "Playing quarterback and wearing number 13 is 'Shamus' O'Rourke's little boy, Johnny." (In Butte, O'Rourke's father was known by his nickname, Shamus.) He received only a splattering of applause from the home crowd. O'Rourke's father was well liked and well respected, but this was football. The captains shook hands, and then O'Rourke was asked to call the coin toss. He chose heads. It was tails. The Maroons elected to receive the ball.

The game began under near perfect conditions. The temperature at kickoff was 72°F, and a light breeze carried a faint smell of fall. With the wind at his back, Mike Walsh, whose play was relegated to kicking duties by his heart murmur, initiated the 1962 Mustangs' season with a thundering kick. The ball was fielded at the five-yard line by the Maroons' returner, who followed his blockers straight up the field and returned the ball all the way to the Mustangs' 45-yard line.

The catcalls from the Butte stands immediately followed Great Falls' inauspicious start. "Hey, Mehrens," yelled one young fan who had started his night off by consuming a little too much beer, "you ain't never beaten us, and you ain't gonna this year." Another yelled, "One play, fifty yards...not bad." Mehrens tried to ignore the comments and sent his defense on to the field. As he did, he slipped the last of his Tums into his mouth.

He could have used more. The defense's performance was scarcely better than the special teams. Butte Central's large offensive line pushed the Great Falls' defenders straight back on five consecutive running plays. Just over four minutes into the game, the Maroons went ahead 7–0.

As Butte lined up to kickoff, Mehrens beckoned his starting quarterback over for some final words of encouragement. "Remember," he said, "I expect you to be an extension of me out there on the field. Now use your head and get us back in this game."

Feeding off of the momentum from their easy first score and smelling blood, the Maroons stormed downfield and pinned down Jerry Kuntz, the Mustangs' kick returner, at the 15-yard line. As the men responsible for holding the chain markers moved their sticks downfield, O'Rourke jogged out onto the field. It wasn't until he got to the huddle that he grasped just how big Naranche stadium was and how loud 2,500 people could sound.

Life in Butte in 1962 was hard. Besides drinking, football was the only sanctioned way for the miners to vent their frustrations. As the roars grew louder, the stadium then seemed to converge on O'Rourke, and for the first time since he been told he was to start at quarterback, he felt nervous. Had not most of his teammates been feeling much the same way, they would have recognized the look of fear in his eyes. The starting defense for the Maroons looked as intimidating as their fathers, who worked in the massive mines.

Mehrens decided to start out easy and called for a simple dive off the right side. After breaking from the huddle, O'Rourke followed his linemen to the line of scrimmage. The voices in the stands melded into a dull roar, and O'Rourke caught sight of Skip Penny. He got the distinct impression, that unlike his own teammates, the ferocious star linebacker could sense his fear. Like a hungry wolf spotting a helpless lamb, Penny narrowed his eyes and coiled himself for the impending attack.

Forgetting that he called the play on a count of two, O'Rourke tentatively barked out the count and was startled when Flaherty hiked the ball into his still clasped hands after this second "hut."

The snap jammed his fingers, and the football ricocheted out and landed with a sickening thud in the loose dirt directly in front of him. Flaherty had pushed out his guy far enough that the only Maroon defender with a chance to recover the ball was the player lined up opposite Dick Kuntz, the Mustangs' right guard. O'Rourke, Kuntz, and the Butte Central defender all instinctively dived for the ball. O'Rourke reached it a split second before everyone else. Butte Central's Penny slammed into his back, and O'Rourke suddenly found himself in the middle of a scrum. One of the other Butte players, out of sight of the referees, reached under O'Rourke's shoulder pad, grabbed a large chunk of his flesh, and twisted it sharply in an attempt to get him to release his hold on the ball. Withering in agony, he held on. Another Butte player grabbed a fistful of dirt and threw it in O'Rourke's direction. It missed its mark and instead blasted Dick Kuntz.

The cheap shot not only missed its mark physically, it had a galvanizing effect on O'Rourke. From that moment on his head was in the game. As he picked himself up, he dusted off the coating of dirt that covered his jersey and, with it, he seemed to whisk away any remaining fear.

Back in the huddle, O'Rourke called his team together, and as they waited for the next play to come in from the sideline, he also recalled Mehrens' words about him being an extension of him on the field. When he spoke, the early tentativeness in his voice was gone. "That was my mistake," he said simply. He then turned to Kuntz, who was still trying to rub the dirt from his eyes. "Are you okay, Dick?"

Kuntz nodded. The fire in his eyes was unmistakable.

"Good. That was a bush-league move. I know these guys, and I know we're a better team. Now, let's cram the ball down their throats and tie this game up!"

The next play was another dive. This time O'Rourke and the rest of the Mustangs executed it flawlessly. Dick Kuntz, still fuming over the cheap shot, leveled the guy who had done it; and Greg Mills, the right tackle, pushed out his defender to create a gaping hole for Wally Berry to barrel through. The play gained 12 yards.

The next play was a dive to the left side. The result was nearly identical. Seven plays later, Berry bowled his way into the end zone for the Mustangs' first touchdown of the season. The score was 7–6. Walsh missed the extra point, but far from deflating the team's renewed enthusiasm, it sparked it further. The Great Falls Mustangs now had the momentum, and they wanted more.

After its shaky start, the defense settled down. The Butte Maroons didn't gain another first down in the half, and by intermission O'Rourke had orchestrated two more touchdown drives. Each ended with runs by Wally Berry of 40-plus yards. The score, though, was only 18–7 because Mike Walsh had missed all of his extra points.

Early in the third period, after two stalled drives, it was clear the Maroons' defense had stiffened and made some adjustments to thwart the Mustangs' inside running game. O'Rourke confided to Mehrens that he felt he could exploit the defense's aggressiveness by running the Belly Series. Mehrens was reluctant to risk a turnover deep in their end but could sense O'Rourke's growing confidence. He gave him the okay.

On the next offensive series, O'Rourke read the defense perfectly and audibled for the play at the line of scrimmage. He handed it off to Berry, but his fake was so good that the defense stayed focused on him. It wasn't until Berry was already 10 yards downfield on his way to a 78-yard touchdown run—his fourth of the day—that Butte Central even knew what had happened.

On the following drive, O'Rourke could sense it was time to put the dagger in the heart of the Butte Central beast. Mehrens had called for a dive, but when he stepped up to the line of scrimmage, he saw that Butte's linebackers had moved forward in anticipation of the play. At the line O'Rourke audibled the play.

This time calling for the "Jackpot Pass"—the play he had been unable to complete in the intersquad scrimmage. With a poise that never manifested itself in practice, O'Rourke dropped back and, in spite of a ferocious rush from the Butte Central defensive ends, evaded them with a simple step forward and zinged a crisp pass to Jerry Kuntz, who had swung out of the backfield and was sprinting across the middle of the field right behind Skip Penny. The pass hit Kuntz in full stride. He galloped untouched for 45 yards. The score was 32–7.

With the game no longer in doubt, Mehrens began to substitute his second stringers in on offense. The last starter he pulled was John O'Rourke. With his parents, siblings, and relatives in the visitors' stands, O'Rourke received an ovation from the small contingent of Great Falls' fans who had made the long trip. The loudest cheering, however, came from his teammates. As he came off the field, Mehrens slapped him on the helmet and said simply, "Well done, Mr. O'Rourke."

On the bus ride home, after the initial euphoria faded and the exhaustion from the hard fought game set in, Mehrens sat down next to O'Rourke. "You played an excellent game. I'm proud of you. I'm proud of your hard work and your perseverance. Mostly though, I'm proud of how you took control and set the tempo for the game. That was true leadership."

He then said something that would influence the rest of O'Rourke's life. "You really have a head for this game."

"Thank you," replied O'Rourke in a soft and humble tone. Mehrens then got up to leave when O'Rourke said, "Coach..." His tone was more suggestive of a question than a statement.

"Yes," replied Mehrens, looking back.

O'Rourke paused a moment before continuing. "Thank you for the opportunity." If he would have had the courage, O'Rourke would have liked to have said, "Thanks for believing in me."

Mehrens just smiled slightly. "You earned it."

Although neither of them recognized it at the moment, O'Rourke's experience in Butte had just set him on the path to becoming a head high school football coach himself.

September 11, 1962

Although the world around her was in turmoil—the day's newspaper announced the Soviet Union was pledging to wage a nuclear war to protect Cuba if America attacked it, and the U.S. Senate was granting President Kennedy the right to call up 150,000 reservists if the situation in Berlin required it—Sister Mary Michelle was upbeat. That was because, as a physics teacher, she was still ecstatic over Kennedy's announcement the day before 200,000 people in Houston in which he promised his fellow countrymen that America would put a man on the moon and safely bring him back before the end of the decade. She intuitively understood that the new "race to the moon" gave her something tangible with which to get kids excited about science.

Sister Michelle was always looking for new ways to reach her students, which is why she found herself seated before Bill Mehrens in the school cafeteria a full hour before the start of the school day to learn about football and watch the game film of the Mustangs' victory the previous Saturday.

At John McMahon's suggestion, Mehrens decided to begin showing the game films to the sisters at Great Falls Central. He did it in part because they were not allowed to attend the games, and he wanted to share this part of school life with them. He also did it because he wanted to convey how football could be used as a teaching instrument and how it reinforced many of the values and principles the school was trying to instill in its students.

Before Mehrens rolled the film, he devoted a good deal of time to explaining the rules of the game. Among his most attentive students was Sister Mary Michelle. The short heavyset nun, with the cherubic face and a peg leg, took copious notes. She immediately grasped that she could use parts of the game to explain some of the fundamental aspects of physics, such as using the arc of a football pass to explain the effects of gravity or how a 190-pound fullback slamming into a defensive end was simply a real world example of speed and mass working in conjunction with one another yielded force.

Toward the end of the film, Mehrens showed the touchdown pass that John O'Rourke threw to Jerry Kuntz. He explained how O'Rourke called an audible at the line of scrimmage and changed the play because of his reading of the defensive alignment of Butte Central.

"What's an audible?" inquired Sister Michelle. Mehrens explained the basic concept and outlined all the factors the quarterback was required to take into consideration before every play and how he was responsible for processing that information in a short amount of time.

Sister Michelle was mesmerized by the complexity of the game. "Wow," she said, before adding almost as an afterthought, "if O'Rourke and the others can absorb that kind of information, it's clear to me that they aren't applying themselves in my class." Mehrens and the others sisters laughed. "I'm serious," she continued. "You ask a lot of these boys."

"We do," replied Mehrens. "We especially ask a lot of our quarterbacks. I expect O'Rourke and Wolf to know not only their position but the position of every other player on the field."

"All eleven?" asked Sister Michelle incredulously.

"Yes, Sister."

"Wolf doesn't surprise me. As his chemistry teacher last year, I came to appreciate how bright he was, but O'Rourke is something of a surprise."

"He's a real student of the game," replied Mehrens. "You're right that he doesn't have Wolf's natural smarts—I don't think anyone on the team does—but he works hard and applies himself."

"Those are the kind of kids who go on to become the best teachers," said Sister Michelle. "They keep working on a subject until it makes sense. And when it does, because of their own struggles, they often seem to develop a special knack for explaining the topic to others."

Mehrens concurred with Sister Michelle's theory and continued to show the rest of the film. Sister Michelle, though, was already processing this new information and changing her approach to John O'Rourke. In addition to her responsibilities as physics teacher, she was also the senior class sponsor, and for the remainder of the year, whenever she had the chance to speak or visit with John O'Rourke, she subtly encouraged him to consider a career in teaching.

1970

Upon graduating from Mehrens' alma mater, Carroll College, in 1966, John O'Rourke accepted his first coaching job at Holy Family Parish in Great Falls. He took over a squad that was coming off a 0–6 season and was so small that it couldn't even scrimmage 11-on-11.

Employing Mehrens' "Standards and Principles of Preparation" and running the exact same set of basic plays his old coach had taught him, which were so effectively put to use against Butte Central, O'Rourke guided his group of eighth graders from "worst to first" and Holy Family's first-ever undefeated season.

As satisfying as the season was, O'Rourke really wanted to coach and teach. And with a new wife, he needed a steady paycheck. So in the fall of 1970, when he was offered a teaching and coaching position at Lewis Junior High in Vancouver, Washington, O'Rourke and his wife packed their bags and moved west. As part of the deal, in addition to coaching football, O'Rourke was also named head wrestling coach.

In his first season he coached a number of kids, but two proved to be more challenging than the rest. The first was an ox of a kid named Lonnie Knotts. Knotts played offensive and defensive tackle and had plenty of talent but was the kind of kid who needed an extra shove to take his game to the next level. O'Rourke gave him that needed push and magnified his talent two ways.

First, he got Knotts to understand that football isn't just a game of strength; it is a game of the mind. He taught Knotts how to read offensive and defensive arrangements as well as how to leverage his size and strength through proper technique. Second, he convinced Knotts not to take his size and strength as a given. He persuaded the kid that he had the potential to be even better through hard work and a disciplined off-season workout regimen. It was O'Rourke who first introduced Knotts to the "Standards and Principles of Preparation."

The other kid was a wrestler named Rick Richart. Richart had a passion for the sport, and O'Rourke realized that with a little coaching and some understanding he had the opportunity to convert the boy into an outstanding wrestler who could perform well beyond his own expectations—not unlike his own change under Mehrens.

A high school wrestler himself, O'Rourke had a solid foundation in the sport and worked with Richart until he, too, had mastered the basics and could do them instinctively. Like Mehrens, his coaching style emphasized repetition.

Over the course of the season, O'Rourke also came to learn more about Richart as a person. He learned that he was the son of a hard-working World War II veteran, who was fond of administering a lot of old-fashioned discipline at home but was incapable of providing any positive reinforcement. O'Rourke sensed Richart was the kind of kid who responded better to carrots than to the stick, and therefore provided him with ample doses of positive encouragement.

O'Rourke also came to appreciate that Richart had a lot of energy and an aggressive personality. He understood that if those traits were not channeled properly, he was the kind of kid who could easily take the wrong path in life. O'Rourke knew wrestling was Richart's salvation and set about giving him some tangible goals toward which to strive.

After a few heart-to-heart discussions, the goal of winning a state championship was settled upon. Although Richart was only an eighth grader at the time, O'Rourke didn't let that fact deter them.

The next best thing was an Amateur Athletic Union (AAU) championship, and in the spring of 1970, O'Rourke, recognizing his own limited wrestling coaching skills could only take the rapidly improving Richart so far, contacted a more experienced wrestling coach and encouraged him to take Richart under his wing. Under the new coach's tutelage, Richart eventually made it to the Western Washington AAU finals, where he finished second in his weight class.

1994

In the summer of 1979, John O'Rourke moved across the river and accepted another teaching and coaching job at Columbia River High School, where he became a social studies teacher and the assistant head football coach. He held the assistant football coaching job for 15 years. It was only in 1994, after the longtime head coach retired, that O'Rourke assumed the top job.

Over the years, amid the flood of kids he coached, Richart and Knotts faded from his memory. Neither man, however, forgot about O'Rourke. Both men stayed in the Portland-Vancouver area and eventually got married and started families. Years later, when both of their sons were ready to play football, there was only one thing they desired for their sons—the opportunity to play under and be coached by John O'Rourke.

Lonnie Knotts' son, Billy, became a three-year starter for O'Rourke and graduated in 1999—a season Columbia River went 10–1 and fell one game short of winning the Washington state championship. Billy went on to play college football at Washington State University and was the starting right tackle on the team that played in the 2003 Rose Bowl.

At the end of the 1999 season, Lonnie Knotts wrote his old coach a short note and framed it with a series of digital pictures of O'Rourke applying his trade on the sidelines of a series of different high school football games. It read:

> *This has been a very special four years for me in many ways. It seems like just yesterday that I was a freshman looking up at Coach O'Rourke. I've been especially excited knowing that my son was living the same wonderful experiences I had with you almost 28 years ago. This last season has been an incredible ride, and it will hold many great memories for all of us, but as the years have gone by, I have to come to realize that the game itself is not important. What is important are the lessons that you have taught us like honor, integrity, the value of hard work, and the will to never, ever quit. These qualities have helped me overcome the challenges of life. These lessons that were given to me over 28 years ago, by the same coach, have now been passed on to my son and is a gift I can never repay. We have been truly blessed to have such a role model for us to look up to. As a young man, those many years ago, I could not possibly realize the true gift you had given me.*
>
> *So, for myself, my son, and the thousands of other young men whose lives you have touched, I say thank you.*
> *Lonnie Knotts*

Richart's son, Casey, purposefully transferred from his high school and friends in Portland, Oregon, to play at Columbia River. A talented but quiet kid, Casey also blossomed and grew under O'Rourke's guidance. The father was so pleased with the results—Casey Richart was twice named to the all-conference team—that he nominated him for the Educator of the Year award in the state of Washington. His letter read, in part:

> *Mr. O'Rourke has been an educator in the Vancouver School District for 35+ years. Thirty-four years ago he was my teacher and wrestling coach during my junior high school days.*
>
> *I am now a 47-year-old man. I consider Mr. O'Rourke's teaching and influence a key element in my life. Myself and others, I'm sure, could have easily chosen a different, less desirable path. Thank heavens for good teachers like John.*
>
> *Looking back, I remember that even as a young man, fresh out of college, he was a teacher who had a calm, loving demeanor. He inspired achievement in both genders then, and does so now. Ask any of the Columbia River kids who have him as a teacher, and the message is clear. He cares, and he loves them.*
>
> *My son now plays football at Columbia River and has Mr. O'Rourke as a teacher and is receiving the same valuable lessons that I did so many years ago. John O'Rourke is truly a man of positive influence and deserving of the Educator of the Year award.*
>
> *Thank you for your consideration.*
> *Rick Richart*

The real testament to O'Rourke's influence as a coach, however, came during Columbia River's annual end of the season football banquet. Casey's senior year was marred by an early season injury and then a severe bout of mononucleosis. Yet, in spite of his limited play and quiet demeanor, he was asked by his teammates to give the final speech at the banquet.

Casey spoke little of the season itself and even less of football. Rather, he spoke in eloquent terms about how O'Rourke and the other assistant coaches—to whom O'Rourke acted as a mentor— had helped him and his teammates become not just better football players but better people.

In his 11 years as a head football coach, John O'Rourke has

compiled a record of 86–30. But as Casey went on to note in his remarks, O'Rourke's real influence is not found in his record; it is found in the fact that although Columbia River is a high school with a student population of just over 1,000, he still consistently gets over 120 kids to come out for football on an annual basis. The reason, Richart said, is because although most players know their playing time will be limited, they understand O'Rourke's real talent is not just turning students into football players, he shapes and molds boys and turns them into men.

WEEK THREE GAME PLAN:
You Can Do This

COACHING FOR LIFE TIP #3:

Identify individual's skills and nurture confidence.

QUOTE TO REMEMBER:

"It is a fine thing to have ability, but the ability to discover ability it in others is the true test."—Elbert Hubbard

KEY QUESTIONS TO ANSWER:

Have you determined how much undeveloped or under-developed talent exists in your organization? Are you willing to accept responsibility for tapping into and harnessing this talent?

Learning You Can Do This

1. How did Mehrens help instill confidence in John O'Rourke?

2. How did the coaches work to "demystify" certain obstacles?

3. What was their secret to getting players to become "overachievers"?

4. How did they use a player's personal goal to help them overcome obstacles?

5. How do you instill confidence in your protégés?

"Our greatest glory

is not in never failing,

but in rising up

every time we fail."

—RALPH WALDO EMERSON

DUST YOURSELF OFF

Jerry Kuntz's, Mike Walsh's, Clark Kochivar's, and
Bob Murray's Stories

November 25, 1961

ore than 40 years later the memory still
lingers—seared into a small crevice deep
in the recesses of Jerry Kuntz's mind. And if asked
about the incident today, it is clear that he is still
not comfortable speaking about it.

In the fall of 1961 after his junior season of
football, Kuntz attended the annual Great Falls
Central football banquet. It was a fun, festive,
upbeat affair—even in a season when the Mustangs
only went 5–3. Father Harvey Livix had pulled his
usual magical strings and arranged for Murray
Warmath, head football coach of the University of

119

Minnesota—winner of the previous year's Rose Bowl—to come to Great Falls and address the members of the team, their families, fans, and members of GFC Roundtable.

Before introducing Warmath, banquet protocol required that Mehrens first distribute the highly sought after "GFC" letter to those players who had contributed enough playing time to earn the award, thus gaining the right to wear the highly coveted letter sweater—the closest thing the high school had to a male status symbol. Before awarding the letter, Mehrens offered up a few remarks about each player's contributions, and if the boy would be returning, he would make some comments about his expectations of the person for the upcoming season.

One by one Mehrens called out the letter winners. When he came to Jerry Kuntz, he began by praising his work ethic and noted that it was as much a product of his upbringing as it was of his personality. As he ticked off a number of contributions Kuntz made as the starting defensive halfback, the tall, lean kid with the over-sized nose and the wide gap between his teeth walked toward the podium and took his place next to the head coach. As he did, Mehrens said he felt that Kuntz needed to bulk up a little and added that he was looking forward to him returning to the starting position as halfback the next season, "provided he sufficiently recovers from his severe case of fumbleitis." Mehrens intended no harm, and the audience laughed at the gentle ribbing, but the comment struck a raw nerve in Kuntz.

To understand the pain, one first had to understand that ever since the seventh grade—when he had watched Mehrens win his first state championship at Great Falls Central—all Jerry Kuntz had ever wanted to do was play football under him. The dream had come true earlier in the year when he broke into the starting lineup on both offense and defense. But after fumbling in two consecutive games midway through the season, Mehrens unceremoniously yanked Kuntz from his running back position and replaced him with Voyd Richtscheid—a sophomore no less.

It was one of the most humiliating things Kuntz had ever had to endure in his short 17 years. As a typical teenager, every moment he stood on the sidelines "warming the bench," he imagined that his teammates as well as the fans were as conscious of his shortcoming as he was.

And now, here on the podium, in front of hundreds of people, his failing was again publicly exposed for all to see.

"Luckily," Mehrens continued, "the disease has a cure. It's called 'hard work,' and I know Mr. Kuntz will take his medicine every day."

In spite of the soft landing his coach provided, the rest of the evening Kuntz burned with a feeling that he had let his coach down and vowed to himself that he was not going to fumble in his senior year—not a single time.

As Kuntz headed out the door of the Rainbow Hotel, where the banquet was traditionally held, Father Livix grabbed him by the arm. Always very sensitive to his students' feelings, Livix knew that the fumble comment probably had the effect of pouring salt in an open wound for Kuntz, and he tried to reinforce Mehrens' message. "Just keep working, Mr. Kuntz, and remember this: If you do your best...angels can do no better."

June 4, 1962

At the end of his junior year, as was true of almost every other teenage boy in Great Falls, Kuntz had to find a job. Unlike most of the other Great Falls Central players, however, he opted for a job outside of town and spent his summer working on a cattle ranch in the Highwood Mountains about 40 miles east of Great Falls.

He did so for a complex set of reasons. First, Kuntz needed the money, and a ranch job was about the best paying job a high school kid from Montana could get in 1962. The Kuntzs were one of the less well-off families at Great Falls Central. They lived on the lower south side that, in addition to being the rougher and poorer section of town, had the distinction of being home to the few black and American Indian families that lived in the city at the time. His father busted his back working a $70-a-week job, stripping zinc at the Anaconda Mining Company, and his mother—when she wasn't busy having kids—worked for tips at The Barrell café, a greasy spoon diner that catered to the workers employed at the smelter.

And while the Kuntzs never considered themselves poor—there was always food on the table, and they were able to set aside just enough extra money to send their kids to Catholic school—Jerry's job out at the ranch meant one less mouth to feed for three months. And for a growing teenager weighing 160 pounds, the amount of food and milk he consumed was not insubstantial.

The extra money that Kuntz earned on the ranch not only meant that he could repay his mother, who had emptied her tip jar—which contained a few weeks' worth of tips—to buy him a letter sweater. The money might also spare Kuntz, at least for a month or two, the humiliation of having to hand deliver the monthly utility bill the day it was due.

The second reason he took the job was because he simply wanted to get out of the house. He was tired of sharing his bed with his little brother; the small bedroom with his other two brothers; and a single bathroom with his entire family—especially his four sisters.

The third reason Kuntz wanted to work out in the country was more practical. Kuntz remained embarrassed over his "fumbleitis," and he wanted to practice running with the football. But that was not something he could do in the city without drawing unwanted attention to himself. The vast and lonely expanse of the Highwood plains, on the other hand, offered the ideal environment for discreetly taking his daily dose of "medicine" and curing himself of his fumbleitis.

And so it was that for an entire summer, Jerry Kuntz, after

working a good 12 hours picking up bales of hay, would spend his evenings carrying an old leather football under his arm. As he jogged along the rolling dirt roads of the ranch at dusk, he would switch the ball from hand to hand and visualize getting hit and holding on to the ball. Occasionally, he would toss it up in the air or flip it behind his back to hone his reflexes.

By summer's end, Kuntz had come to know the feel of the football as well as the back of his well calloused hands, and after lifting thousands of bales of hay, his once lean body had been transformed into a solid, sinewy combination of strength and speed.

August 22, 1962, 9:15 a.m.

Mehrens continued his policy of meeting with four players every day after practice to discuss their goals for the upcoming season. He smiled as he reviewed Kuntz's note card before calling the quiet halfback into his office. The first personal goal Kuntz listed— even before earning a college scholarship—was "No fumbles."

Upon being called in, the boy nervously placed himself opposite Mehrens' stark steel desk, which was barren except for a football that sat motionless on the corner. "I'm happy to see that you don't intend to fumble this year," said Mehrens, refusing to engage his players in idle chitchat when the more pressing matters of football needed to be discussed. "But it is expected, as a matter of course, that running backs on my team will *not* fumble." Kuntz's throat drew tight, and his face turned a brighter shade of red. He summoned every ounce of courage he possessed and continued to look squarely into Mehrens' eyes. He held the coach's stare.

"Let's discuss the other two goals," said Mehrens finally, letting him off the hook. For the first few minutes, Mehrens outlined his expectations for Kuntz and made it clear that he expected him to play a major role on offense, defense, and special teams. Kuntz was surprised at how much time and attention Mehrens devoted to his responsibilities as a punt returner, but he listened intently.

123

The coach then, as he had done with so many of his other players, honed in on Kuntz's third goal—winning a college scholarship. "How you perform in the next three months could well determine your future," said Mehrens. "It could be the difference between going to college or," tossing his head in the direction of the smelter plant, "working over there." Kuntz understood exactly what he meant. "You don't have the speed or size to play at a big college, but you do have the skills and work ethic to succeed at a school such as Montana or Montana State." Kuntz figured as much himself, but it was still gratifying to have his coach confirm his feelings.

"But you can't let up," continued Mehrens. "Someone like Berry is going to earn a scholarship on sheer talent alone. You can't count on that. You have to bust your hump on every play and use every practice to get better. I can tell already that you must have spent a lot of time lifting weights this summer."

"Baling hay," said Kuntz, softly correcting him.

"Even better," replied Mehrens, "but you can't afford to let up even for a single moment. It might be unfair, but people like you—and by that I mean most people—only succeed through hard work."

Mehrens knew exactly what he was talking about. Like Kuntz, he had been an undersized halfback in high school before going on to star at Carroll College.

May 1964

Aided with a strong recommendation from Mehrens, Kuntz received a scholarship to play football at Montana State starting in the fall of 1963. After he arrived at Bozeman, the combination of too much freedom and tougher than expected academic requirements caused his grade point average to dip below the standard necessary to stay eligible. He did not return for the spring semester.

Three thousand miles away in Miami, Wally Berry was having an equally hard go of it, and his more heralded college football career came to an equally ignominious end.

And so it was by spring of 1964, Kuntz and Berry both dropped out of college and returned to Great Falls. The two old friends reconnected and went to work for the Montana highway department, where they helped construct the new interstate highway system going across the state. Both, however, recognized that with things heating up in Vietnam, it was only a matter of time before the draft board caught up with them, so one day the pair went down to the Air Force recruiter in town to enlist.

Together, they took the standard physical and suffered through the usual assortment of small indignities. They were halfway through the mechanical aptitude test when an older doctor called Kuntz back into his office.

"Young man," he said after a few pleasantries, "you're a walking time bomb. Your blood pressure is 210 over 120, and that makes you ineligible for military service." Kuntz was stunned. "I don't know if that makes you happy or sad," continued the doctor, "but at the present time you have more serious issues to think about. High blood pressure is treatable, but you've got to start taking care of yourself." The doctor then suggested the name of a local doctor and brusquely escorted Kuntz out of his office.

For the third time in less than a half year, Kuntz's future had suffered a serious setback. First, his football career had ended, then his college career, and now even the military—a sure thing in the mid 1960s—had been denied him.

Kuntz returned to his job with the highway department, but his life seemed adrift. The feeling of failure—the feeling of "fumbleitis"—and the nagging thought that he had let both his family and Coach Mehrens down began to weigh on him.

A chance assignment landed him out near the Highwood Ranch where only two years before his life and his future had seemed so bright. As he labored under the hot Montana sun, he often found his mind wandering back to the evenings he had spent jogging and practicing holding the ball. He recalled with some pride how his hard work had paid off—he began the season with a touchdown, added six more during the regular season, and capped it off with a spectacular finish.

A second chance encounter reinforced the message. One early morning as he was preparing to leave for work, he bumped into Mehrens, who was working his summer job of delivering milk. Embarrassed at his present status, Kuntz confessed to his old coach that he wouldn't be returning to Bozeman in the fall.

He could tell Mehrens was disappointed. In fact, Mehrens did little to hide his displeasure. He understood better than Kuntz himself the great opportunity he had been given, but rather than harp on the negative, Mehrens chose to offer his old player one more coaching lesson.

"We all make mistakes," he said, "but our mistakes only become failures when we refuse to change them."

As the summer construction season wore on and he continued the tedious task of spreading hot boiling asphalt, Kuntz reflected on Mehrens' remarks. He thought about the 1962 season and, specifically, why he had succeeded. He came to realize that it was nothing but hard work. He decided that if he could do it in football, he could do the same thing in college.

Armed with a scholarship from the highway department, Kuntz returned to Montana State in the fall of 1964 with a new attitude. He graduated with honors in 1968 and soon landed a job at an elementary school in Great Falls, where he coached football, basketball, and track.

In 1973, he returned to Montana State for his master's degree in educational administration and went on to continue his teaching and coaching career at a local junior high in Great Falls. In 1981, he became a counselor at Charles M. Russell High School. He also became the head golf coach, a sport he had taken up in college.

August 22, 1962

Only at the end of his goal setting session with Kuntz did Mehrens return to his first goal and the topic of fumbling. He had heard through the grapevine—actually it was a very sophisticated network of GFC Roundtable members from whom Mehrens gathered and dispersed news and information on the progress and development of his players—that Kuntz had spent his summer practicing holding the football. Mehrens knew the problem was now more mental than physical.

"You and I both know that you had trouble holding on to the ball last season. That season is behind us. Your job is now to focus on *this* season. As a senior, you need to lead by example. What that means is that it is time for you to stop thinking about yourself and start thinking about the team. The issue of your fumbling has less to do with you—and more to do with the success of the team. If you concentrate on executing your running and blocking assignments and less on holding on to the ball, you'll be fine. In fact, I'm confident you will achieve your goal." Mehrens paused to assess whether his message was sinking in. "What I'm saying is this: Just concentrate on playing football. I have watched you play since you were a seventh grader at Lady of the Lourdes. You're a fine athlete and a good player—a very good player. Now just go out and have some fun. The greatest mistake you can make is being afraid of making another one." For the first time, Kuntz smiled.

"Now call in Mr. Walsh," said Mehrens. It was his way of saying that their conversation was over. As Kuntz walked out of his office, Mehrens called his name and tossed the football that had been sitting on his desk directly at Kuntz's back. By the time he turned around, the ball was already on top of him and thumped off his chest. Instinctively, he reached out and pulled it into his chest like an old pro. "Nice catch," said Mehrens. "Just remember this—you have got everything you need to meet all of your goals.

Everything is right in there," said Mehrens, tapping lightly on his own chest, "in your heart."

May 2003

Jerry Kuntz had just started his twenty-second year as the head golf coach of the Charles Russell High School in Great Falls. During that time he had coached hundreds of kids, won two state championships, and was named Montana Golf Coach of the Year three times.

A few matches into the 2003 season, his team was again performing well, especially the star of his team. The boy had been the team's top performer since his sophomore year, and at great expense to his parents who had devoted a considerable portion of their discretionary income to private golf lessons over the past summer, he had become even better. He was widely expected to lead Charles M. Russell High School to its third title and to challenge for the state's top individual honors.

In late April, however, his game began to unravel, and a week before the state team championship tournament he was in a full blown slump. The pressure was becoming intense, because it was always the boy's goal—as well as his parents'—that he would become the state golfing champion of Montana. As his slump continued, the dream appeared to be in serious jeopardy. The boy felt pressure from everyone, especially himself and his family. In the process, he forgot that he was still a member of the team. He was only concerned with his personal goals.

Kuntz continued to work with the boy, but whenever he thought he had made some progress, the following day the teenager would come back with a new glitch in his game—the result of his father's well-intentioned but counterproductive dinner table advice.

The first round of the Kalispell Invitational, the last tournament before the State AA Championship, was played under cool and extremely gusty conditions. After bogeying the eighteenth hole, his star golfer finished a disappointing nine-over par. Before Kuntz could reach him, the boy was buttonholed by his less than pleased father. "I could've saved a boat load of money and just had you practice your short game at the putt-putt!" Kuntz instinctively stepped between the pair and shot the father an icy stare before he could inflict anymore psychological damage to the boy—who was already in a fragile condition.

"Let's go get a Coke," Kuntz said, putting his arm around the discouraged boy, steering him away from his father and toward the clubhouse. After the staff delivered two Cokes, Kuntz began the conversation, "Do you remember Mike Hansen?"

"Of course, he won the state individual championship the year I was a freshman."

"That's right. You know I saw him a few weeks ago while he was home on spring break. You know what he told me?" The teenager just shrugged his shoulders. "He said that while he was proud of his individual championship, the greatest disappointment of his high school career was losing the team championship twice to Billings by a single stroke. He said he would have gladly given up his individual championship for the team championship."

"Really?" The boy's tone suggested he didn't quite believe it.

"I'm not kidding. He said what still gnaws at him is the putt he missed on the first hole in sudden death. If he would have hit that five footer for a birdie, Charles Russell—and not Billings—would have won the team championship. To this day he feels as though he let his teammates down—think about that. How well would you sleep at night knowing you soured a lifelong memory for five of your teammates?" Kuntz paused to let the statement sink in.

"I can tell you from experience that the accomplishments you will look back on in your life with the greatest sense of pride aren't your individual achievements—and you're going to have a lot, believe me—they are the team victories."

A spark seemed to register in the kid's eyes, and Kuntz sensed it. "Look, I know you're under a lot of pressure—I heard what your father was saying to you out there. First, let me tell you that it's just not true. Second, you've just got to forget it—put it behind you. What you have to do is stop thinking about yourself and start thinking about the team. This is your senior year. You are the undisputed leader of this team. You still have 54 holes of golf left, and your teammates are still out on the course. You can either wallow in self-pity, or you can take some initiative and act like a leader. The choice is up to you."

The boy finished his Coke and was about to depart when Kuntz leaned over the table and said, "You know what happened to that kid who won three straight tournaments last month? Well," said Kuntz thumping the kid's chest, "he's still right there." A slight smile crept across the boy's face. "You've got everything you need to help this team win the championship *and* obtain your personal goal." Kuntz tapped the boy's chest again and said, "It's all right there—just where it's always been."

For the first time in his career after a less than stellar round, the boy stayed behind and greeted his teammates as they completed their rounds. After the first round was complete, the Charles M. Russell Rustlers were well within striking distance in third place. And, much to his surprise, his nine-over par left him only three shots off the individual lead.

The next day, the boy found his game again. He shot a one-under par 71 and won the tournament championship.

The following week, he shot an amazing 66 the first day and not only won the individual championship, but in an exciting playoff that had a bit of poetic justice, he sank a 15-foot putt on the eighteenth hole to give the Rustlers a one-shot victory over the same Billings team that had beaten them for the state championship only a few years before.

August 22, 1962

Mike Walsh silently walked past Jerry Kuntz and took his place before Coach Mehrens. "How do you feel?" asked Mehrens, who kept a close eye on Walsh and was concerned that the warm afternoon temperature and two-a-day practices might be placing too much strain on the player and his ailing heart.

"I'm fine, Coach. All I'm doing is kicking the football." Which, by doctors' orders, was all he could do since he had been diagnosed with a heart murmur the previous year.

"I know it's frustrating, especially for an athlete of your caliber, but until Doc MacGregor gives me the okay, your playing time is going to be limited." Walsh nodded his head in understanding. "That doesn't mean your contributions to this team are going to be limited though. You'll be doing all the kicking this year—kickoffs and extra points. And I can almost guarantee you that at least once this season you will be the difference between us winning and losing a game. The question is: Which do you want that to be?"

"A win, sir," replied Walsh with great sincerity.

"I know. And that's why I expect you to devote all your time and energy to kicking. It might get repetitive. It might get boring, and I'm sure you'll feel that no one appreciates your contributions—but you have a responsibility to your teammates."

"It's just that I can contribute so much more. I have been kicking all summer. I could play scout team quarterback, or I could—"

"I know it's hard," said Mehrens, cutting him off, "but this is what being a member of a team is all about. Now, just do your part, practice your kicks, and believe me, your teammates will know that you did everything in your power to help them win."

September 18, 1962, 9:55 a.m.

Clark Kochivar, the sophomore backup halfback, was storing his books in his locker between his second and third hour class when he spotted Bob Kuntz. "Nice photo in today's paper," he said. Kochivar was referring to a large photo on the front page of the *Great Falls Tribune*. It pictured Jerry and Dick Kuntz, their cousin, Bob Kuntz, and Bob Kunz, and it ran under the headline of "Confusing, isn't it?"

"I guess my cover is blown," said Bob Kuntz. "I've been telling all the girls that it was me and not Jerry who was our starting halfback." Kochivar just laughed. He had been friends with Bob since grade school, and the two often teased each other.

"Where are you off to?" he then asked.

"Religion III," replied Kuntz.

"With Mother Mary James?"

"Yup."

"Good luck. What's she pounding into your thick skull today?"

"A discussion of the Ten Commandants."

"Sounds fascinating...you'd better pay attention."

Mother Mary James, like the majority of other instructors at Central, wasn't interested in rote memorization. She wanted her students to reflect upon topics in the light of the Bible. "Did you know," she said to her class, "that a lawyer once asked Jesus this question: 'Which is the greatest commandment in the law?'" She allowed her class to consider the question for a moment. "And what, Mr. Kuntz, do you think he said?"

Kuntz stared at his hands for a moment and then replied, "I'm sorry, Sister, I don't know."

She turned her attention to Mike Walsh. "And what about you, Mr. Walsh?" His response was the same as Bob Kuntz's. She asked a few more students and received the same result.

"Jesus said, *'Thou shall love the Lord thy God with all thy heart, and with all thy soul, and with all thy mind.'* And for the second greatest, Jesus said, *'Thou shall love thy neighbor as thyself.'* He then added, 'On these two commandments hang all the law.' I start today's section on the Ten Commandments with this story, because if you follow these two simple commandments, all the others will fall into place." It was a lesson Mother Mary James repeated often.

September 18, 1962, 4:00 p.m.

"Punt receiving formation!" Mehrens yelled after an hour and 15 minutes into practice. Jerry Kuntz ran to the south end of the field and awaited the kick from McMahon, who was acting as surrogate punter. The former Carroll College football player booted a long, low kick, and Kuntz caught it on the fly. He got only five yards before being drilled by Clark Kochivar, a scrappy sophomore. "Nice hit, Kochivar," said Mehrens, before launching in a scathing assessment of the first team's performance.

To no one in particular and everyone in general, Mehrens yelled, "Let's do it again." He blew his whistle, and the players sprinted to get back into punt formation. McMahon booted another high punt, and Kuntz was barely able to get under it before members of the coverage team were on top of him.

"No! No! No!" hollered McMahon. "The second team was all over Kuntz like flies on..." Tossing the ball to Tom Strizich, the team's third-string quarterback, McMahon ordered him to throw the ball in lieu of him punting so that he could stay on the sidelines and assess the performance of his linemen.

For the third time the whistle was blown. Strizich arched the ball as far as his 145-pound frame could heave it. Kuntz received the ball and after juking two defenders was tackled for a modest seven-yard gain.

"Murray," McMahon screamed at Bob Murray, the team's starting left guard, "we're in punt receiving formation. Your job is to get downfield and set up your blocking assignment. What are you trying to block the punt for?" McMahon could see that Murray was actually going to answer his rhetorical question so he grabbed him by the face mask and said, "Look, all I want you to do is get your butt downfield and take up your proper position in the wall." The "wall" was a standard blocking scheme for punts and kickoffs that required the offensive line to fall back and, depending on whether it was a right or left formation, post themselves five yards apart from the other linemen and about five yards from the sideline, creating an alley for the kick returner to run down.

"Punt formation left," called Mehrens. Strizich heaved the ball again, this time sending it over to the left side of the field. Kuntz easily fielded the ball and raced up the sideline before getting hit.

This time it was Mehrens' opportunity to do the critiquing. "Kuntz, what are you doing?" The tone clearly suggested his comment was more a criticism than a question. "If you run immediately to the left, the defenders are going to know you're going that way, and you make it that much harder for your linemen to construct a solid wall. You also make it harder on yourself because it allows the defenders to get a better angle on you—so if you want to get your bell rung, just keep doing what you're doing. If you don't, I suggest you try breaking toward the middle. If you do that, you'll do two things: one, you'll give your linemen a decent chance to set up the wall; and two, you'll spread out the defense because they have to respect the possibility you might run up the middle." Finishing his brief tutorial, Mehrens cried out, "Let's do it again!"

As Wally Berry jogged back to the line, he muttered, "We've got better things to do than practice this punting. Punting is for babies," in a tone not loud enough to be heard by the coaches but loud enough to signal his discontent.

"What did you say, Berry?" asked McMahon.

"Nothing, Coach."

"I don't believe you," said McMahon, who knew enough about Berry to know that it was some type of smart-aleck comment. "Drop and give me 25!"

Berry casually went to the ground. "Make it 35, pretty boy,

and keep your head up and your butt down. If I catch you rubber-necking your push-ups, I'm going to make you do it again, and you'll be doing 50—on your fingertips!"

Picking up on Berry's sense of frustration, Mehrens chimed in, "We're going to keep doing this until we get it right, and when we do, we're then going to practice our extra points." The last comment was directed at Mike Walsh, who provided the only sour note in the previous week's impressive victory over Butte Central by missing three extra points.

For the remainder of the week, Mehrens devoted a disproportionately large portion of each practice to both the punting and the kicking game. Often, the coaches would run the play as many as 11 times so they could isolate on each player at least one time.

Finally, the day before the Glasgow game, the players had taken about all they could of the punt practices. A number of linemen got together and decided to take out their frustrations by blocking one of McMahon's punts.

McMahon, who had resumed the punting duties in an effort to give Kuntz a more realistic experience fielding punts, took the snap, but before he could even take a step and get his foot on the ball, Murray and Flaherty broke through the middle of the line as two others crashed in from the sides. The ball—along with McMahon's legs—was driven backward. Suppressing a grimace, McMahon flashed a smile. (Only 40 years later did he admit his leg was severely bruised on the play.)

Mehrens couldn't help but smile at his players' aggressive attitude and decided that it was an appropriate time to switch to practicing extra points. Eleven times the first team lined up to kick the extra point, and 11 times Mike Walsh kicked it straight through the crossbars. After the final kick, Mehrens concluded that that was a sufficiently positive note to wrap up the final practice before the Glasgow game. He called for his team to gather around him. After they unstrapped their helmets, Mehrens told them to take a knee. "This is the best Glasgow team we've ever faced. They have not yet allowed a touchdown this season. Their 13–0 victory over Wolf Point was expected, but they beat up on Laurel last week, and that tells me these guys are tough. We can't afford to look past them. One of the reasons I have had you guys practicing punts, kickoffs, and extra points so much is because that is where close games are won and lost. I want all of you to focus on your assignments and your jobs, especially on special teams. If you do that, we'll win."

September 21, 1962

The Great Falls Central Mustangs were still riding high after their decisive season opening victory over Butte Central. It was the Mustangs' first-ever victory over the larger school, and by a rare scheduling quirk they had a bye the following week. They were confident, well rested, well prepared, and had every reason to be motivated. In short, everything looked promising for a second victory over the Glasgow Scotties.

The Mustangs, however, came out surprisingly flat, and although they moved the ball effectively, they were unable to put any points on the board. At halftime the game was tied 0–0.

During the intermission, Mehrens gathered his team in the small hut at the south end of the field. He then took the unusual step of asking Father Livix, who had come to offer the team some encouragement, to leave. He was afraid he might use some language that would offend the priest's sensibilities. Once Livix was gone, he proceeded to lambaste his team. "This is *our* home field. This is *our* first home game. Your parents, your teachers, and your classmates deserve better! And the members of the Roundtable deserve better! Do any of you realize how much effort the Roundtable puts into this team to get it on the field?" The room was silent. "Well, let me tell you. Romeo Ranieri spends his entire two-week vacation every year going door-to-door to every business

in Great Falls in order to get them to advertise in the football program—and he doesn't even have a kid playing on the team. Mr.
Dywer spent a week remodeling and installing new lockers in the
locker room. Mr. Flaherty painted every one of your helmets, and
Mr. Kochivar busted his back to raise the funds so that we could
take a nice coach bus to all of our away games. Why do they do it?"
Mehrens paused. "I'll tell you why...because they believe in you.
Now, the least you can do is to give 100 percent! You have a
responsibility to your parents and our community supporters to do
that!" By the time he was done, Mehrens had dropped a few
unsanctioned words but had succeeded in whipping up his
Mustangs into a wild frenzy—perhaps too much so.

Great Falls opened the second half by kicking off. Mike Walsh's
short kick was caught by the Scotties' fastest runner, Charlie Parker,
at the 15-yard line. Parker darted to the right and a mass of adren-
aline-rushed Mustangs flowed in his direction. In their zealousness, they over pursued, and when Parker cut back toward the middle, a huge hole had developed. Parker broke one tackle and then
simply outran Walsh, who, while athletic, could not match his
speed. Eleven seconds and 85 yards later, the score was 6–0. The
successful extra point made it 7–0.

In the third quarter, the Mustangs twice moved the ball down
within Glasgow's 20-yard line. But both times they came away
empty-handed. Once a touchdown was called back after Byron
Weber, the right end, had uncharacteristically lined up offside. A
second time, the drive stalled when the Mustangs were unable to
push the ball across for a score after having a first-and-goal from
the seven-yard line. Part of the problem was the Scotties' tena-
cious defense. Another part of the problem seemed to be that John
O'Rourke, the team's second-string quarterback who was still starting in place of the injured Gary Wolf, seemed to have used up all
of his potential in the previous game against Butte Central.

As the game moved into the fourth quarter, the home crowd

began to grow restless as the Mustangs failed to move the ball any closer than the 20-yard line. With just over two minutes left, and only one time-out remaining, the crowd fell silent as the home team was again forced to turn the ball over on a punt. The Glasgow Scotties needed only one first down to run out the clock and secure its third victory of the season.

On their first play from the line of scrimmage, Glasgow tried a sweep around the right end, but the fleet Charlie Parker ran smack into the outstretched arms of Bruce Campbell, who hammered him to the ground. On second down, after running off as much of the clock as possible, the Scotties called for a play right up the middle. Flaherty, sensing the conservative play, blitzed up the middle and caught the runner three yards behind the line of scrimmage. The home crowd stirred back to life.

As the clock ticked under 30 seconds, the defense knew their moment had arrived. If they could keep the Scotties from getting a first down and then call a time-out, it was possible that they would have a shot at getting the ball back.

Again, the Scotties played it conservatively and attempted a sweep around the left side. Berry, who had keyed in on Parker, broke through a block and drove him into the ground for another three-yard loss. Jumping up, he signaled for Great Falls' final time-out. Twelve seconds remained on the clock.

Positioned at their own 13-yard line, Mehrens and McMahon both realized all Glasgow had to do was have their punter take the snap and run out of the end zone for a safety. If he did, the game would end in a 7–2 Glasgow victory.

On the sideline, McMahon took a moment to pray that the Scotties' head coach would punt the ball and give the Mustangs a remote chance at salvaging a tie.

Mehrens and McMahon then conferred and agreed on "punt formation right." McMahon called his linemen to gather around him. "As soon as they punt, I want you to haul your butts back as fast as you can and set up the wall." He grabbed the thin, plastic face mask on Bob Murray's helmet and, nearly lifting him off the ground, asked, "Do you understand me?" Murray nodded. "Good, then I want you to nail the first guy you see in a red uniform."

Turning to the rest of the line, McMahon said, "That goes for all of you. I want each of you to put someone on the grass. Now listen, we're going to score a touchdown, and you're the ones who are going to make it happen! If anyone here doesn't believe that, then sit down and I'll put someone in who does." No one sat down.

A few feet away, Mehrens had pulled Kuntz aside and, in a calm voice that was the polar opposite of his excited assistant coach's, said, "Don't get ahead of yourself. Just catch the ball, head toward the middle of the field, and then veer back right. The wall will be there for you, okay?" Kuntz said nothing, but Mehrens could see that his punt returner didn't have the necessary confidence that the situation required.

Mehrens put his hand on Kuntz's shoulder pads and said, "Just do it like we've been doing it in practice all week." Then, just as Kuntz was about to leave to take up his position at the 50-yard line, Mehrens added, "There's no one I would rather have returning this punt. Now go get us a touchdown."

On the opposing sideline, Darrel Hueth, the head coach of the Scotties, called his team together. "We're going to punt," he said simply. He offered no explanation, but his reasoning was simple—after shutting out his first two opponents and holding Great Falls Central scoreless for the entire game, he had no intention of allowing two meager points to blemish his perfect record and ruin his chance for a third consecutive shutout. "Get downfield and make the tackle," he said in an even voice, "just like you've done all season."

Time seemed to freeze for a moment as both sides squared up against each other. The referee blew his whistle to signal that the play could start. Forty yards downfield Jerry Kuntz reflected on all the hours he had spent holding and catching the football over the previous summer and thought to himself, *I can do this.*

The Scottie punter held on to the ball for a moment before unleashing a long, low punt. The extra second gave the Mustang linemen that much more time to get downfield and in their positions. On the sideline, McMahon breathed a sigh of relief. "They actually punted," he muttered, shaking his head in disbelief.

The ball sliced through the warm air of the Montana evening, and its sharp angle and low trajectory gave Kuntz no time to think. He sprinted toward the ball, caught it in full stride, and headed toward the middle of the field. Then, whether it was Mehrens' last minute advice or pure instinct after running the play dozens of times in practice, Kuntz slashed back and headed toward the right side of the field. By the time he reached the 40-yard line, the clock read :05. To his immediate left, Wally Berry leveled a vicious block on an oncoming Scottie. The hit allowed Kuntz to get behind the first man in the wall. As he did, he marveled at what he saw. His teammates had constructed the perfect wall. A Glasgow defender tried to breech the wall but ran into Murray, who let out a primordial scream worthy of his nickname, "The Animal," and savagely repelled him back. Every other Mustang player laid a hit on someone in a red uniform, and the wall held up.

As Kuntz approached the goal line, the clock turned to :00, and a referee fired a small cap gun whose sound was drowned out in the screams of the home crowd. A second later, Kuntz galloped into the end zone untouched.

On the sideline, while everyone else celebrated, Mehrens calmly pulled Mike Walsh aside. "We're kicking it." At the time, an extra point, regardless of whether it was kicked or run in, was only worth one point. (If the two-point rule would have been in place, Mehrens would have undoubtedly gone for it.) As it was, his decision was a supreme vote of confidence in the junior who had missed three of his five kicks against Butte Central.

Mehrens' instructions were simple. "Just punch it over the bar like you have been doing all week in practice." Walsh confidently nodded, and Mehrens slapped him on the helmet. Mehrens then grabbed Billy Sprinkle, the holder, and ordered him out to the field with the instruction that they would be using a silent count.

Any elation the players felt at Kuntz's touchdown quickly subsided when the reality hit them that they still needed the extra point to tie the game.

The Scotties, however, stood paralyzed by the sudden turn of events and struggled to line up to block the kick. Their perfect season had just burst. From his crouched position as holder, Billy Sprinkle flicked his fingers to signal that he was ready. He didn't want to make Walsh think about the kick any longer than necessary, and he certainly didn't want to give Glasgow any more time to get set up. Flaherty, as he had since his freshman year, hiked a tight, perfect snap to Sprinkle who, with the crisp precision of an automated assembly machine, placed it down. Walsh moved purposely toward the ball, swung his right toe into the underbelly of the football, and watched as it sailed straight through the crossbars. The scoreboard turned to reflect the new score: 7–7.

The hours of practicing the punting and kicking game had proved critical—but the resulting tie left a bitter taste in everyone's mouths. Mehrens and McMahon intended to make sure the taste lingered for a good while. They were livid at their team's overall performance. Their stellar performance in the final 12 seconds only highlighted how little effort they had exerted in the first 47 minutes and 48 seconds.

In their temporary euphoria, the players didn't know it, but a week unlike any that they had ever experienced was about to descend on them.

July 14, 1985

When the call came at a little after 1 a.m., it was not totally unexpected, but it still came as a shock. Mike Walsh set the phone down by his bed. The voice on the other line was the head night nurse at a veterans' hospital in Pittsburgh. She said Bob Murray was dead and apologized for delivering the news but said Walsh's telephone number was the only contact information Murray left. The nurse added that he died of a failure of the liver.

Walsh knew that years of hard drinking had finally extracted the ultimate toll on his old teammate and friend. He tried to fall back asleep that night but couldn't. He lay awake and wondered what else he could have done.

The problem had started in high school. Although Murray never drank during football season—it was the only thing that seemed to have a higher place on his priority list—the same could not be said for the rest of the school year. There was hardly a Friday night or a school dance at which he didn't have a case of Rainier Beer in the trunk of his car. He even kept a sharp pointed can opener in his pocket at all times so he could easily crack open the all-steel top on the beer cans.

His drinking grew worse during his freshman year of college at Western Montana, and by the end of two tours in Vietnam, it was a chronic problem.

When Murray returned to Montana after his military service, he dropped out of sight until 1979 when he reappeared on the front door step of Mike Walsh.

Walsh could see that his teammate was in need of help, even if he was too proud to ask for it. He offered him a small room in the basement of his house and helped him find his first gainful employment in nearly a decade. The arrangement only lasted a few months until Murray resumed his battle with the bottle. He again disappeared.

But rather than waiting for him to reappear this time, Walsh went out in search of him and found his old friend in a rundown bar on the lower south side. Murray was at the end of a three-day drinking binge. It took some convincing, but Walsh persuaded his old buddy to seek treatment at a VA facility in Oregon. He made the arrangements himself and drove Murray to the clinic.

Murray returned to Great Falls three months later looking as fit as ever. With Walsh's help, he again found employment and was successful enough to move out of Walsh's basement into an apartment of his own. He even resumed playing softball, an old favorite recreational hobby.

Unfortunately, a small thing can lead to dire consequences for an alcoholic. A meaningless victory in a weekend softball tournament led to a celebration at a local bar, and what started as "just one beer" didn't end until days later when he landed in the local detox facility.

Walsh started working the phones again, and although it was harder this time, he was able to get Murray placed back in the VA facility in Oregon. The same cycle repeated itself the following year, but after contacting almost every VA hospital in the country, Walsh was able to give Murray a third chance at turning his life around by persuading the VA hospital in Pittsburgh to accept him.

After buying Murray an airline ticket to Pittsburgh, Walsh drove him to the airport. As the two sat silently in the airport lounge waiting for his plane, he looked at Murray and said, "You remember the Glasgow game?"

"Yeah, what about it? I can still hear your blood-curdling scream before you leveled that Scottie. He was the last guy who had a chance to tackle Kuntz, and you just knocked him flat. Or, as McMahon would say, you 'put him on the grass.'" For the first time all day, Murray smiled.

"That was nothing," replied Murray. "If I didn't do that, McMahon would have killed me." He then stopped and reflected for a moment. "But you, on the other hand, you were the one who had all the pressure. But you did it...you came through."

Just then the overhead speaker announced the final call for

flight 667 to Pittsburgh. The two stood up. Walsh stuck his hand out to shake his old friend's hand, but Murray, instead, gripped him in a big bear hug. He pressed his unshaven face against Walsh's cheek and said, "Thank you, Mike. You were always there for the team, and you've always been there for me."

Neither man wanted to let go, but another announcement came over the system. Walsh then watched him board the plane. It was the last time he saw his old teammate alive.

May 1, 1989

After high school, Clark Kochivar went into the seminary for a short period of time. He thought the priesthood was his calling because his friends so often came to him with their problems. An excellent listener, Kochivar found that he could usually help his friends with whatever was troubling them.

In time, he came to realize that he didn't need to be a priest to practice his unique skill. He returned to Montana in the early 1970s, got married, and started a family. In 1980, after his father died in a car accident, he took over the family ranching business. Back in the Great Falls area again, he rekindled his friendship with many of his classmates, including Wally Berry's younger brother, Fred.

In 1989, tragedy struck. Kochivar, whose wife only months earlier had been diagnosed with multiple sclerosis, was himself diagnosed with cancer of the esophagus. He was informed by his doctor that he had a five-percent chance of survival.

Kochivar called Fred Berry from the hospital and told him the news. "Don't worry," he said. "I've always been in the top five percent of everything I do, so I'm sure I'll beat this too."

Berry admired his friend's optimism and courage and actually believed him for a while. As the chemotherapy began to take its toll, though, it was clear that his friend needed help. The weekly trips into the hospital in Great Falls for treatment were clearly extracting a physical toll on Kochivar, so Berry invited his friend to move in with him and his family. He moved in with the Berrys in February 1989.

A month later, tragedy struck the Berry household. Fred Berry's 17-year-old daughter, Tracy, suffered a massive stroke. It left half of her body and all of her speech functions in need of serious rehabilitation. Even though the Berrys were in no financial position to handle the situation, the family didn't despair, and neither did Kochivar.

Kochivar, who spent his days at the Berrys' house, immediately began working with the daughter on her speech and even helped her learn to write with her left hand. Tracy, in turn, helped Kochivar deal with his pain and aided him in taking his daily drug regimen.

On a regular basis, a number of old teammates, including Bob Kuntz, Barry Newmack, Jerry Kuntz, Wally Berry, and Mike Walsh, would also take turns in stopping over to visit. They would drive Kochivar to the hospital while another would watch over the daughter or just spend time talking with him.

Often, when it was just Kochivar and his old teammates, the conversation would turn to their days at Great Falls Central. Sometimes, though, more difficult topics, such as where he wanted to be buried or how he intended to provide for his children, would need to be discussed. Kochivar, who still had a knack for putting people at ease, always took the lead in discussing these matters. And when it was just him and Fred Berry and the discussion turned to Tracy, it was Kochivar who was the strong one. "I know she's in there, Fred," he would say. "I see it in her eyes. Her soul is stronger than ever, and she's growing more vibrant every day." Berry marveled at how Kochivar, even in his pain and suffering, could be such a source of strength. He was glad his friend was with him.

One day in early May, Berry went to his room. It was almost 9 a.m., and Kochivar was always an early riser. He knocked softly on the door. There was no response. Fearing the worst, he pushed the door open. Berry was surprised to find Kochivar just staring out the window.

"It's beautiful, isn't it?" he asked. Berry said nothing. He could see from his friend's face that he had had a rough night. "Isn't that robin absolutely beautiful?" Kochivar repeated. Berry looked at the bird out the window and nodded.

"I thought I was going to die last night," Kochivar said matter-of-factly. "I was really scared—all alone in the dark—my wife and children miles away. I started to cry, and then I must have drifted off to sleep. When the sun rose this morning, it was as though I saw things in a new light—literally. I see God's grace everywhere. I see it in that robin. I see it in Tracy's eyes, and I see it in all of my friends." He stopped to reflect on his newfound vision. "Do you remember Mother Mary James?" he asked.

"Yeah."

"Do you remember her religion class?"

"Not really," replied Berry after a moment of reflection.

"Well, I do. I now know that she really got it. She understood that for all of the Church's focus on scripture, the Beatitudes, the commandments, everything could be boiled down into this one simple thing: *Love your neighbor as yourself.*

"You, Newmack, Walsh, Kuntz, and all the others from Central are living that lesson. And it makes me thankful that I'm around such beautiful people." He had tears in his eyes. They were not, however, tears of sadness. They were tears of joy.

Clark Kochivar died the following week on May 7, 1989. He was 42 years old and left behind his wife and three children, Terje, Shaun, and Collette. His friends continued to live by those words. After his death, they raised thousands of dollars to ensure his three children all had the opportunity to go to college.

WEEK FOUR GAME PLAN:
Dust Yourself Off

QUOTE TO REMEMBER:
*"Our greatest glory is not in never failing, but in rising up
every time we fail."*
—RALPH WALDO EMERSON

KEY QUESTIONS TO ANSWER:
Are there members of your organization who are not ful-
filling their individual potential? Have you identified how
every individual member of your organization can contribute to creating a more effective team?

Learning to Dust Yourself Off

1. How did Mehrens help Jerry Kuntz turn a weakness into a strength?

2. How did the coaches balance constructive criticism with positive encouragement?

3. How did the coaches handle those individuals
who had a limited playing role?

4. What role did the coaches' expectations play in
individual player development?

5. Discuss the role that repetition played in individual development?

6. How did the coaches utilize the players' responsibility to their school and community to reinforce their messages?

CHAPTER 5

"He who lives without discipline

dies without honor."

—OLD ICELANDIC PROVERB

TOUGH LOVE

Byron Weber's Story

August 20, 1962

The decision to attend "Boys State," the annual program sponsored by the American Legion of Montana to foster an interest in state government and promote an appreciation for the finer intricacies of democracy, was not an easy one for Byron Weber.

Ed Flaherty and Wally Berry had both declined because the convention conflicted with the first week of two-a-day practices. As the two players most likely to be elected captains, their decision was straightforward—as Coach Mehrens let it be known in none too subtle terms when he learned both were considering attending.

149

For Weber, who was the presumptive starting right offensive end and the starting defensive left end, the decision was not quite so cut and dried. To begin, unlike Flaherty and Berry, he wasn't a captain, and he didn't harbor notions of receiving a college football scholarship. Second, he was the student body president-elect for Great Falls Central High School, and, as he was constantly reminded by Father Livix, he had responsibilities far greater than football.

Still, football was so big in Great Falls that for those who played the game, it was often the primary way that they were thought of by their peers—and often how they thought of themselves. This was even true for someone who was student body president. Therefore, the decision to miss the beginning of practice to attend the event represented a real conflict for Weber.

In the end, he sought the advice of Father Livix, who was also Weber's drama coach. Livix, a devoted football fan and probably the school's top supporter, empathized with his decision. In his theology class, Livix often liked to pose moral dilemmas to his students because he felt young people only honed their ethical decision-making process by applied use. "Ethics are like a muscle," he always told his students. "They'll get stronger only if you use them."

Livix listened to Weber's dilemma but offered him only this advice: "The noble man makes noble plans, and by noble deeds he stands." Livix said it with such flair that Weber figured it was a quote from Shakespeare. He didn't know it was from the Bible.

Weber reflected on the advice of his mentor and chose to attend Boys State. In doing so, he became a small part of the program's history. The 1962 convention was the first ever to elect a black "governor." Luther Garris was from Billings, and Weber cast his vote for him. As he did, he again reflected on Livix's advice. It was not an easy decision. A good friend of Weber's, Mike Pichette, was the other candidate. He was an outstanding student and an even better person. But Weber was also aware that as they were preparing to vote, Catholic schools in New Orleans were being forced to close due to bomb threats from segregationists who wanted to keep blacks and whites apart. In his own small way, Weber wanted to show his convictions for a cause greater than friendship.

September 20, 1962

Immediately following the Glasgow contest, even before the players reached the school gym for the regular post-game dance, the film of the game had been placed in a metal canister and was enroute to the local airport for express service to Salt Lake City—the only town within 500 miles capable of processing the film and returning it within two days. The cost of the service was high—particularly by 1962 standards—but it was a cost the Great Falls Roundtable incurred with little complaint because it allowed Mehrens and McMahon an extra day to identify and remedy the mistakes of the previous week.

More so than most weeks, the Great Falls coaches were happy they had the express service. As the Glasgow game aptly demonstrated, the Mustangs had a lot of mistakes to correct. The seriousness of the situation was compounded because their next opponent was Havre—the returning Montana Class A champions—who, in its first two victories of the season, had shown no signs of letting up in its pursuit of another state championship.

Over the weekend, as they waited for the game film to be returned, Mehrens and McMahon were hardly idle. On Saturday morning at Gordon's Restaurant and Supper Club, Mehrens held court for an hour on the local radio station where he dissected his team's play on a program called "Coffee with the Coaches."

He had little that was positive to say about his team's performance. His main conclusion was that his team had suffered a mental breakdown following its resounding victory over Butte Central, and they failed to give Glasgow enough respect. Mehrens assumed a lion's share of the responsibility and vowed to his listeners that it was not going to happen again. He went on to express concern

COACHED *for* LIFE

about Havre's "offensive machine" and spent the better part of the hour paying homage to the skills and talents of their two stars, Glenn Havskjold and Lowell Gorseth—the dreaded "Gold Dust Twins." Only near the end of the program did he offer a hint as to how he hoped to contain the dynamic duo.

Following the program, Mehrens, along with McMahon, made their way to Eddie's for a hearty breakfast of steak and eggs. They rehashed the game with some of the town's most vocal supporters, who offered only vague or painfully obvious insights. Still, Mehrens, who as one of the city's two head football coaches, had to perform this day-after ritual with all the magnanimity of a politician running for reelection and patiently heard out his supporters. Only near the end of the discussion did Mehrens explain how he intended to assign his two best athletes—Wally Berry and Ed Flaherty—to track the Gold Dust Twins relentlessly throughout the game. He had refused to go into any such detail on the radio for fear that a Havre supporter, in an attempt to glean some small insight into his game plan, was serendipitously listening to the program.

After downing a second cup of coffee, the two coaches politely excused themselves. They knew the conversation would go on for the better part of the morning, but they had more pressing things to do, such as reviewing the scouting report from Havre's most recent game.

For the better part of the afternoon, they drilled Jim Trudnowski about every Havre player, every formation the Blue Ponies used, and every play they ran. Ostensibly, Trudnowski was also an assistant football coach. In reality, he was the school's new basketball coach and merely moonlighted as an assistant football coach in order to supplement his modest income. And because he was not particularly skilled as a football coach, Mehrens relied on him to scout only those games that he and McMahon were not able to attend themselves.

The remainder of the day, with the exception of taking a short break to listen to the fourth quarter of the Notre Dame football game on the radio, was spent preparing for Havre. Mehrens paid special attention to how and where the Havre defensive players lined up. If they were on the inside, head to head, on the outside shoulder, or far wide, Mehrens wanted to know.

Sunday was much the same only more intense. By the time Mehrens and McMahon had returned from Mass, the film of the Glasgow had been deposited outside the front door of Mehrens' modest house. Mehrens had long ago dispensed of any guilt about working on the Lord's Day. He did so by convincing himself that since he enjoyed it so much, it could hardly constitute work.

Shirley, Mehrens' wife, instinctively began preparing for the long day's work. Now in her seventh year as a football coach's wife, she knew, based on the unsatisfactory outcome of the Glasgow game, that her husband's schedule—and his life—would not return to anything even remotely resembling normalcy until after the Havre game. In fact, she knew that her husband wouldn't really be reengaged with the family in any meaningful way until after the end of the season. With the tie to Glasgow and the Havre game approaching, she also understood enough about football—and enough about her husband—to know that the upcoming week was going to be more stressful than most. The Havre game was either going to make or break the Mustangs' 1962 season, and she knew that her husband intended to do everything in his power to ensure that his team would "make" the season.

So after she put the finishing touches of mayonnaise, lettuce, and tomatoes on the ham sandwiches that would feed her husband and John McMahon for the next 12 hours, she expertly set up the projector, pulled the shades in the dining room, and shut the door behind the pair. For the rest of the day the room was off-limits to her and the two daughters, because it had been temporarily converted into a makeshift football study, where the two coaches would immerse themselves in the film and identify every mistake and miscue the Mustangs made the previous Friday. They also scanned the film for any additional weaknesses that might be exploited by Ralph Frank, the wily veteran Havre coach.

As was their custom, Mehrens and McMahon reviewed the film once in its entirety without interruption. Watching it a second time, they made notes of the most obvious errors. Mehrens focused on the play of the offensive and defensive backs, while McMahon directed his attention to the performance of the linemen. They watched the film a total of six more times that evening. On each showing, McMahon focused on one individual lineman, while Mehrens concentrated his considerable attention on the backs. On the sixth and final showing, together, they keyed in on the performance of Byron Weber. They were not pleased with what they saw.

The multiple viewings allowed Bill Mehrens to be in complete control for the showing of the film that was conducted for the benefit of the members of the Roundtable—the financial supporters of the Great Falls Mustangs—at an early morning breakfast. The ritual, which preceded America's obsession with the Monday Night Football by more than a full decade, was institutionalized by Mehrens during his first year at GFC. He did it as a way to build long-term support for the program in the community and to show his appreciation to the team's financial backers.

For the next hour—play by play—Mehrens walked his audience through a critical assessment of his team's performance. The first time he stopped to replay the film was on a successful touchdown pass in the first half that had been called back. On the play, Byron Weber executed a crisp five-yard down-and-out and, after catching the pass, neatly lateralled it to Wally Berry who sprinted 20 yards for a score. The touchdown was called back because Weber moved a split-second early and was flagged for being offsides. The infraction was clear on the film, but Mehrens said nothing. It was never Mehrens' policy to openly criticize a player. Any negative comments were offered in private sessions with the player.

The next miscue occurred at the beginning of the second half when Charlie Parker, the Glasgow runner, returned the opening kickoff for an 85-yard touchdown. While obviously displeased with the play, Mehrens acknowledged his own culpability. He confessed that in his zeal to fire up his players at halftime, he may have unwittingly encouraged them to over pursue.

Mehrens saved his greatest wrath for his team's failed attempt to punch the ball across the goal line after having a first-and-goal at the Scotties' four-yard line in the third quarter. "Inexcusable," he said. McMahon used more colorful terms to describe his linemen's tepid performance. "It won't happen again," the assistant coach promised.

As the film wound toward the end of the game, the members of the Roundtable eagerly awaited the game's only redeeming play—Jerry Kuntz's last second punt return for a touchdown. It was not to be. The film ran out halfway through the play—a victim of the football program's modest budget that allotted only two canisters of film per game.

"I know you're all disappointed in not being able to see the end of the play," said Mehrens, "but it is important that you know Coach McMahon and I are not interested in what went right last Friday night...because, in reality, that play and, maybe, the performance of the defense were about the only things our team did well. I'm more interested in correcting what went wrong. And, as you just saw, there was a lot that went wrong."

Mehrens paused to contemplate what he was about to say next and then plunged ahead. "I should warn you this week is going to be hard—very hard. Coach McMahon and I intend to work your boys—our boys," he said correcting himself, "like they have never been worked before.

"We should never have allowed ourselves to be put in the position we found ourselves in Friday night. We were the better team, and, but for the grace of God, we were lucky to escape with a tie. If we want to compete for the state championship—and I still believe we can—we have to do a heck of a lot better than we did against Glasgow. I don't have to tell any of you, Havre is an excellent team, and we're going to be playing them on their home field." The men in the room all knowingly nodded their heads. "We're going to find out this week what the '62 Mustangs are made of," continued Mehrens. "Our boys aren't going to have a fun week. Tell their mothers to keep their suppers warm because they're not going to be coming home early this week. Coach McMahon and I are going to work them like dogs, and, in the process, we're either going to break 'em," said Mehrens, looking around the room, "or make 'em into a real team." The men in the room conferred their approval of this approach by again nodding their heads.

A few questions were raised about the status of Gary Wolf's return, and Mehrens, to the relief of all in the room, informed the men that since the cast was off his star quarterback's arm, Wolf was slated to start against Havre. The meeting adjourned on that positive note, and the members of the Roundtable departed.

September 24, 1962

Since the beginning of the season when he showed up a few days late for the start of two-day practices because of his participation at Boys State, Byron Weber had been behind the proverbial eight ball and under the close scrutiny of Coach Mehrens.

It was not that Mehrens had anything against Boys State. In fact, as a social studies teacher, Mehrens encouraged all of his students who were interested in the program to apply for the prestigious summer camp. But when the student also happened to be a football player and the camp coincided with the beginning of the practice, Mehrens took a somewhat different view of one's involvement in the program. However, because Weber was a model student-athlete and came to practice in excellent shape, Mehrens only needled him occasionally about his decision. One such time occurred when Weber finished first in a wind sprint, and Mehrens called out to everyone within earshot, "Well, look at that, perhaps everyone should have gone to Boys State!" It was his way of not too subtly reminding Weber that his case of mistaken priorities was not entirely forgotten and that his complete commitment to the team remained in question.

Following their review of the Glasgow film, the coaches had renewed reason to question Weber's commitment to football. As was his style, Mehrens broached the topic privately with Weber. After attending Mehrens' social studies class, Weber was on his way out the door when the head coach called out to him. "I'd like to see you for a minute, Mr. Weber." The boy walked back to Mehrens' desk and stood silently as students from the next class began taking their seats. "I want to see you back here after your last class," said Mehrens. Weber responded with a simple, "Yes, sir," and then departed after seeing that Mehrens wasn't going to elaborate.

The directive only served to heighten the anxiety that had been building up in Weber's stomach. His first inkling of a problem came right after Kuntz had returned the punt to tie the game. He had jubilantly tossed his helmet high in the air but noticed that neither of the coaches seemed to share in his excitement. It didn't take him long to figure out why. Mehrens and McMahon understood that they never should have been placed in a situation that required a near miracle to salvage a tie. It then dawned on him that one of the reasons why they were in that situation was because of his mistake on the touchdown that had been recalled earlier in the game. Bit by bit, he soon began to recall other mental errors he had committed during the game.

The rest of the day was a kind of slow agony for Weber. It had all the pleasure of waiting to go to the dentist to have his wisdom teeth extracted. He knew Mehrens wanted to talk with him about his performance, and he knew he wasn't being called to his office to be praised. When the final bell rang, it brought a small sense of relief. At last his moment of reckoning had arrived. He deposited his books in his thin steel locker and nervously peered through the frosted glass window of the solid oak door that led into Mehrens' room. He knocked on the door and then entered. He found Mehrens grading a pop quiz that he had given the students in one of his classes earlier in the day. Mehrens motioned Weber in but refused to extend an invitation to have him take a seat. Too polite to presumptuously assume such an offer, Weber remained standing and waited for Mehrens to finish slashing his red pen across the paper he was grading. When he was done, Mehrens looked up, settled his cold eyes on Weber, and said without emotion, "We don't need you on this team."

The comment hit Weber like a ton of bricks. He felt dizzy, and he struggled to process the comment. "Your performance last Friday evening was inexcusable. Absolutely inexcusable," continued Mehrens. "Football is a team sport. As a senior and one of the leaders on this team, I thought you grasped this simple concept. After reviewing Friday's game film, it is clear you don't." The disappointment in Mehrens' voice was sincere. Weber was too smart to attempt to respond. "I have to get the room ready to show the film," Mehrens said. "I want you to think long and hard about whether you want to join the team for this afternoon's practice or, instead, if you want to clear out your locker and turn in your equipment."

"I want to be on the team," replied Weber earnestly.

"Fine, but you're now on the second team. Pete Rice will be starting on both offense and defense. You're dismissed." The news was a considerable blow to Weber. The Havre game was the biggest of the year, and the thought of not playing in it was almost too much for him to bear.

By 3:00, all the members of the Great Falls Central Mustangs, including Byron Weber, were seated in Mehrens' second floor classroom. Normally, the room was filled with laughter and the gentle ribbings that so often accompany a group of young boys—especially testosterone-filled athletes—but today the room was deathly quiet. The only sound was the hum of the large fluorescent lights that hung overhead.

Word had gotten around from some of the players whose fathers had attended the morning film session that it was going to be a tough week. One father even called it "Hell Week"—a term the players still use four decades later when referring to the week.

The coaches' demeanor during the school day seemed to validate the rumor.

And it was confirmed when Mehrens, always a stickler for punctuality, purposely delayed his entrance to give his players a few more minutes to contemplate their sins from the previous Friday. At 3:05, the two coaches walked into the room. Without saying anything, McMahon pulled down the shades and shut the door. Mehrens flicked off the lights. With the room dark, he brought the old projector to life and started the film.

The first frames of the grainy black-and-white game film appeared. On the screen was the opening kickoff. The silent film seemed oddly out of place because it captured none of the sights, sounds, or emotions so evident only 72 hours earlier. All it captured were the cold, hard facts.

From the opening kickoff, it was clear the Mustangs did not play well. In fact, the opening kickoff wasn't even done before McMahon, in his loud, gravelly voice, began ripping into the performance of his line. "Mills, Murray, and Campbell, what are you guys doing? Once you see that it's not an onside kick, all of you should be busting your butts to get downfield and set up the wall! For Pete's sake, the Glasgow linemen almost beat you downfield. We never stood a chance of getting decent field position because you never gave Kuntz a chance to get past the 20! Apparently," McMahon added ominously, "we need to work on our wind sprints!"

The film then abruptly cut to the first play from the line of scrimmage. As instructed, the person who filmed the game from his perch high above the Memorial Stadium press box captured only the plays. Any film expended after the referees blew the whistle was considered a waste. Mehrens, however, gave explicit instructions to the man filming the game to never stop shooting until the whistle blew because he wanted to evaluate whether his players followed through on their assignments until the very end.

"Look at how we're getting beaten off the ball!" Mehrens said, stopping the film. "If I didn't know better, I'd think that Glasgow was in our huddle and knew the snap count!" On the next play, it was McMahon's turn to let it rip. "Why is it that the whole offensive line isn't moving in unison? Look, only one player has his head up."

"Probably Weber looking to see if his girlfriend is in the stands," said Mehrens. Nobody laughed, and Weber cringed. School policy, in fact, prohibited students from dating. So strict was the policy that students were not allowed more than two dances with any one partner during school social functions, and if a pair was believed to be dating, they were sent to the principal's office and told in no uncertain terms to end the relationship. Mehrens, however, knew that his players sometimes thwarted this policy, and his comment to Weber was meant as a thinly veiled suggestion to everyone in the room that they were to put all relationships on hold until after the season.

"How the heck can you know where the man you're supposed to block is if you don't have your head up?" asked McMahon rhetorically. The comment was directed at all of his linemen. He continued his commentary as the play unfolded. "And Weber, look at you, why did you stop blocking? Is the play over?" Weber meekly acknowledged that it wasn't. "You're right," replied McMahon. "I bet you didn't stop dancing with your girlfriend in the middle of a song at the post-game dance. You owe me four laps as soon as we get out on the field."

160

On the third play, Mehrens critiqued the quarterback and running backs. While his style was more quiet and thoughtful than McMahon's, his assessment was no less biting. "You guys look timid, like you're afraid to get hit. If you're not going to run hard on every play, I'll find someone else who can," said Mehrens, directing his comments at Wally Berry and Jerry Kuntz.

And so it went for the next hour as the two coaches stopped and dissected a limited number of plays for special attention. McMahon was especially critical of Fish's failed tackle, but every player was singled out at least once for a specific failure. A few unfortunate souls were selected a few times. And then there was Byron Weber, who held the distinction for having his name called the most times. By the end of the film, he understood why Mehrens had questioned his commitment. His performance was even worse than he had imagined. If there were a rock in the room, he would have gladly crawled under it.

But rather than wallow in pity, Weber began to mentally prepare himself for the week ahead. He knew it was going to be tough, but he figured he deserved whatever the coaches threw at him— and he correctly surmised that they were going to throw a lot.

The first tangible sign of what was to come came when Mehrens ordered everyone to suit up in full gear and report to the practice field behind the school. Normally, the Monday practice following a game was short in duration and the players wore only their helmets and shoulder pads. The purpose was to give the players an extra day to rest their bodies. Mehrens and McMahon were in no such gracious mood this week.

By 4:15, everyone was on the field, and following the usual routine of calisthenics and stretching exercises, McMahon directed the captains to join their ranks. He assumed a place at the front of the squad and, like a Marine Corps drill instructor, began putting the team through their paces.

"Start chopping," he barked. In unison, the entire squad

began furiously pumping their legs, while holding out their arms at a 90° angle. "Hit it!" McMahon screamed. Every player dove to the ground and promptly jumped back into his upright position. They kept their legs pumping. "Hit it," McMahon yelled again. The drill continued uninterrupted for what seemed ages. Soon, the players' legs began to burn, and each successive trip up from the ground became progressively more difficult. Often the slowest players were still getting up when McMahon ordered them to hit the ground again. As the players' fatigue increased, the squad's precision further deteriorated. Both Mehrens and McMahon began to single out players and accuse them of a lack of effort. "Get your butts up," McMahon bellowed. "It's the fourth quarter against Havre!" The latter comment was his way of reinforcing why this conditioning was necessary.

Finally, McMahon blew the whistle and ended the drill. The players felt he had made his point. They were ready to get on with practice. But before anyone could even catch his breath, McMahon barked out another drill. This time it was the crab drill. That was followed by a series of other drills. Each one with a simplistic name, such as the "wave" or the "grab grass" drill, that belied its difficulty. As the hour approached six o'clock—a full half hour after the usual finishing time for practice—Mehrens ordered everyone to run four laps.

The squad released a collective sigh of relief at what they assumed was the end of the day's practice. But today was no ordinary day, and after everyone had completed their laps, Mehrens directed his players to get some water and report back to the field where he proceeded to subject them to a series of 40-, 60-, and 100-yard wind sprints. By 6:30, the late September sun had finally begun to set, and even the best conditioned athletes gave thanks for the impending darkness.

The players, however, had once again underestimated their coaches' resolve. A simple obstacle such as the lack of natural light was not going to deter the coaches today. As the last rays of twilight faded into the dark sky, McMahon called over Chucky Boyle, a red-headed wisp of a boy and one of the team's two student managers, and tossed him his car keys. Mehrens did the same to the other manager, Pat Penbernathy, and ordered the boys to go fetch their cars and drive them onto the practice field.

When the reality of what the coaches were doing dawned on the players, their hearts sank. The coaches were going to use the car headlights to light the practice field. They now had no idea when practice was going to end. One pair of headlights was directed down the width of the end zone in order to provide McMahon enough light to work the linemen on the blocking sled, while the other car's lights were pointed down the end zone at the opposite end of the field so that Mehrens could work the running backs. The coaches continued as though practice had just begun—which, in their minds, it had.

While Mehrens worked the backs on the tackling dummy—a large canvas bag tethered, via a pulley system, to a heavy slab of concrete—McMahon ordered the starting offensive line to fetch the massive, iron-cast blocking sled and position it along the side of the end zone nearest the rectory—the official residence of the Bishop of Great Falls. McMahon then perched himself atop the device and ordered the first group to line up. "Hit it on one," he said coolly. The exhausted linemen positioned themselves in front of the steel monstrosity and awaited McMahon's command. Upon hearing the count, Bruce Campbell, the left end, fired out and was the first to hit the sled. His quick reaction had the effect of twisting the sled in a counterclockwise motion. It also had the unintended effect of highlighting Byron Weber's lackadaisical effort. Had Weber hit it quickly enough and with a force equal to Campbell's, the sled would have been driven back in a parallel fashion.

McMahon became unglued. The veins in his neck bulged as he unleashed a stream of profanities at Weber that caught even himself off guard. After his choice words were spent, McMahon zeroed in on his target. "Why are you even out here, Weber? After watching your performance on Friday, I would have thought you would be dying to redeem yourself. In fact, that's why I allowed you to line up with the first team—I thought you'd give me everything you had. Instead, how do you respond? You let Campbell beat you off the snap by a mile!" He ordered Pete Rice to replace Weber on the starting line.

McMahon gathered his thoughts and then unloaded on Weber again. "Weber, you let your teammates down on Friday, and you're doing it again here today. You might think you can cheat—or glide—your way through life, but you can't. On the football field, players are exposed for what they really are. And the same thing is going to happen in life. You can't hide from your opponents, you can't hide from your teammates, and you certainly can't hide from yourself. Oh, you might be student body president, and you might be able to coast along on smarts, good looks, and limited talent for a while; but, at the end of the day, only those who are truly committed and work the hardest are going to be the ones to persevere! The others will be exposed as frauds." Weber dropped his head.

Taking the Lord's name in vain again, McMahon screamed. "Don't you drop your head on me, Weber." In the eerie glow of the headlights, McMahon looked less than human. "And don't you ever drop your head on your teammates. Now, get out of my sight," he said, spitting out the last phrase. "Give me five, and while you are running laps, I want you to use the time to get your head back in the game. To give you a little more time, take the blocking dummy with you."

Weber picked up the tall, slender 50-pound canvas bag and began circling the dark field. Then, as if to add insult to injury, McMahon yelled after him that he was to take his place with the second team when he returned.

As Weber struggled to position the dummy in such a way that he could find a comfortable stride, Father Livix made his way out of the rectory and, in his black cloak, moved along the shadows of the darkened field. He walked unseen past McMahon, who had turned his wrath toward a number of other players whom he felt were providing him with less than 100 percent.

As Livix came into the light at the opposite end zone, where Mehrens was watching his players slam their bodies into the tackling dummy, driving it back until the heavy cinder blocks reached the top of the pulley and could go no farther, a number of players silently rejoiced because they assumed Livix had come to deliver them from this torturous practice. As the priest approached, Mehrens halted the drill and ordered the running backs to join Weber on his laps.

"Working 'em pretty hard aren't you, Bill?" said Livix, watching the players trot off into the darkness.

"Yes, and we're not done."

"That's fine," replied Livix, a proponent and practitioner of strict discipline. "My only concern is that the volume and nature of John's language is unbecoming to our Catholic heritage." Since he was an entire football field length away, Mehrens hadn't actually heard what McMahon was saying, but it didn't take much imagination to figure it out. "What I'm saying, Bill, is this—just move John away from the end of the field nearest the rectory. His foul language is filtering up through the windows, and while I can handle it, I can only imagine how offensive the Bishop finds it— not to mention the sisters," continued Livix, referring to the Sisters of the Ursaline Academy, whose convent was only slightly farther away from the practice field than the rectory.

"It has probably got them working overtime on their Rosaries, praying for your and John's souls," he said with a laugh.

"Ask the sisters to say a few more for the team against Havre this Friday," replied Mehrens with a slight smile, before adding on a more serious note that he would speak with McMahon. "He's a screamer, Father. But he's also a teacher."

"I know he is, Bill. Keep up the good work. I agree with your approach. If we are going to beat Havre, more 'Hail Marys' aren't the answer—our boys just have to play better than they did last week."

"They will."

"I know," replied Livix, before slipping back into the shadows.

Mehrens sent his backs for a few laps and strolled down the field to speak with his assistant. The pair quickly struck a workable compromise. Rather than pushing the blocking sled along the length of the end zone near the rectory and the convent, McMahon mandated his players to push the sled up the field—away from the sensitive ears of the priests and nuns.

As the linemen labored to move the sled up and down the field in 10-yard increments, McMahon exhorted each player to perform better, and when he found them wanting—and on this day he found them all wanting—he either made them perform again or he sent them for a lap or two.

After the second complete trip up and down the field, the first signs of distress began to appear. Glenn Fish was the first to crack. He collapsed at the base of the sled. "What are you doing, Fish! Who said you could quit? How many times do I have to tell you to hold your block until you hear the whistle? Now do it, again!"

"I can't," responded Fish meekly. His legs had turned to rubber.

"Yes, you can!"

"I can't," Fish replied, his voice now breaking. "I try and I try...but whatever I do, it just isn't good enough for you." The combination of fatigue, anger, and stress caused tears to well up in his eyes.

"Go," said McMahon, signaling for the boy to take a lap. He realized that for the moment he had probably pushed Fish and the rest of the linemen about as far as he could. "Everybody else join him."

After pushing the sled for 200 yards, the laps were a welcome relief, and the players jumped at the opportunity to escape the monstrous steel contraption. One by one, as his teammates ran by Fish, they offered him their encouragement. Flaherty, the team captain, was the first. "Hang in there, Glenny. You're doing fine. We'll get through this. Just tough it out." Bruce Campbell, Fred Zadich, and Greg Mills said much the same thing, and Dale Roos, who often shared the bench with Fish, simply ran alongside him in a quiet sign of solidarity.

McMahon was pleased at how Fish's teammates had come to his support, but he was still concerned about the boy's emotional condition. At some point, he knew that players such as Fish had to realize on their own that their ability to endure hardships was not so much a physical characteristic as it was a mental one. McMahon wished he could coach them through it, although he knew it was something that they did—or didn't—learn the hard way.

Upon their return, McMahon offered Fish the day's only laudatory remark, when he said, after they returned to the blocking sled and the boy slammed hard into the canvas bag, "That's it, Fish. Now you're hitting like a football player. In fact," he continued, "now you're all starting to hit like a team.

"If we're going to beat Havre on Friday, we have to play together as a team—through the good and the bad. Go hit the shower." The first day of Hell Week was finally over.

September 25, 1962

Sister Helen Paul's biology class was the one hour of the day Byron Weber truly enjoyed himself. After the previous day's practice and what he was sure would follow later in the day, that was especially the case this particular day.

From the very first moment Weber had stepped into Sister Helen Paul's class, he was captivated. The young nun of the Sisters of Charity of Providence radiated enthusiasm. But more than that, she was the first person to ever validate Weber's interest in the natural sciences. Weber had collected bugs and insects since he was a young boy, but he had kept his interest a secret since being teased by his classmates years earlier.

Since the beginning of the semester, Weber had been engaged in the behavioral study of grasshoppers. He was partnering with Bob Bailey, a fellow football player who thought the project a complete waste of time and was more than happy to sit back and leave all the work to Weber. Sister Helen Paul, however, took a genuine interest in the project. She listened intently as Weber rattled off the variables that shaped a grasshopper's behavior.

"It's a combination of plant availability, environmental conditions, competition from other insects, as well as the number and type of predators," said Weber. "All four factors affect what, when, and how the grasshopper eats."

"And why is that important, Mr. Bailey?" Sister Helen Paul asked Weber's partner.

It was clear from Bailey's expression and the tone of his response that he didn't much care. "I don't know, Sister."

"It's because the study of the grasshopper—or any insect or animal for that matter—can give us insights into how we can better manage our natural resources and help devise strategies for conserving those resources." Sister Helen Paul was way ahead in her appreciation of the importance of conservation, and she found an attentive student in Weber.

"From grasshoppers?" replied Bailey skeptically.

"Yes, Mr. Bailey, from grasshoppers. The natural world around us is full of important information. For those who wish to leave something behind in this world, there are few areas more rewarding than biology. We have only begun to scrape the tip of the iceberg in terms of our knowledge and understanding of the world around us. For those who take the time to study the small things around us, I am confident they will be rewarded with an even clearer understanding of God's beauty and His greatness."

Sister Helen Paul's message fell on deaf ears with Bailey, but it captivated Byron Weber.

September 27, 1962

Practices on Tuesday and Wednesday were much the same as Monday's. Every night—well past sunset—Mehrens and McMahon pushed and drilled their team to the verge of exhaustion. Only on Thursday, the day before the big game, did they halt practice at the regular time of 5:30. As Mehrens blew his whistle and signaled for everyone to come over, he didn't bother to give a speech about what his team needed to do to beat Havre. He knew he had something better than words.

Before the beginning of practice Byron Weber had approached him and requested the right to "challenge" Pete Rice for the honor of earning his starting spot back. A challenge provided any player the right to request an opportunity to win a starting spot by beating the starter in a best-of-five contest on the "meat grinder"—a full contact drill that consisted of one running back, one offensive lineman, and one defender. The job of the offensive lineman was to block the defender. The defender's job was to tackle the running back. What made the drill so helpful for the coaches was that players had no place to hide. Success and failure were as plain as black and white.

The challenge was the first of the year, and the team excitedly huddled around Weber and Rice as they lined up. Weber desperately wanted his starting job back. He also wanted to earn back the respect of his teammates. He knew McMahon was right—he had let his teammates down, and he wanted a shot at redemption. Moreover, Weber firmly believed he was better than Rice and felt he owed it to his teammates to be in the starting lineup against Havre.

The first meat grinder had Weber in the offensive position. McMahon blew the whistle, and Weber fired out to his right,

pushing Rice wide to the side. The running back ran by untouched. On the following play, Weber assumed the defensive position. Rather than attempting to guess which way the back might run, he used the rage that had been building up within him the past few days and, upon hearing the whistle, drove Rice back into Billy Sprinkle—the unlucky running back assigned to carry the ball on the play—and knocked him flat. The score was 2–0, and Weber needed only to deliver the knockout punch to regain his starting job.

Rice was a good athlete and, feeling humiliated by the first two drills, redoubled his efforts. In his exuberance, though, he sprung up too high, and his aggression worked against him. Weber caught him squarely in the midriff and smashed him into the ground. The violence of the hit knocked the wind out of him. As Mehrens crossed out Rice's name from the starting lineup on his clipboard, a small smile slipped from the corner of his mouth. Even McMahon couldn't contain the smile that crept across his face. He knew that Weber now understood what it meant to be a team player.

August 29, 1968

After graduating from the College of Great Falls in 1967, Byron Weber decided to join the Marine Corps. The decision was not nearly as complicated or difficult for him as it was for so many other young men of his generation. Weber had always considered himself a patriot, and with the draft looming over him, he chose to present himself at the Marine Corps recruiting office in Great Falls for the simple reason that he wanted to serve his country. He selected the Marines because he liked their mystique—he felt they were the toughest branch of the military.

Weber endured the four months of Officer Candidate School at Quantico, Virginia, in large measure because the experience— especially after having practiced a season under Coach John McMahon—didn't seem nearly as difficult in comparison. When the drill sergeants got in his face and unloaded their endless barrage of four-letter words, Weber took it all in stride. As a result of his Hell Week experience with McMahon, he realized better than most of his fellow officer candidates that the drill instructors were not attempting to tear them down; they were trying to build them up by demonstrating that they could perform at a level higher than they ever expected. And, like McMahon and Mehrens, the drill instructors wanted each officer candidate to understand that there was greater strength when they performed together as a team than as individuals.

Weber easily survived the four long and often humid months at Quantico and was commissioned a second lieutenant in November 1967. After spending six months at the Basic School and Infantry School, where he trained to become an infantry officer, he asked to attend the Army Civil Affairs School at Fort Gordon, Georgia. He was intrigued by the politics of the war in Vietnam and was interested in working with Vietnamese civilians. While there, he also took some courses in Vietnamese on his own initiative.

In July 1968, Weber received his orders to report to Vietnam, where he was slated to serve as an infantry officer in charge of a platoon of 50 Marines. Within two weeks of his arrival, Weber was thrust into an even greater leadership position and was put in charge of a company of 200 Marines.

It was an extraordinary responsibility for a second lieutenant, and Weber would recall years later that he "had no business doing some of the things he was doing." But just as his high school football coaches had trained him to take out much stronger and more physically talented players by focusing on fundamentals and by constantly repeating certain techniques, the Marine Corps used the same themes to help him perform under great stress.

Just one week into his new duties, Weber was ordered to secure a piece of land near the infamous "Dodge City"—a few miles southwest of Da Nang. Because the job was limited in nature, Weber took only 42 members of his company. As they waded through the dense bamboo forest and the thickets of elephant grass—whose serrated edges posed a constant threat to any exposed human flesh—Weber's radio man, an experienced enlisted man nicknamed "Speedy" who had been in the country for some time, said to Weber that he sensed something bad. While inclined to agree, Weber had been given his orders and directed his men forward.

Without warning, a single shot rang out. Because the five-foot high elephant grass made it impossible to see, Weber didn't know his radio man's shoulder and chest had exploded into a bloody mess of sinewy tendon.

A few more isolated shots were fired, but by the time the second Marine was hit a few seconds later, it was clear Weber's unit was under a vicious and coordinated attack. They had walked directly into a horseshoe-shaped ambush and were under fire from every direction. There were snipers hiding in the bamboo trees, others were located in ground level bunkers, and still others were firing at their knees and ankles from well concealed tunnels.

Weber's unit returned fire as best they could, but they were at a distinct disadvantage—the enemy could see them, but they couldn't see the enemy. It would be days later before Weber would find out that his unit had stumbled upon the headquarters of a North Vietnamese battalion leader, who, as a result of his prominent position, was afforded an unusually high level of protection.

Weber's M-60 crew quickly set up their heavy machine gun and began returning fire. The viciousness and scale of their response was able to disrupt, although not entirely deter the enemy. When the shooting finally stopped a half hour or so later, Weber's Marines had suffered 21 causalities. Seven of his men lay dead, and another 14 were seriously wounded. The results would have been far worse but for the quick actions of some of his men. In addition to the professionalism of the M-60 crew, another Marine tossed a hand grenade into a bunker only to have it tossed back out—where, but for the grace of God, it exploded harmlessly. The Marine who threw the first grenade then grabbed another one and, after pulling the pin, coolly held on to it for a few seconds before lobbing it back into the Vietcong bunker. The delay ensured the Vietcong had no time to repeat the trick, and the device exploded inside the bunker, killing everyone inside. A number of other lives were saved by the scale of the Marines' response. The sheer volume of the hot lead that the Marines pumped out of their M-60 and the M-16s forced the enemy to remain hidden behind protective cover a great deal of the time.

In the ensuing two days, after Weber called in additional air and armor support, the Marines expertly retrieved 13 of their wounded comrades. For their heroics, one was awarded the Navy Cross and another the Silver Star. Only one Marine—a young enlisted man named Garcia—remained beyond their reach. The sound of his anguished cries was muffled by the thick dense forest.

Recognizing the tenuousness of their situation and fearing that the Vietcong were only allowing the soldier to survive because they wanted to use him as bait to kill additional Marines, one of Weber's more experienced men pleaded with him, "Lieutenant, we have to get him out of here." Weber ordered the man to take the remaining members of the unit and move back to a more secure area, where they could set up a defensive perimeter until additional reinforcement could arrive and the wounded men could be safely evacuated. Weber, however, stayed behind with his sergeant and patiently waited for the right moment to attempt a rescue of Garcia.

As he waited, Weber was filled with a flood of emotions—a combination of fear, anger, and the awesome feeling of responsibility that comes with knowing that you were in charge of a group of men who were placed in harm's way. At times, he wanted nothing more than to retreat to the safety of the defensive perimeter, but he knew he couldn't.

It would be too much to directly attribute his refusal to leave to the direct influence of John McMahon or his experience at GFC. Weber did it, in part, out of his own sense of honor; and, in greater part, out of the loyalty to the Marine Corps who had instilled in him the code that Marines never left their fellow Marines behind.

Still gnawing somewhere deep inside him, however, was the same empty feeling he had felt after he watched the game film of the Glasgow game and realized he had let his team down. He knew he never again wanted to experience the pain that is associated with letting down one's teammates.

And so, with his sergeant at his side, Weber made a mad dash through the elephant grass. The pair struggled to roll Garcia onto Weber's poncho. Then, with Vietcong firing their AK-47s in their direction, each man grabbed a corner of the makeshift stretcher and labored to drag Garcia's limp, pale body back to safety.

Just as they had picked up some momentum and were beginning to make progress, Weber found himself flying through the air. When he landed, he was dazed but not in pain. He felt a warm liquid running down his entire left side. He felt faint—as if he were going to pass out. He reached his hand down to assess the damage, but was perplexed when he found no wound or blood. Again, he reached down and, again, found no sign of blood.

Confused, it took Weber a few moments to realize that his canteen had been hit and punctured by an AK-47 bullet, and that it was the force of the tumbling bullet that had propelled him through the air. The wetness he felt was nothing more than water. In stunned disbelief—the bullet had just missed shredding his hip by a single inch—he turned back to the task at hand and, with the help of his sergeant, pulled Garcia to safety.

Later that evening, one of his Marines, to whom he had once confided his interest in insects, brought him a beautiful moth that had been attracted to the light in his tent. Weber studied it for a while and was surprised that he was able to find a moment of peace among the pain, suffering, and confusion he was feeling. He recalled Sister Helen Paula's comments about finding God's beauty in insects and marveled that it was even present in the jungles of Vietnam.

For the remainder of his time in Vietnam, Weber collected moths and butterflies. Much to his astonishment, and in spite of the rather un-Marine Corps-like nature of the hobby, he was surprised to encounter a few other Marines who shared his passion.

1970s

In 1971, First Lieutenant Weber received his honorable discharge. Like so many other young men of his generation, his experiences in Vietnam had left him confused and bitter. In an attempt to get away from it all, he decided to use the money he had managed to save and took up a friend on his invitation to travel to South America.

As he hitchhiked south from Montana toward South America, he stopped in Arizona to visit Harvey Livix, who much as Weber was now doing, had done some soul-searching in the late 1960s and decided to leave the priesthood to start his own business. Livix graciously offered to put his former pupil to work, but Weber politely declined. After a day together, Livix drove Weber back out to the freeway so he could resume his hitchhiking adventures. As the pair said their good-byes, the old priest in Livix just couldn't resist and he offered up a verse from Proverbs:

Blessed is the man who finds wisdom,
the man who gains understanding,
for she is more profitable than silver
and yields better returns than gold.
She is a tree of life to those who embrace her;
those who lay hold of her will be blessed.

In keeping with the rebellious spirit of those late Vietnam war years, Weber split with his friend after a few months. He wanted to navigate the entire Amazon River and study its people and biology. Weber spent a year and a half living, working, and traveling along the Amazon River and, in the process, was able to put some distance between himself and his experiences in Vietnam.

In 1973, he was ready to return to Montana and worked at various odd jobs, including stints as a miner, bartender, and rancher. In the mid 1970s, he reentered the University of Montana to become a science teacher. He also became actively involved in the environmental movement.

He taught for five years before he felt a strong urge to write. With no family to support, Weber left the teaching profession and spent two-and-a-half years living a "Thoreauean" existence along the Bitterroot River in Montana. He was still looking for wisdom and trying to gain understanding. Most of his days were occupied by traveling the rugged terrain and recording his findings on the natural environment in his journal. For subsistence, though, he sometimes found it necessary to take an odd job in town.

In the fall of 1984, one of those jobs found him working as a bartender at a small bar just outside of Florence, Montana. Late one afternoon, near the beginning of the school year, the superintendent of the local school district, who was familiar with Weber's past experience as a teacher, came into the establishment and told Weber his talents were being squandered and he "needed to get his head back in the game." The man told Weber he knew he was a skilled teacher and that he had an opening for him as a second grade science teacher at the Florence-Carlton Elementary School just down the road.

The superintendent's comment was not unlike McMahon's admonishment some 22 years earlier when he chastised Weber for failing to perform to his potential on the blocking sled. Weber realized the man was right.

The following day, he accepted the offer to teach, and for the last 20 years Weber has made the topic of science come alive for hundreds of wide-eyed students and influenced a generation of students. He found he has the ability to capture students' attention through the natural sciences.

So enthusiastic is Weber for the field, especially that of the study of bugs, that he now has his own regular monthly program on Montana Public Radio entitled "The Pea Green Boat." It is just one of the many ways he has found to fulfill Sister Helen Paul's advice to "leave something behind."

2000

In the spring of 2000, Weber attended the graduation ceremonies of Florence High School and watched with a small sense of pride as one of his students gave the valedictorian speech. After the student thanked his mother and father, he went on to cite Byron Weber—his second grade teacher—as the person who had the greatest influence on his life. It was a memorable moment, and it offered Weber all the validation he needed to know that he had made the right decision to get his "head back in the game."

It was, however, the passing comment of a mother that had the greatest effect on him. One day, as he was browsing the aisle of the local grocery store, a woman came up to him and, with the pride that only a mother can properly express, related the accomplishments of her three children—all of whom had the honor of having Weber as a teacher. She thanked him for his efforts and told him how often her children still brought up his name. She then parted by saying, "Don't think that you are ever forgotten...or that what you do isn't important. You've made a huge difference in my kids' lives, and I know you've done it in a lot of others."

WEEK FIVE GAME PLAN:
Tough Love

Discipline is a form of love.

QUOTE TO REMEMBER:
"He who lives without discipline dies without honor."
—ICELANDIC PROVERB

KEY QUESTIONS TO ANSWER:
What is your philosophy regarding discipline? Do your own personal actions adequately reflect this philosophy?

Learning Tough Love

1. Did the coaches consistently apply discipline to all the players?

2. Did the coaches take disciplinary action for a player's failures, or rather because they were not living up to their potential? What is the difference between the two approaches?

3. How did Mehrens and McMahon use discipline to reinforce the concept of team?

4. Were there—or could there have been—some negative outcomes from the coaches' use of discipline?

5. How could the coaches have modified or improved their disciplinary tactics?

CHAPTER 6

> *"We are what we repeatedly do.*
>
> *Excellence, then,*
>
> *is not an act,*
>
> *but a habit."*
>
> **—ARISTOTLE**

SWEAT THE SMALL STUFF

Billy Sprinkle's Story

December 15, 1960

Billy Sprinkle's father was a big man. He stood 6'1" and weighed 250 pounds. The weight was an unfortunate side effect from his service in World War II. As a young man living in Seattle when the U.S. was attacked at Pearl Harbor in 1941, Bill Sr. opted to enlist in the Royal Canadian Royal Air Force (RCAF) because he could earn his wings in one year as opposed to the two years it would take in U.S. Army Air Corps.

By early 1943, he was flying B-17s in combat. On his way back from a bombing run over Germany, his aircraft was hit and seriously damaged. The plane was forced to make a crash landing in a farm field in the south of England. Upon impact, an engine exploded, and Sprinkle was violently expelled from the cockpit. The accident shattered his right leg, severely burning his buttocks and back. Still, Sprinkle was lucky. Of his eight-man crew, he was the sole survivor.

It took him over a year to recover, but in 1945 he eventually left the hospital and was honorably discharged. He returned to the Pacific Northwest and soon married a Canadian woman whom he met while training for the RCAF. They settled in Great Falls, Montana, and raised a family of five children while he worked his way up the corporate ladder to become the vice president of a local bank.

The job and his family life left Sprinkle little time for exercise, but even if he had wanted to, his war injuries—especially the shattered broken leg that had left him with a noticeable limp—hampered his mobility. It was this lack of mobility that led to his heavy weight and, in turn, the massive heart attack that took his life on December 15, 1960. He was 43.

Billy Sprinkle, then 14 years old and a freshman at GFC, received the news after basketball practice that day. Father Arbanas invited Sprinkle into his office and asked him to have a seat. As gently as possible, he broke the news to the young boy that his father was dead. Sprinkle was devastated.

The death of a parent at any time is difficult. It is that much harder when it comes around the Christmas holidays. But it was especially hard on Billy. Not only did he lose his greatest teacher and role model, he also lost the one person who understood his greatest challenge—his stuttering problem. Sprinkle's father had also been a stutterer and had overcome the problem through years of therapy and a fierce willingness to confront the problem head-on.

Because the death occurred at the height of Billy's formative teenage years, his mother worried about the effect it would have on his self-confidence. Who, she wondered, would help him with his studies, his sports, and his stutter. She would not have the time. Now a single mother with five kids under the age of 17, she had to find employment in order to support her family.

Into this painful void stepped Bill Mehrens. After the holidays, when Sprinkle returned to school, Mehrens—who was also the freshman basketball coach—took him under his wing. He understood the boy was at a critical juncture in his life. Sprinkle had lost the person most responsible for shaping his character, and Mehrens knew that even a few poor decisions at this stage could alter his life.

Mehrens became the boy's surrogate father. He channeled Sprinkle's time and energy into athletics, starting with basketball. By his freshman year, Sprinkle's natural athletic talent was beginning to emerge. It was first exposed on the basketball court where his speed, athletic coordination, and smooth jump shot made him a natural.

Mehrens encouraged Sprinkle to stay after practice each day and work on his outside shooting game and his free throws. He did this not so much because Sprinkle needed to—although Mehrens was constantly reminding him that he had room for improvement—but rather because he knew that the basketball court was one of the few places where Sprinkle could escape the loneliness his father's death had created.

As winter turned to spring, Mehrens directed Sprinkle's attention to track. His decision to recruit the speedster to the sport was easy. In addition to keeping Sprinkle's mind occupied, Mehrens had his own selfish reasons. During the basketball season, it had become evident that there was no one faster at pushing the ball up court than Billy Sprinkle, and Mehrens was convinced that he could translate that speed into success on the track. He also felt that, in time, he could make Sprinkle "football fast." In short, Mehrens saw an emerging three-sport star in Sprinkle.

All that season Mehrens encouraged Sprinkle to work on both his speed and his endurance. He made him run countless sprints and laps. He taught him how to fire out of the blocks and introduced him to isometrics—which in the early 1960s foreshadowed today's emphasis on weightlifting. Mehrens often pushed him so hard that by day's end Sprinkle only had enough energy to eat his dinner and do his homework—which Mehrens also closely monitored—before collapsing exhausted into bed.

Under his coach's tutelage, Sprinkle's times on the track improved considerably. The isometrics worked to unleash the power in his slender legs, and the endurance work ensured that his legs kept churning like two highly powered and well lubricated pistons. By the end of Sprinkle's freshman year, the times he was clocking in the 100-, 220-, and 440-yard sprints in the junior varsity track meets exceeded those being run by the upper classmen in the varsity meets. Mehrens, however, did not believe in lettering freshmen and was content to watch Sprinkle improve, knowing that for at least a few hours each day, his mind was occupied on things other than his home life.

The following summer, Mehrens made it a point, during his regular rounds of delivering milk, to check in on Sprinkle and his mother. Often, the boy had already gone to his job at Buttrey's, the local grocery store, by the time Mehrens reached his house in the morning.

One day, though, he found Sprinkle at home doing nothing. When Mehrens asked him why he wasn't doing something useful—such as practicing—Sprinkle muttered that he was tired. Mehrens was smart enough to know that wasn't the truth. He suspected Sprinkle was lying around because he figured he was already good enough. Mehrens resolved to get to the bottom of the situation before it calcified into a bad habit, and the surrogate father in him knew he had to nip such a problem in the bud.

Mehrens took the unusual step of asking Sprinkle over to his house that evening to grill hamburgers. The invitation surprised the boy. Mehrens typically maintained distance from his players that, in turn, created an aura of aloofness. It was not a trait Mehrens consciously tried to cultivate. It was a byproduct of his era. He simply felt that discipline was more easily administered if a formal barrier between coach and player was maintained. Mehrens realized that Sprinkle's situation required a different tack. He understood that the boy could benefit by time away from the pressures of his home life and was pleased when Sprinkle accepted his invitation.

After Sprinkle arrived at Mehrens' home, he was introduced to Mehrens' wife and his two young daughters. Over hamburgers, corn on the cob, baked beans, watermelon, and lemonade, Mehrens gradually—and artfully—turned the conversation from sports to the topic of what Sprinkle needed to do to develop his full potential.

"What do you hope to accomplish this season in football?" Mehrens asked.

"E-e-easy," stuttered Sprinkle. "I w-w-want to play in enough games to letter in football."

"What about basketball and track?"

"I want to start on the b-b-basketball team and, in track, run the 220 in under 23 seconds."

"You need to write those goals down," said Mehrens matter-of-factly. *"A goal undocumented is a goal that isn't accomplished."* Mehrens could see that his comment hadn't fully registered with Sprinkle, so he continued. "Everyone has dreams and aspirations, Billy, but few people are willing to make a public commitment to achieving those goals. The reason is because they're afraid of failure. People feel that if they don't achieve their goals, they'll be branded a failure." Mehrens paused to let the boy absorb the message. "But remember this. The greatest failures are not the defeats or setbacks that are suffered on the football field, basketball court, track, or elsewhere. They are the dreams that die inside you because you never had the courage to admit them either to yourself or others. As Theodore Roosevelt once said, 'It is better to have tried and failed than to have never tried.'

"All the goals you listed are realistic," continued Mehrens, taking a sip of his lemonade. But before Sprinkle could begin to feel pleased with the positive affirmation, Mehrens added, "But you aren't going to reach them at your current skill level. Don't get me wrong, you're talented—in fact, you're very talented—but you have to keep getting better *every* day, and the *only* way to do that is to practice. Now, if you're really serious about those goals, you have to make a commitment to get better, and then you have to put in the time. Your natural talent will only carry you so far; it is practice—and practice alone—that will get you your letter sweater, land you the starting job on the varsity basketball team, and allow you to break 23 seconds in the 220."

Mehrens could see in the young boy's eyes that he was receptive to the message, so he offered to help draw up a training regimen for him to follow. For the remainder of the summer, when Sprinkle wasn't helping his mother put food on the table by working at the grocery store, he was following the schedule Mehrens had created for him.

February 10, 1962

The regimen worked to perfection. Sprinkle played in enough games in the fall of 1961 to letter in football. And not only did be become the starting guard on the varsity basketball team, he was also the team's leading scorer—averaging 20 points a game.

Late in the season, Great Falls Central traveled to Lewistown for a game. By midpoint in the second half, Sprinkle had 23 points and the Mustangs were coasting to an easy victory. In the stands, Bill Mehrens was watching the game when a Mustang defender slapped away a pass. The ball rolled toward center court and was halfway between Sprinkle and a Lewistown player. Sprinkle made only a half-hearted attempt to get the ball, and the Lewistown player easily beat him to the ball.

The play had no impact on the outcome of the game, which GFC won handily, but it caught the attention of Mehrens. After the game, as the players were loading onto the bus, Mehrens pulled Sprinkle aside outside the locker room and said, "Mr. Sprinkle, you're better than that." Sprinkle knew instantly that Mehrens was referring to his failure to hustle after the loose ball. "Just remember this," continued Mehrens, "if you're standing still, you're not getting better." The coach said nothing else and walked away. Sprinkle knew he had disappointed his fatherlike coach. He would not do it again.

September 25, 1962

Day Two of Hell Week was about to begin. Sprinkle grabbed the gray T-shirt off the hanger in his locker and slipped it on—it was still damp from the previous day's long, late practice. The discomfort of its cool dampness was obviated only by its pungent smell.

Next, he strapped on his bulky leather shoulder pads and then laced up his high-top cleats. He was sure to double tie them as Mehrens instructed all of his players. Mehrens hated it when his players had to come out of a game or practice due to something as simple as an untied shoelace or an unstrapped shoulder pad. Sprinkle lugged his lean 140-pound frame, still stiff from the previous day's session, out to the practice field.

The first person he saw outside was Bill Mehrens. The coach was gazing across the practice field like a lion eyeing a herd of sheep. "Afternoon, Coach," said Sprinkle.

"Good afternoon, Sprinkle. Are you ready to get better today?"

"Yes, sir," replied Sprinkle, who knew from his two-and-a-half-year association with Mehrens that it was more than a rhetorical question.

"What's your plan?" he asked.

Sprinkle, by now well accustomed to Mehrens' near obsession with goal setting, replied, "Win every wind sprint and not fumble the ball."

COACHED for LIFE

Mehrens nodded his head. "You write 'em down?"

"Yes, sir," said Sprinkle, who didn't realize until years later that this habit of writing his goals down on a piece of paper had given his life some much needed structure.

As Mehrens turned his attention to another player coming out onto the practice field, Sprinkle stole a glimpse at Mehrens' clipboard. He was hoping to get an idea of what the day's practice held in store. His cursory review yielded no reason for excitement. The entire three-hour session was organized into small, compartmentalized blocks of time ranging from four minutes for a torturous drill called "burpies" to 30 minutes for practicing a prescribed set of plays. The structure of compartmentalizing his practices down to the minute was a habit Mehrens had picked up from his former college coach, John Gagliardi.

After the obligatory two warm-up laps around the field, the three captains called the team into formation for calisthenics and began putting the squad through its regular paces. They proceeded on schedule until the leg lifts, when Mehrens suddenly intervened. About 45 seconds into the exercise—which required players to lift both legs six inches off the ground and then hold them stiff as a board—Mehrens, in a conversational tone, urged everyone to keep his legs up. "I'll tell you when you can stop," he said nonchalantly.

For another 30 seconds everyone struggled to hold his legs aloft. "Keep 'em up!" he barked as soon as he saw the first pair of legs hit the ground. As their stomach muscles slowly gave way to the stress, a number of players attempted to sneak their arms—which had been at their side—under their buttocks to artificially prop up their legs. But both Mehrens and McMahon cracked down on such violators. "No cutting corners!" yelled Mehrens. "We tried that last week against Glasgow, and we know it doesn't work." McMahon picked up on the theme and added, "If I catch anyone cheating, I'll double the length of the drill." It was his way of fostering the idea that every player had a responsibility to the team.

Finally, just when most players thought they couldn't go any longer, Mehrens blew his whistle. "You've got to get better," he said, shaking his head. "The only way we're going to beat Havre is by outworking them, and that requires we push ourselves even when you don't think you can go any further."

To the players, it seemed that Mehrens was just being a masochist and punishing them for their lackadaisical performance the previous week. The latter was true only in part. What he was really doing—and what he would continue to do throughout the week and for the season itself—was gradually instilling in his team a belief that they could sustain more pain, overcome greater adversity, and perform at a level higher than even they thought possible.

And more often than not, Mehrens concluded such exercises not with effusive praise but rather a simple reminder that they could—and were expected—to do better. He subscribed to the belief that people, especially young people, rose to the expectations that their parents, teachers, and coaches set for them.

Following calisthenics, Mehrens took the running backs and began practicing what he considered to be the core of his offense—the dive series. On this day, he wanted to perfect the 71 counter. He had seen something in the scouting report that led him to believe it might be effective against Havre's aggressive defense. The play, because it was a misdirection play and required precise timing, was more complicated than most of the plays in the Mustangs' playbook and hadn't yet been used because John O'Rourke had problems executing it. Now that Gary Wolf was returning to the starting lineup, he intended to run it until he was convinced everyone had it seared into their brains.

The play called for the fullback to line up directly behind the quarterback, while the halfback positioned himself behind the guard. The other halfback was flanked out behind and on the

opposite side of the other halfback. On the snap, the fullback was tasked with charging into the line, and the quarterback would fake a handoff to the halfback who, after a short delay, was to follow immediately behind the fullback. The quarterback would then quickly swivel and hand the ball off to the wingback who, after also delaying, would be coming down the line from the opposite side.

If the linemen did their job—a pulling guard was supposed to block the defensive end, while the offensive end was to crack down on the defensive tackle—there would be a large hole between the tackle and the end.

Because of the faking and the delaying, the play was more complicated to execute than it appeared on paper. The first few practice plays bore this out. Gary Wolf, still rusty from his injury, had a difficult time turning around in time to get the wingback the ball in a position where it hit him securely in his stomach— or his "breadbasket," as Mehrens liked to call it.

The first time they ran the play, Wolf was slow in his delivery, and Sprinkle had to reach back for the handoff. He fumbled.

"There's no room for mistakes, Sprinkle," said Mehrens before meting out his usual punishment of two laps. Sprinkle bristled at what he considered his unfair treatment. He felt Wolf should also have to run, but bit his tongue and ran his laps. He knew Mehrens despised players who made excuses and often made them run extra laps. When he returned, Sprinkle took his place with the running backs and proceeded to run the play again and again. In fact, they ran it so many times that Sprinkle began to think he could run it with his eyes closed—which is precisely what Mehrens wanted.

When the drill finally ended, Mehrens called all of his backs into the huddle and said, "I know some of you think I'm picking at you when I critique how wide apart your feet are or where your hands are—or how you have to look the ball into your stomach, or how you need to protect the ball with both hands, or how to keep your head up when you hit the hole. But when game time comes, all of these things must be second nature. I don't want any of you thinking about the basics during the game. I just want you to do them. These might seem like small details that I'm harping on—and they are—but in a close game, they're what will give you that extra split second to read your block or elude a defender. And, believe me, against Havre, we're going to need every second and every advantage we can get.

"This evening after you've soaked your feet in brine and studied your playbook, I want each of you to thoroughly think through everything you're supposed to do on every given play— right down to the smallest detail. It's not enough for you to know where you're supposed to run; you have to know how, when, and why you're doing what you're being asked to do on every play. The better prepared you are, the better you'll play.

"There are some teams that may be more talented than us, but we can beat them if we're better prepared." Mehrens paused to let his players reflect on the comment and then said, "Now go get some water and come right back, we're going to run the 71 counter to the left side."

November 17, 1961

Bill Mehrens was a straight shooter and so was Father Harold Arbanas. It was just one of the many reasons why the two men respected each other. Still, as Mehrens sat in the principal's office for the meeting he had scheduled, he didn't quite know how to broach this particular topic. The 1961 football season had just ended, and the team's record was a disappointing 5–3. Mehrens wanted to make some changes.

Arbanas could see that Mehrens was holding something back, and he broke the tension, "I can see something's troubling you, Bill. What's on your mind?"

Mehrens let out a deep breath and said, "I don't quite know how to say this Father, so I'll just be blunt. We're doing too much praying before our games, and it's distracting our boys from the task at hand." Mehrens was quick to add that he wasn't opposed to all prayer and then said, "It's just that I think the Lord has bigger things on His mind."

"I see," replied Arbanas, not showing any emotion.

"Let me give you an example," continued Mehrens. "Last month we had to play in Sidney, which, as you know, is over 400 miles away. That meant we had to leave on Thursday. Father Gregori accompanied the team, but he had to say Mass before we left. That meant the whole team also had to go to Mass with him. We then stopped in Glasgow for the night and went with Gregori to Mass on Friday morning. We then said the Rosary with him later that afternoon, and on Saturday morning, before the game, we again attended Mass with him. I have no problem going to service on Holy Days of Obligation and, of course, on Sundays...but three times in three days seems a little excessive."

Arbanas nodded his head.

"I'm the coach," continued Mehrens, "and it is my job to see to it that our students do their best. It is my opinion that we could make better use of the time we've been spending at the extra Masses by either working on our game plan or allowing our boys an extra hour of sleep on the morning of a big game. It's those little things that will make the difference on the field."

Arbanas, who was always deliberative, replied, "Let's call a moratorium and talk about it in the morning." It was the best that Mehrens could hope for, and he thanked the priest for his time.

The following day, Arbanas pulled Mehrens aside and said, "I've given a good deal of thought to our conversation yesterday, and I'm in general agreement with your point. You've now been here at Central for five years, and you're 27 years old. I don't think a priest needs to chaperone the team on every trip any longer."

"Thank you, Father."

"I'd still like to have a priest present on certain occasions, such as when we play our Catholic school rivals or when we have a big game." Arbanas then looked directly at Mehrens and said, "I want you to know that I agree with your point that God is not much interested in the outcome of a football game. It is just that there are certain times when I want to remind our students that Great Falls Central is a community and our faith is vital component of who we are."

September 26, 1962

The following day's practice was a mirror of the previous two days, only the temperature was about 10°F warmer. The combination of the heavy leather shoulder pads, wet cotton T-shirts, and humid conditions were causing blisters to develop, and this, in turn, required Mehrens and McMahon to spend the better part of their time before practice cutting out donut-shaped patches of mole cloth to place over the players' blisters. Billy Sprinkle's blisters on his shoulders were so bad that Mehrens had to place two swaths of the thick cloth over his boney shoulder blades.

Mehrens, who ran his practices as though they were an extension of the Swiss train service, ended practice at precisely 5:00. "Let's go everybody, line up on the goal line." It was a phrase that all of the players had come to anticipate with a curious feeling of relief and dread. They were relieved because they knew it meant the end of practice was near. They dreaded it because it also meant one thing—wind sprints.

"We're only going to run 18 this afternoon," said Mehrens in a tone that conveyed the sense that he was somehow granting them a great reprieve from the 20 sprints they had run the previous day. Still, the players were grateful for any kind gesture—however small. "In fact," he continued, "the first two are going to be 10 yarders."

On Mehrens' whistle, the whole team sprinted to the first hash mark. Most of the players reached the line within a fraction of a second of one another. They then lined up and ran the 10 yards back to the goal line. On the next set, Mehrens ordered them to run to the 20-yard line and back again. The next set of sprints was 40 yards. This was followed by a pair of 60 yarders. Each time more distance separated the fastest and slowest runners.

As the team's swiftest runner, Sprinkle came across first but just by a hair. He was avoiding running all out because it exacerbated the blisters on his shoulders. As he jogged back to the line, feeling satisfied with his first-place finish, he ended up close to where Mehrens was standing. Out of earshot of the other players, the coach said, "Sprinkle, I expect you to win every one of these sprints. I expect you to finish first by a healthy margin, and I expect you to run through the finish line. I don't ever want to see you let up at the end. *The difference between winners and losers is that winners run hard all the way until the end of the race.*"

After progressing to two 100-yard sprints, Mehrens then reversed the process with pairs of 60-, 40-, and 20-yard sprints before finally finishing with two 10 yarders. In each one, Billy Sprinkle finished first. Mehrens had been true to his word—they had run only 18 sprints, but far from being easier than the previous day, the net effect of the progressive sprints was that it nearly doubled the total yardage the players had to run.

As Sprinkle stood with sweat dripping off his face, trying to catch his breath after the final sprint, Mehrens approached him and said, "I'm going to continue to push you. For one thing, I know you can do it. Second, you still have a lot of room for improvement. You've been blessed with a God-given talent, and it's your obligation to foster and nurture that talent. But the real reason I'm doing it is because you *owe* it to the team."

Mehrens could see from the expression on Sprinkle's face that he didn't understand his comment. "You owe it to your teammates," he

Montana State High School Class "A" Football Championship

MEMORIAL STADIUM — 8:05 P.M.

NOVEMBER 9, 1962

GREAT FALLS, MONTANA

Great Falls Central Mustangs
vs.
Havre Blue Ponies

Souvenir Program — 50c

GREAT FALLS TRIBUNE

Associated Press

MONTANA'S BEST NEWS GATHERER

VOL. 77, NO. 131   GREAT FALLS, MONTANA, FRIDAY, SEPTEMBER 21, 1962   *United Press International*   PRICE 10 CENTS

THE MUSTANGS — Pretty Cheer ...'Loughlin typifies the hundreds of ...entral students and fans who will be ...r a victory in tonight's Mustang home ...gainst Glasgow at Memorial Stadium. In front row are three of coach Bill Mehrens' top linemen this season. From left are end George Leffler, center Ed Flaherty and end Byron Weber. Game time is 8 p.m. Tribune photo.

1962 Football Schedule

GREAT FALLS CENTRAL

MUSTANGS

Sept. 8 Butte Central T
Sept. 15 Open
Sept. 21 Glasgow H
Sept. 28 Havre T
Oct.   5 Hardin H
Oct. 13 Billings Central T
Oct. 19 Bozeman H
Oct. 27 Livingston T
Nov.   3 Laurel H

JERSEY GOLD FOODS, INC.

Great Falls, Montana

(STICK OTHER SIDE TO WET WINDOW. TO REMOVE, USE RAZOR BLADE.)

1962 GREAT FALLS CENTRAL

GREAT FALLS CENTRAL MUSTANGS

TOM STRIZICH
Quarterback

BILL SPRINKLE
Halfback

MIKE WALSH
Quarterback

JOHN O'ROURKE
Quarterback

DALE ROOS
Guard

DAVE HAVERLANDT
End

BOB KUNTZ
Halfback

CLARK KOCHIVAR
Halfback

GREG STECKLER
End

JERRY KUNTZ
Halfback

DICK KUNTZ
Guard

VOYD RICHTSHEID
Halfback

FRED ZADICK
Guard

GARY WOLF
Quarterback

BYRON WEBER
End

JIM GOLDSWORTHY
Guard

PETE RICE
End

FRANK DURAN
Quarterback

GENE OULLETTE
Tackle

BARRY NEWMACK
Tackle

JIM NEUFELDT
Center

BOB MURRAY
Guard

WALLY BERRY
Fullback & Quarterb'k

BOB BAILEY
Fullback

GLEN FISH
Guard

BRUCE CAMPBELL
End

ED FLAHERTY
Center

BOB KUNZ
Tackle

TOM HEATH
End

ED KRALICH
Tackle

MUSTANGS FOOTBALL

GREAT FALLS CENTRAL MUSTANGS

GREG MILLS
Tackle

DAVE NASH
Tackle

GEORGE LEFFLER
End

JIM LOVE
Tackle

MIKE DONOVAN
Tackle

JOE GILSOUL
End

GREAT FALLS CENTRAL MUSTANGS COACHING STAFF

BOB BREWER
Tackle

JOHN McMAHON
LINE COACH

BILL MEHRENS
HEAD COACH

Not pictured—Raymond Mehrens, Junior Varsity Coach and Paul Ferda, Freshmen Coach

GREAT FALLS CENTRAL MUSTANGS CHEERLEADERS

BARBARA THEISEN

CHARI PAT DALE

MARIAN McKAY

SUE BEAULAURIER

PATTY O'LAUGHLIN

GREAT FALLS CENTRAL MUSTANGS MANAGERS

PAT PENBERTHY

TOM MINCKLER

DENNIS MORA

BILL FURMAN

CHUCK BOYLE

1st Practice Aug. 24

Rebuilding Mustang Line Presents Big Problem for Mehrens at GFC

"We'll be light and inexperienced in the line. If we can lick this problem the Mustangs may shape up as a darkhorse in the Western Division race," was the summary offered by Great Falls Central coach Bill Mehrens this week as he charges to open football drills Aug. 24 at GFC.

Mehrens faces the task of rebuilding nearly his whole line this season—center Ed Flaherty is the only returning starter. The grid mentor feels he will have a good backfield, with quarterback the question mark since letterman Gary Wolf fractured his wrist this week.

Coach Ray Mehrens, and Freshman Coach Paul Ferda.

The Mustang mentor said he feels there won't be a real standout team in the Western Division this season. Bozeman — which dominated the loop last ... probably will rem... favorite but the Ha... rather heavily by gr... spring. Livingston ... proved club at the ... season and probably ... darkhorse role.

"I think we'll c... be tough. We and Bill ... could scramble thi... bit," Mehrens comm...

The Mustangs open their season Sept. 8 against a traditional Class AA foe—Butte Central—in the Mining City. They have an open date Sept. 14-15, then host Glas... home opener Sept. 21. ... y travel to take on ... Havre Sept. 28, ... tion opens Oct. 5

Great Falls Central Has Turnout of 70 Gridders

Roughly 70 candidates answered the grid call at Great Falls Central High School Friday and head Coach Bill Mehrens says his charges have plenty of work to do this week.

The Mustang me... uled a full-scale ... Saturday. "Then ... the mistakes and ... proving ourselves ... 8 opener against B... Butte," Mehrens sa...

Emphasis on offe... is being stressed, al... ditioning and fundam...

Mehrens said ... back Gary ... a b...

Mike Wade, Tom Zadick, Jim Riley, Fred Berry, Clark Kochivar, Bill Medved, Tim Furlong, Glen Fish, Frank Kitchingma... John Bronco...

...unde...
...sea...
for c...
Mehr...
gener...
o pla...
or fo...
field...
acks...
hisch...
erry—...
n duty...
en back...
inkle,...
and f...

nen in...
Weber...

...MENT ANYWHERE as Maroon and Mus...
this against action. In the center fore...
...throwing a block, is Butte Central's Ray

Robins, Beh...
5 of the same

Mustangs

In Scrimmage . . .

Mehrens Is Satisfied With GFC Defense P...

...ent about as we ex-... sired. He added that li...
as expected, showed th...
of the men up fro...
e White team won ...
13-7 over the Blu...
s were considered ...
nal, and Mehrens str...
...n't have an actual fir...
... the field. "I ...

GREAT FALLS CENTRAL MUSTANGS
vs
BOZEMAN HAWKS
FRIDAY, OCTOBER 19, 1962

GREAT FALLS CENTRAL CATHOLIC
HIGH SCHOOL
HOME GAMES SCHEDULE
(Memorial Stadium)

GLASGOW .... SEPT. 21
HARDIN (Homecoming) .... OCT. 2
BOZEMAN .... OCT. 19
LAUREL .... NOV. ...

Billings Central Rams
vs
Great Falls Central Mustangs

GFC Has Little Trouble With Hardin

Great Falls Central Mus-
muffed and puffed through
first half performance,
ne back strong to tally an
7 win over Hardin Fri-
t at Memorial Stadium.
he first Class A western
game of the season for
s,
ustangs gave away an
hdown to the Bulldogs,
d with numerous

Hardin, deep in a hole late in
the second quarter, quick-kicked
out to their own 41. From here
GFC drove to a score on eight
plays, despite two damaging penalties. A 12-yard pass from quarterback Gary Wolf to Kuntz was
the payoff, although the big gainer
was Richtsheid's 17-yard sprint
that cancelled out a 15-yard pen-

alty. Walsh's kick again was
good.
Berry, who played only briefly
in the first half because of a
leg injury, sparked the two Mustang drives in the third period.
It started when end Bruce
Campbell intercepted a pass on
the Hardin 15 and carried it to
the Bulldog 7. Berry scored from

2 yards out and Walsh again boot-
ed the point.
Then, three minutes later, the
Mustangs blocked a punt on the
Hardin 36. Berry, on the first
play, went straight up the middle
on a delay play for another TD.
He had good blocks from center
Ed Flaherty and guard Dick
Kuntz.

A Wolf-Richtsheid pass g
for 43 yards set up the fou
Mustang score in the fou
This carried to the Hardin
Halfback Bill Sprinkle went
the way on the next play with
nifty bit of outside running.
Walsh's five good extra-po
kicks in the game gave him
string of 10 straight successes
his past three encounters.
Coach Bill Mehrens' cle
wasn't impressive in the fir
half. But a good defensive effo
throughout the game kept Hard
from threatening seriously.
Coach Dick Imer did get
good running performance fror
Wolfe, while Egnew's passes t
Darrell Hill and Pat Kronmille
were effective.
Next Saturday things ge
tougher for the Mustangs. They
travel to meet arch-rival Billings
Central in an afternoon game in
Billings. Then, on successive
weekends, GFC must meet Bozc-
man at home, Livingston on the

RUGGED LINE
Central grid clash
play came on the

Stopping Hav
ard-Nosed Defense
ppears Only Solution

blem: Stop Glen Havskjold,
Gorseth, Dave Taft, Har-
py and other assorted Blue
s.
tion: 48 minutes of hard-
defensive football.

That's what faces the Great
Falls Central Mustangs when they
journey to Havre to meet the
high-powered Ponies in a Class
A nonconference game t

"We know we have a t
game ahead of us, and m
that will help," was the
ment of Mustang mentor
Mehrens Thursday. He expla
his men were inclined to
Glasgow lightly last weeker
and the Mustangs conside
themselves fortunate to pull
7-7 tie with the

Mustang Schedule

Coach McMahon

Conference Games

Oct. 5—Hardin .... Homecoming
Oct. 13—Billings Central .... There
Oct. 19—Bozeman .... Here
Oct. 27—Livingston .... There
Nov 3—Laurel .... Here

ower Maroons, 32-7

GREAT FALLS CENTRAL MUSTANGS
Vs.

ustangs Trounce Laurel for
entral Will Host East Champion
for State Title Friday

Central High
aturday night
Western Di-
onvincing 41-0
urel Locomo-

re a warm-up
te Champion-
ntest. In win-
entered the
ill be played
against the

l a y night
hopes of

a 7-7 nonconference tie with Glasgow.
In their five conference games,
Coach Bill Mehrens' Mustangs
have rolled up 162 points, allowing but 13.
The clincher Saturday night
was all GFC. The Mustangs won
the toss, received, and marched
from their own 36 to the Laurel
goal in six plays, Bill Sprinkle
going over from four yards out
and Mike Walsh booting the con-
version.
That took less than five min-
tes. The Mustangs kicked to
the Locomotives

and it was 27-0 with 8:15 left in
the third quarter.
On the ensuing kickoff, the
Laurel safety man had trouble
finding the handle and by the
time he had the ball securely and
started to run, several Mustangs
were in the way and he barely
kept from being tackled behind
the goal line, falling on his 1-
yard-line.
A quarterback sneak got six
yards, but on the next play, the
ball slipped loose, with the Mustangs recovering on the 10. It
took Jerry Kuntz two tries at the
line, each netting five yards, to
et the ball across. The Walsh

Get Havre-Got STATE

Enjoy that REFRESHING NEW FEELING!

GREAT FALLS CENTRAL MUSTANGS

No.	Name and Class	Pos.	Wt.
10	TOM STRIZICH—Sophomore	QB	143
11	BILL SPRINKLE—Junior	HB	147
12	MIKE WALSH—Junior	QB	150
13	JOHN O'ROURKE—Senior	QB	135
15	DALE ROOS—Senior	G	150
16	DAVE HAVERLANDT—Junior	E	150
17	BOB KUNTZ—Junior	HB	165
18	CLARK KOCHIVAR—Sophomore	HB	155
19	GREG STECKLER—Senior	E	150
20	JERRY KUNTZ—Senior	HB	170
21	DICK KUNTZ—Junior	G	160
22	VOYD RICHTSHEID—Junior	HB	170
23	FRED ZADICK—Senior	G	140
24	GARY WOLF—Senior	QB	150
25	BYRON WEBER—Senior	E	160
26	JIM GOLDSWORTHY—Junior	G	159
27	PETE RICE—Junior	E	150
28	FRANK DURAN—Junior	QB	135
29	GENE OULLETTE—Junior	T	160
30	BARRY NEWMACK—Junior	T	160
31	JIM NEUFELDT—Junior	C	163
32	BOB MURRAY—Junior	G	173
33	WALLY BERRY—Senior	FB & QB	182
34	BOB BAILEY—Senior	FB	154
36	GLEN FISH—Senior	G	150
37	BRUCE CAMPBELL—Senior	E	168
38	ED FLAHERTY—Senior	C	190
39	BOB KUNZ—Senior	T	
40	TOM HEATH—Junior	E	1
41	ED KRALICH—Junior	T	1
42	GREG MILLS—Senior	T	1
43	DAVE NASH—Junior	T	1
44	GEORGE LEFFLER—Senior	E	19
45	JIM LOVE—Junior	T	17
46	MIKE DONOVAN—Junior	T	19
47	JOE GILSOUL—Junior	E	16
48	BOB BREWER—Junior	T	170

HAVRE BLUE PONIES

No.	Name and Class	Pos.	Wt.
11	DAVID TAFT—Senior	QB	155
12	BOB STROMBERG—Senior	QB	150
21	JOHN DANELL—Senior	E	153
22	LOWELL GORSETH—Senior	B	166
23	TOM ANGSTMAN—Senior	B	130
24	HARRY LIPPY—Senior	E	168
30	JUPE COMPTON—Junior	B	175
31	FRANK PASSON—Sophomore	T	200
41	GREG ANGSTMAN—Sophomore	B	145
42	GLENN HAVSKJOLD—Senior	B	178
40	JACK McLEOD—Junior	B	155
52	JIM KRAVIK—Senior	E	148
53	JOHN HEBERLY—Senior	E	147
51	KEN WARWICK—Sophomore	E	172
50	BILL SEABERG—Senior	E	152
62	RICHARD DAVEY—Senior	G	160
61	DAVID HALIVKA—Junior	C	165
63	RICHARD PRIETE—Junior	G	170
60	JIM	G	170
70	TERR	T	205
71	STEV		
72	DON		
73	JOH		
81	RIC		
80	RI		

PROCEDUR

legally kicking or
batting a loose ball.

Pushing, helping
runner or
interlocked interference.

FOUL SIGNALS

Touchdown or
field goal.

Ball is dead.
For touchback,
wave sidewise.

Clock starts.

First down.

Officials time out.

Safety.

Ball ready
for play.

Incomplete forward pass.
Penalty declined. No play
or no score.

Mustangs Defeat Havre 34-6 for Championship

Great Falls Central's fighting Mustangs fractured Havre's passing attack with four key interceptions Friday, and the rest of the job was relatively easy.

The Mustangs raced to a 34-6 win over the outgunned Blue Ponies to capture the second Class A championship in the history of the school. The tussle wasn't close after GFC ran up a 27-0 halftime margin over the Havre club.

Although fullback Wally Berry and halfback Jerry Kuntz ripped the Pony line to shreds with their torrid runnings, it actually was the Central defensive unit that keynoted the win.

GFC's defensive team limited Havre passers Dave Taft and Bob Stromberg to seven completions in 21 attempts for 89 yards. What's more, the Mustang line rushed the Pony throwers unmercifully — which led to the four passes the Mustang secondary picked off.

In the touchdowns-prevented category, full credit should go to Mustang linemen Byron Weber, Bruce Campbell, George Leffler, Greg Mills, Dick Kuntz, Bob Murray and Ed Flaherty.

The Mustangs wasted no time in scoring. They drove 62 yards on 14 plays on the opening series of the game, with Berry's 24-yard ramble on a delay the key

then Kuntz blasted over for the TD. Mike Walsh booted the extra point.

Then GFC scored again, this time late in the period. They took the ball on their own 16 on a punt. Quarterback Gary Wolf went 4 yards and Berry 3. This set the stage for the most explosive run of the game.

With the ball on the GFC 23, Kuntz took the leather on a belly play, slashed off tackle and rambled 77 yards for the second TD. Havre's speedy Glen Havskjold almost caught him, but Kuntz ducked into the end zone with Havskjold hot in pursuit. Walsh again kicked the point.

The first of GFC's four interceptions started the Mustangs rolling again early in the second period. Bill Sprinkle picked off a pass on his own 40. Berry blasted 16 up the middle and Sprinkle ran 9 to the Havre 36.

Then Wolf lofted a short pass to Weber, who took it on the Pony 25 and threaded his way into the end zone. Havskjold again just

Continued on page 10

Soviet Subs Prowled Caribbean

GREAT FALLS CENTRAL

Home of the State Champion Mustangs

Mustang Varsity Letterman Football Banquet

November 24, 1962 —
Great Falls Central Gym

HONORING
THE MONTANA STATE CLASS A FOOTBALL CHAMPIONS

Toastmaster .... Allen Donohue

Guest Speaker .... Dr. Michael J. Pecarovich

Banquet Chairman .... Fred Jones

Invocation .... The Most Reverend Eldon B. Schuster, D.D.
Auxiliary Bishop of Great Falls, and Supt. of Schools

Welcome address .... Father R. James Reitz
Principal, Great Falls Central High School

Introduction of the Mustangs .... William A. Mehrens
Athletic Director and Head Football Coach

Introduction of Coaches .... William A. Mehrens

Introduction of Cheerleaders .... Toastmaster

Introduction of Special Guests .... Toastmaster

Thanks to the Coaches ...... Co-Capts.: Wally Berry, Ed Flaherty
and Gary Wolf

Entertainment .... The Elk Choraleers

Most Valuable Player Award .... Father R. James Reitz

Principal Address .... Dr. Michael J. Pecarovich

Benediction .... Father Harvey D. Livix

MENU

Juice   Roast Beef   Salad
Mashed Potatoes   Buttered Peas
Rolls and Butter   Choice of Beverage
Ice Cream

GREAT FALLS CENTRAL VARSITY FOOTBALL TEAM

Name Position	Year	Name Position	Year
Bob Bailey—Fullback	Sr.	Dave Nash—Tackle	Jr.
Wally Berry—Fullback and Co-Capt.	Sr.	Barry Newmack—Tackle	Jr.
Bruce Campbell—End	Sr.	Jim Neufeldt—Guard	
Glen Fish—Guard	Sr.	Gene O	
Ed Flaherty—Center and Co-Capt.	Sr	Pete Ric	
Jerry Kunts—Halfback	Sr.	Voyd Ric	
Bob Kunz—Tackle and Guard	Sr.	Bill Spri	
George Leffler—End	Sr.	Mike Wa	
Greg Mills—Tackle	Sr.	Clark Ko	
John O'Rourke—Quarterback	Sr.	Tom Stri	
Dale Roos—Guard	Sr.		
Greg Steckler—End	Sr.		
Byron Weber—End	Sr.	Head Foot	
Gary Wolf—Quarterback and Co-Capt.	Sr.	Line Coac	
Fred Zadick—Guard	Sr.	End Coac	
Bob Brewer—Tackle	Jr.	J. V. Coac	
Mike Donovan—Tackle	Jr.	Frosh Coa	
Frank Duran—Quarterback and Halfback	Jr.		
Joe Gilsoul—End	Jr.		
Jim Goldsworthy—Guard	Jr.		
Dave Haverlandt—End	Jr.		
Tom Heath—End	Jr.		
Ed Kralich—Tackle	Jr.		
Bob Kunts—Halfback	Jr.		
Dick Kunts—Guard	Jr.		
Jim Love—Tackle	Jr.		
Bob Murray—Guard	Jr.		

CENTRAL ROUND TABLE OFFICE

Al Kochivar ....

Romeo Ranieri ....

Mel Schneider ....

Rev. Harvey D. Livix ....

307

"I know the plans I have
for you," declares the Lord.
"Plans to prosper you and not
to harm you, plans to give you
hope and a future."

THE BOOK OF JEREMIAH

GFC Banquet Tonight Honors Grid Champ

HERE FOR BANQUET — Dr. Michael Pecarovich,
second from left, is greeted by representatives of

state champion football team in the Centr
torium. From left to right are Al Zarony, l
friend of the speaker; Pecarovich; Bil
CFC grid coach and athletic director;

GFC Central Mustangs

STATE
CHAMPIONS
CLASS A
1962

"Forty years from now you will still remember this game. You'll tell your children about it. Make the most of this opportunity. Coach McMahon and I know you are champions."

COACH MEHRENS

"It is a privilege to coach another man's son. Think about it. How many men get the opportunity to spend two or three hours a day with their sons during the most formative period of their lives? It is sad . . . but not many. Only a person who has coached can understand the special relationship and bond that occurs between a coach and his players. Well, John and I had the privilege of coaching all of you."

COACH BILL MEHRENS
OCTOBER 26, 2002

Flaherty, Ber

Athletic Gr

Sweeping S

Both Falls Grid Mentors Picked Coach of Year

Montana Coaches Name G. Carlson, W. Mehrens

Continued from page 1

All-Staters and both had their championship teams of the season well represented on the All-State squads.

Carlson, a graduate of Great

After serving two years in the Air Force, Carlson joined the Great Falls Bison coaching staff in 1957 and was named head coach in 1958. In 1961 his team placed second in the conference

GENE CARLSON

Falls Public, played varsity fullback at Montana State University and was All-Skyline for the Grizzly baseball team. He was graduated from the Universit...

BILL MEHRENS

to Butte Public on the strength of a 7-6 loss that gave Butte the championship.

Mehrens w...

Clay-Moore Fight Sets Money Mark

LOS ANGELES (UPI) — While youthful Cassius Clay went on a shopping spree Friday, the promoters of bout with Archie Moore tallied up the financial reports and announced it was the most successful indoor fight in California ring history.

The crowd of 16,400 which turned out to see the 20-year-old youngster knock out his aging foe in four rounds resulted in a gross gate of $182,599.76 at the Sports Arena.

The previous California high mark for an indoor fight was $167,870 grossed by the Ezzard Charles-Pat Valentino heavyweight title bout at the Cow Palace in San Francisco Oct. 14, 1949.

Dodgers Return Omaha Lease

OMAHA (AP) — The Los Angeles Dodgers will turn back their Omaha franchise to the Am... Association...

---

olf on AP Class A All-State Football Listing

repares Changes

6 Great Falls Leader
Monday, Nov. 12, 1962

Kennedy Pushes AAU-NCAA Peac

By THE ASSOCIATED PRESS

Dawson of Glendive, Great Falls Central, Havre and Glasgow dominated the first team of The Associated Press Class A All-State football selections.

Dawson placed three men on the first squad, Havre, Great Falls and Glasgow two each and Park of Livingston and Custer of Miles City one each.

Selections were determined on the basis of a mail vote by coaches, sportswriters and sportscasters throughout Montana.

The only repeater on the AP all-state first eleven was Havre senior... Gorseth, a Havre senior...

The only junior on the first string is tackle Jerry Jimison, a solid 6 feet even at 185 pounds, who starred for Dawson. On the other side of the line is Lew Cooksey of Custer, the biggest all-stater who stands 6-2 and weighs 205.

Doug Crum of Dawson, 5-6 and 152 pounds, and John Zavalney of Glasgow, 6-0 and 170 pounds, hold down the first string guard positions.

Ed Flaherty of Great Falls, 5-9 and 178 pounds, won the nomination for center going away.

Second Team

Glasgow and Park accounted for more than half of the second

With Havskjold at second-team halfback is Al Monte of Dawson. Havskjold is heavier than many of the linemen named at 185 pounds. He stands six feet even. Monta's dimensions are 5-9 and 168 pounds.

Gary Wolf, a 150-pounder from Great Falls, was the pick for quarterback.

Filling out the second team backfield is Bob Knapp of Dawson, relatively small for a fullback at 5-9 and 165 pounds. He was picked for honorable mention last year.

Honorable Mention

Just behind those four ends who tied for second team honors was Darrell Hill of Hardin. Ties... al points resulted in some

NEW YORK (AP)—Under direct pressure from Pres... Kennedy, the AAU and NCA... expected to sign a pact tod... ing the bitter, 2½-year w... control of amateur sports... United States.

The President's four-... ney General Robert Kenn... here to sit in as media... meeting called by Kenn...

present district plan/ following exceptions:
(now in Class B) would to District 11 C com...

Top two teams in each division would advance to the state basketball tournament.

This sets up the possibility GFC... and GFHS could meet in the

"FOUR YEARS OF FOOTBALL

are calculated to breed in the average man

more of the ingredients of success in life

THAN ALMOST ANY

academic course he takes."

KNUTE ROCKNE

John "Poncho" McMahon   Paul Ferda (deceased)   Ed Flaherty   Bill Mehrens   Ray Mehrer

repeated, "because the only way they can get faster is if *you* push them to get faster. If you slack off and just barely come in first, the others will feel that they can also let up. But if you don't, they can't either. And although you're only a junior on this team, you have a responsibility as great as any senior or captain—you have to help drag people up. That's right—drag people up. By challenging yourself to become even faster, you'll force others to do the same. As a result, the whole team will not only become faster, they'll become better conditioned. And that, in turn, is going to make us a better team."

As Sprinkle absorbed the lesson from the man he would later consider his mentor, Mehrens said, "Now, go get showered up." Exhausted, Sprinkle walked to his locker and hung up his pants, shoulder pads, and soaking wet T-shirt. He then gingerly pulled off the bloodstained mole cloth from around his now enlarged blisters.

1978

After college, Sprinkle, like his father, went into the banking business. The job, though, did not provide him the personal satisfaction he craved. He found himself wanting something more enriching—something more rewarding. And he knew exactly what he wanted to do. He wanted to follow in the footsteps of Bill Mehrens, the man who next to his own father had done the most to shape his life. He wanted to be a coach.

Sprinkle just didn't know how to go about it. As luck would have it, John McMahon, his old assistant football coach at GFC, had moved up the coaching ranks and was the head football coach at Montana Tech University in 1972. A chance encounter with his old assistant coach led to a discussion about his desire to get into coaching.

McMahon, after just one interview, offered Sprinkle the job of assistant backfield coach. McMahon knew Sprinkle had the experience, knowledge, and temperament to be a good coach. After

GFC, he had gone on to earn an athletic scholarship to the University of Washington. He could have starred in either basketball or track, but he chose football and spent two years as the Huskies' starting right cornerback.

Sprinkle spent two years as an assistant coach, and when McMahon left to become an assistant coach at the larger University of Idaho, he was promoted to the head coaching position. Sprinkle served in that capacity for two seasons before following McMahon to Idaho, where he accepted the position of backfield coach.

Sprinkle stepped into some big shoes. He replaced Jack Elway, the future head coach at Stanford and the father of Hall of Famer and Superbowl MVP John Elway. And before Elway, Dennis Erickson—the future head coach of the Miami Hurricanes and the San Francisco 49ers—had held the same position.

The job was definitely a steppingstone, so after two successful years at Idaho, it took the football community by surprise when Sprinkle left and opted to take a position not at a bigger college— as Elway and Erickson had—but, instead, decided to accept a high school coaching position.

In 1978, Billy Sprinkle became an assistant coach at Charles M. Russell High School in Great Falls. His reasoning was simple. He wanted the opportunity to mold young men just as Mehrens had helped mold him. Sprinkle knew from firsthand experience the positive effect a coach could have on the lives of young men during their most formative years, and he simply wasn't getting that satisfaction at the college level, where coaching was focused more on improving a player's technique and less on the development of his moral character.

Equally important, as a father himself, Sprinkle no longer wanted to put in the grueling 18-hour days that college football coaching required. He wanted to spend more time with his wife, Danette, and their two children. Growing up, he and his siblings had been robbed of time with their father by death, and he didn't want his children to be shortchanged through negligence.

September 28, 1962

Game day had finally arrived. The players' excitement and adrenaline masked the fatigue from Hell Week. At mid afternoon, the GFC student body gathered in the school gym for a pep rally. The cheerleaders were dressed in their pleated skirts and waving their blue and gold pom-poms. The school band was pounding out a rendition of the school fight song, which was played to the plagiarized melody of "On Wisconsin."

When it quieted down, Father James Reitz, the new school principal who had replaced Father Arbanas, called the rally to order with a short prayer and then turned over the microphone to Mehrens. The head coach began by reminding everyone that Havre was the defending state champion, and they were returning "The Gold Dust Twins." Furthermore, Havre had in Dave Taft and Harry Lippy arguably the best quarterback-receiver tandem in the state. Despite these facts, Mehrens radiated confidence. He told the jazzed up student body that their boys were coming off a great week of practice and were ready.

After a rousing send off, the Mustangs boarded the deluxe Greyhound—rented with funds raised by the Roundtable to transport the team to away games—and began the long drive to Havre.

Midway through the trip, the team—in deference to the Catholic Church's policy of refusing to allow practitioners of the faith to eat meat on any Fridays—stopped at a diner that was serving salmon steak. The players washed the meal down with milk so that it would be properly digested by game time. Just as the sun was setting, the bus inched its way up the snaking road to Havre's unique canyon bowl stadium where only 10 months earlier six of the Mustangs had set their sights on winning a state championship. As the bus parked, Mehrens and McMahon silently

195

wondered whether they had pushed their team too hard during Hell Week. They were concerned that their team wouldn't have enough "gas left in the tank" to be competitive.

Following warm-ups, Mehrens gathered his team in the locker room for a few final words and a prayer. "We had a setback last week—no doubt about it. But setbacks are not defeats, nor are they failures. They only become so when we refuse to change in response to them." He then looked at Sprinkle and then at Weber. "We got knocked to the ground last week, but it matters less that we allowed it to happen. What matters is how we respond. We can either repeat our errors and mistakes, or we can dust ourselves off and play to the level I know we're capable. It's now in your hands." Mehrens then nodded toward Livix who, because of the importance of the game, had been allowed to accompany the team. He opened with a prayer.

> *The Lord gives strength to the weary*
> *and increases the power of the weak.*
> *Even youths grow tired and weary,*
> *and young men stumble and fall;*
> *but those who hope in the Lord*
> *will renew their strength.*
> *They will soar on wings like eagles;*
> *they will run and not grow weary,*
> *they will walk and not be faint.*

Livix and Mehrens then called for the team to draw closer, and they prayed the "Hail Mary."

The coaches' pregame worries about the team's strength were partially alleviated on the game's opening drive. After receiving the opening kickoff, led by Gary Wolf, who had returned to the starting lineup, the Mustangs systematically marched downfield. Wally Berry opened with a solid seven-yard gain. He then ripped off a 12 yarder. After a week of McMahon working them on the blocking sled, the linemen crisply fired off the line in unison and drove their men back until the whistle blew. The efficient seven-play, 65-yard drive was capped by a 10-yard sweep by Jerry Kuntz, who followed Weber's block right into the end zone.

Any remaining worries about their team's energy level were put to rest on its first defensive series. On the first play from the line of scrimmage, Dave Taft, the Blue Ponies' quarterback, faked a handoff to Gorseth and then spun and pitched the ball to the streaking Glenn Havskjold, the fastest runner in Montana. As Havskjold swept toward the end, Bruce Campbell, who had been reminded all week by McMahon that he needed to help keep the Havre running backs contained and "keep 'em running sideways," blew past his blocker and delivered a forearm shiver that dropped Havskjold to the ground. From the sidelines, McMahon could barely contain himself. "I love it!" he screamed. "I love it!"

Campbell coolly walked back to the huddle and announced to his fellow defensive end, Byron Weber, "Better get ready, Webs, because they aren't coming to my side again." Campbell's hit and his infectious attitude had the effect of gasoline being poured on an open fire. A week's worth of pent-up frustration was about to be unleashed on the unsuspecting Havre Blue Ponies.

Responding to Campbell's comment, Bob Murray excitedly suggested to his teammates that they "pretend they are McMahon!" The brutal week of practice had left the players with no positive feelings toward their assistant coach.

On the second play from scrimmage, Havre tried its other star, Lowell Gorseth, up the middle. Ed Flaherty took Murray's advice to heart and, after correctly diagnosing the play, made a beeline straight at Gorseth. With the advantage of a five-yard running head start from his position at inside linebacker, he lowered his shoulder and crashed so hard into the Havre running back that the force of the collision knocked both players out.

Flaherty's father, who had made the trip to Havre, heard the tooth-rattling hit high up in the stands and rushed to the sidelines to check on his son. It was the only time in his son's football career that he had ever made such a visit.

McMahon watched from a distance as Flaherty's father hovered over his son while Doc McGregor, the team doctor, administered smelling salts and ran through a battery of questions designed to check for signs of a concussion.

"Do you know where you are?" he asked. "Who are we playing? Who's the president of the United States?" Although visibly shaken, Flaherty answered all the doctor's questions correctly, including the last one that required him to tell McGregor how many fingers he was holding up.

As Flaherty regained his wits, McMahon strolled over to him. "It's a long way from your heart," he said. Flaherty, who had heard the comment before and would hear it a great many more times before the end of the season, interpreted the comment to mean, *Don't be a baby...get your butt back in the game*—which was exactly how McMahon intended it to be interpreted.

Back on the field, with the left side of the line being controlled by Campbell and Gorseth temporarily out of the game, Havre decided to go to the air. Their best receiver was Harry Lippy, who lined up opposite Weber.

Suspecting a pass, Weber chucked Lippy hard as he fired off the line. The hit delayed Lippy's route out to the flat. Weber then rushed the quarterback and sacked him for another significant loss. It was the first of many such plays for Weber, who had pledged to himself that he was going to atone for his unsatisfactory performance the previous week against Glasgow.

Havre's "Gold Dust Twins" were held to a negative three yards rushing in the first half, and its heralded passing attack was completely silenced. By the middle of the third quarter the score was 21–0, when Billy Sprinkle came out of the game and rushed over to Mehrens. "C-c-c-coach," he said excitedly, "I th-th-think a 71 c-c-c-counter will work." Mehrens looked at the kid whose team-mates teasingly called him "B-B-B-Billy" and smiled. He figured that it was time to drive the nail into Havre's coffin. He was also anxious to find out if Sprinkle was ready to collect a dividend on his hard work. "You think you can beat Havskjold?" he asked. Sprinkle nodded confidently.

Mehrens called for the play, and Sprinkle ran it into the huddle and told Wolf, "71 c-counter, r-r-right." The team executed its trade-mark clap in unison and broke from the huddle. Sprinkle lined up on the far left side in the wingback position. His feet were shoulder-width apart, and his eyes were focused straight ahead. After the snap, he delayed a split second while Berry crashed into the left side of the line and Wolf faked the handoff to Kuntz. Sprinkle then shot down the line and felt Wolf punch the ball squarely into his "bread-basket." With both hands protecting the ball, he looked up and saw a massive hole. Byron Weber had cracked down on the defensive tackle and pushed him far inside. Further inside, Flaherty adminis-tered a devastating block that collapsed the entire left side of the Havre defensive line; and Dick Kuntz, from his pulling guard posi-tion, kicked out the defensive end. Sprinkle burst through the hole and eluded Havskjold by a whisker. The long hours he had spent practicing, building up his speed, and pushing himself past the fin-ish line in every sprint made the difference. Once past Havskjold, Sprinkle switched the ball into his right hand and with the grace of a gazelle sprinted 70 yards downfield and into the end zone.

After he breathlessly returned to the sidelines, Sprinkle ran up to Mehrens and said, "Coach, I l-l-l-laughed in Havskjold's face and r-r-ran r-r-r-right by him." In a testament to Havskjold's speed, the Havre defender eventually caught up to Sprinkle but only after it was too late—he was already eight yards deep in the end zone. (The following spring, Havskjold would gain a measure of revenge by besting Sprinkle in the 100-, 200-, and 440-yard sprints at the Montana State Track championships.)

By game's end, Havre's 12-game winning streak, which had started the year before, was over. Only a long touchdown pass late in the third quarter and a meaningless touchdown near the end of the game prevented the score from being an embarrassment. The Mustangs defeated Havre 28–13, and Mehrens and McMahon now were convinced that their team had the dedication, persistence, and confidence it would take to challenge for a state championship.

December 16, 1962

"Come here, Sprinkle," said Father Livix. The junior halfback cringed at the directive and cursed his bad luck. For the first time in his life, Patty O'Loughlin, the pretty senior cheerleading captain, had initiated a conversation with him, and now Livix had to come along and ruin the whole thing. As he walked over to the priest, he wondered what he had done to earn the priest's wrath.

He was, therefore, taken aback by Livix's comment. "I want you to start taking my speech class at the beginning of the next semester," he said. Livix knew Sprinkle had just passed the second anniversary of his father's death. "With just a little help, I know we can overcome your stuttering problem. You just need to apply the same principles that you have applied to your success on the football field this year. Repetition. The more public speaking you do, the sooner you'll overcome it."

Sprinkle thanked Livix for his suggestion then begged his pardon before rushing off. He raced back to find O'Loughlin, but the moment was gone. Whatever spark of interest he had imagined the Cheer Queen had in him was never reciprocated.

May 20, 1963

The touchdown against Havre the previous fall—the first of Sprinkle's varsity career—had infused his confidence. He adhered to Mehrens' training regimen and got faster. He listened to his advice about the importance of paying attention to the small details, and the habit produced the results his coach had promised.

The following spring, Sprinkle applied Mehrens' advice to a new interest. He decided to run for student body president. The decision, in and of itself, was not particularly courageous. What made it impressive was that Sprinkle had to give a speech before the entire 900-member student body. Such a challenge, intimidating for any high school student, could be downright debilitating for one with a speech impediment.

To make matters worse, Sprinkle's opponent was David Wells, captain of the debate squad and a member of the drama club. Wells was far and away the most eloquent speaker at GFC. If mishandled, Sprinkle knew his performance could subject him to a good deal of public ridicule. However, he chose to do it because he recalled Mehrens' earlier advice about the benefit of making one's goals public. He knew he might fail, but he figured that was better than never trying.

Sprinkle approached his speech in the same fashion that Mehrens had taught him to prepare for a football game. He outlined and wrote down his goals. He organized his remarks and then practiced relentlessly. Sprinkle spent hours in front of his mirror at home reciting his speech.

Then, on the day of his speech, he walked on stage with the same confidence he had demonstrated when he told Mehrens he could score against Havre, and he delivered his remarks. After he was done, his friends and teammates sat in stunned silence for a moment. Sprinkle had delivered his remarks without stuttering once. They jumped to their feet and gave him a rousing ovation.

His remarks, while flawlessly delivered, failed to persuade a majority of the student body that he was the best candidate, and he was defeated in the ensuing election. But for Sprinkle, the defeat was not a setback, because he had defeated a far more difficult opponent—his stutter.

The following fall, on the same day that President John F. Kennedy visited Great Falls and gave a speech before a packed audience at Memorial Stadium, Sprinkle was sworn in as the president of his senior class.

Today, while an occasional hint of a stutter can still be discerned if one listens closely, Sprinkle, an accomplished public speaker, is regularly called upon in his official capacity to give talks before large audiences.

1986

After a year coaching at Charles M. Russell High School in Great Falls, Sprinkle coached five years at Billings Central and then moved to Helena High School. In 1985, in his second season as the head coach of the Helena High Bengals, he coached the team to its most successful season in school history. The following year, they were looking to improve upon their 7–2 record and make a run for the state championship. In most polls, they were picked to finish in the top five. The Bengals were led by Dave Nyland, a modest-sized senior quarterback, who had started the previous season only because the team's starting quarterback was caught at a beer party before the season began and was kicked off the team by Sprinkle.

Nyland was just the kind of kid that had caused Sprinkle to forsake the allure of a college football coaching career and made him instead go into high school coaching. Nyland came from a broken family and lived on the east side of Helena—the blue-collar side of town. He had some rough edges. Many weeks he would alternate between wearing two different shirts in a feeble attempt to give the illusion that his wardrobe had more variety than it really did.

Sprinkle saw in Nyland shades of himself 25 years earlier. The kid had some athletic talent but lacked the discipline and self-esteem to get him to the next level. Sprinkle, who modeled his coaching style after Mehrens, knew what he had to do, and he strove to provide Nyland the same structure Mehrens had given him. He made Nyland write down his goals, gave him a training regimen, and pushed him to work as hard as possible. Sprinkle realized, though, he had to go beyond and really reach out to him. So just as Mehrens had done with him years earlier, he invited Nyland over to his house on occasion.

Other times, knowing that Nyland didn't have much money, Sprinkle would treat the kid to a meal at an upscale restaurant in Helena. Their last meal occurred near the end of Nyland's senior season. The early promise of a run at the state championship had faded. The Bengals were 2–6 after losing the second to last game of the season in overtime. It was their second overtime loss of the year, and five of their losses had been by a combined 13 points. To make matters worse, Nyland had suffered a season ending injury in the game. In reality, it was also a career-ending injury, because Nyland didn't have the talent to go on and play at the collegiate level.

The boy's confidence was shattered, and his dream of salvaging the season with a season-ending victory over the Bengals' arch rival, the Helena Capital Bruins, was no longer possible because of the injury. The starting job was turned over to Sean Downs, a junior.

"I know you're disappointed, Dave," said Sprinkle, whose only tangible difference from Mehrens' coaching style was that he called players by their first name, "but don't think that all of your hard work and effort has been for nothing."

"But look at our record, Coach. I was supposed to lead the team to a conference championship," he said as his wispy hair fell over his eyes. "We were expected to finish near the top of the polls." The disappointment was evident in his voice, and his reply was hard to hear because he had dropped his head.

"Look at me, Dave. You have nothing to hang your head over. We lost a lot of close games, and I, as a coach, am more responsible for that than you. You should be proud of all you've accomplished. You've come an incredible distance in a short amount of time. You set high expectations for yourself and for our team this season, and we almost obtained them. We have lost five games by a total of 13 points. Football, like life, can be that way. Had the ball bounced differently a couple of times, or had a few of our players not gotten hurt, we could easily be 6–2 or maybe even 7–1 at this stage. Unfortunately, we're not."

"I'm sorry, Coach," replied Nyland, not buying into what he thought were just platitudes from Sprinkle. "I let you and the team down."

"Hold on," interrupted Sprinkle. "You haven't let anyone down. I can't tell you how proud I am of you. Look at me," he said, pausing until Nyland looked him in the face. "Over the last two seasons you have come a long, long way. Your teammates respect you because you're a leader, and I trust your judgment—I wouldn't have let you call plays and audible if I didn't." Nyland silently acknowledged his progress and the confidence Sprinkle had shown in him. "But remember this," continued Sprinkle, "wherever life takes you next, it's better that you set high goals and fall a little short than to have never set any goals in the first place. Now, get your head up and keep it up," Sprinkle said with a smile. Nyland looked up and returned the smile. "But you know what," continued Sprinkle, "your team still needs you. You've got to help Downs this week. If we're going to beat the Bruins, he needs your help. We beat these guys last year with you at quarterback, and we can do it again. But Downs needs to benefit from your experience. You're still a member of this team, and I expect you to help this team win."

Nyland did his part and supported Downs throughout the week of practice, and that Friday night he was his greatest supporter on the sideline. Unfortunately, as often happens in football, things don't always favor the better or more prepared team. For the third time that season, the Helena High Bengals lost in overtime. They finished the season a disappointing 2–7.

Following the conclusion of the season, Sprinkle received one of the greatest shocks of his coaching life. When the final season polls came out, the Bengals, despite their record, were ranked sixth in the final statewide poll of the Double A conference schools. It was an implicit acknowledgment that Nyland and his team had just run into some bad luck.

That small recognition, however, was not nearly as satisfactory as what happened next. At the end of the season, Sprinkle announced he was leaving coaching to accept a leadership position with the Montana High School Athletic Association. As he was clearing out his office and reflecting on whether his years of coaching had been worth the effort, the school receptionist brought him a small, poorly wrapped present. "It's from one of your players," she said. Sprinkle studied it for a moment and then unwrapped it. He stared at the contents, and tears welled up in his eyes. The gift was a mocked up copy of a *Sports Illustrated* cover with a picture of him roaming the sidelines during a game. The headline had been doctored to read, "Coach of the Year." Attached to the gift was a two-word note that simply read, "Thanks, Coach." It was signed by Dave Nyland.

It was all Sprinkle needed to know that he had made the right decision to go into high school coaching. He had made a positive impact in a player's life—just as Mehrens had made an impact on his life. To this day, the gift holds a prominent place on Sprinkle's office wall. It is among his most prized possessions, and it is a daily reminder of what coaching is all about.

Sweat the Small Stuff

COACHING FOR LIFE TIP #6:
The difference between winning
and losing can be found in the details.

QUOTE TO REMEMBER:
*"We are what we repeatedly do. Excellence,
then, is not an act, but a habit."*
—ARISTOTLE

KEY QUESTIONS TO ANSWER:
Do you adequately know all of the strengths and weaknesses
of the members of your team? What are you doing to maximize the former and minimize the latter?

Learning to Sweat the Small Stuff

1. When did preparation for the 1962 season begin?

2. How did Mehrens and McMahon apply "attention to detail" to their own coaching habits and techniques?

3. How did the coaches use this trait to reinforce some of their other coaching principles, such as goal setting, preaching persistence, and building confidence?

4. Aside from individual player development, what ancillary benefits were derived from "sweating the small stuff"?

5. Discuss the role that repetition played in focusing players on the smaller details of the game.

6. Was attention to detail stressed only in regard to physical activities?

7. What were some of the benefits of this coaching principle?

CHAPTER 7

"Talent is God-given:

be humble;

Fame is man-given:

be thankful;

Conceit is self-given:

be careful."

—JOHN WOODEN

THIS IS YOUR RESPONSIBILITY

Wally Berry's and Bruce Campbell's Stories

September 1962

At 190 pounds and 6'2", Wally Berry was the epitome of a football player—at least by 1962 standards. He was nearly the largest player on the Great Falls Central team and ran the 40-yard dash in 4.6 seconds. To top it off, he could lower his shoulder and punish defenders with his solid size.

It was this combination of size, speed, and strength that made him the team's best player and its most potent offensive force—as he so ably demonstrated when he scored four of the team's five touchdowns in Great Falls Central's impressive victory over Butte Central in the season's opener.

But Berry also possessed something else. He had that certain intangible trait that separates the great athletes from the very good. Berry had an unshakeable aura of confidence. He'd had it ever since grade school, but it really began to flourish in his freshmen year when, after being put into his first varsity game—a rarity for a freshman under Bill Mehrens—he scored a 75-yard touchdown the first time he touched the football.

His confidence transcended football and carried over into every aspect of his life. It was conveyed in the way he walked—he was the kind of guy who seemed to not so much walk as strut. It was also there in the way he spoke to adults, and, of course, it was there with girls as well. With his wavy brown hair and slightly darker complexion—the result of a hint of Indian blood he had inherited from his father's side of family—he was as successful with the opposite sex as he was on the gridiron.

As a result of his immense skill and confident demeanor, Berry was selected as one of the three team captains. While Ed Flaherty was the designated "ass-kicker," and the cerebral Gary Wolf was the "brains" of the team, Berry was the kind of guy who let his play on the field do his talking.

Following the Butte Central game, life was good for Wally Berry. His four touchdown performance had caught the attention of a number of college recruiters in the region. And while it was too soon for them to begin contacting him, he was marked as a definite "Big-Time" college prospect.

The week following the Butte Central game, Great Falls Central had a bye, and after a relatively relaxing week of practice, Berry spent the first Saturday of the college football season in front of the family television—a concession his mother had extracted from his father when he relocated the family from Havre to Great Falls a few years earlier.

The only televised game that day was the University of Miami versus Pittsburgh. The Hurricanes surprised the heavily favored

Panthers by a score of 23–14, led by the efficient passing of George Mira, an emerging college superstar. Berry thought little of the game or Mira's performance, but a seed had been planted.

Following the bye week came the Mustangs' miraculous last-second tie against Glasgow. The only silver lining in Berry's otherwise average performance was the devastating block he laid on the Glasgow defender that helped spring Kuntz for his last-second heroics. Berry literally laid the guy flat on his back with a hit that reverberated far behind the sidelines.

In a sense, it was felt all the way down in Miami. That is because although the game film inexplicably stopped just a second before capturing Berry's hit on film, a report of the hit was duly recorded by Al Zarowny, a Roundtable supporter who had some contacts with the University of Miami. He promptly fired off a letter to the head coach and told him he should request some game film of Wally Berry, "the hardest hitting fullback in the West."

During Hell Week, Mehrens rode Berry as hard as he had ever ridden him. The head coach wasn't a screamer, and Berry was not the type of player who needed to be prodded by such methods, but in his own way, Mehrens pushed Berry to step-up his game a notch. His typical tactic was to talk with Berry about his responsibilities as he taped him up every day before practice. As coaching goes, it was pretty subtle. But because Mehrens had the opportunity to talk with him one-on-one for at least five minutes a day, the sheer repetition had a positive effect.

Mehrens would increase the intensity of his lectures to Berry on game days. This was especially the case before the game with the defending state champs, Havre. After the other players had already dressed and gotten on the bus to drive to Havre's stadium, Mehrens reminded Berry of his responsibilities. "This is a big game for us," he started. "I know I don't need to tell you that, but I do want to remind you that it's games like this that separate the boys from the men, or put a little differently, the big-time college players from the in-state players." The latter was a reference to the University of Montana and Montana State.

"You're going up against Glenn Havskjold. He's the fastest player in the state, and he scored three touchdowns last week. I know there are a few college recruiters who have come here to get a look at him and Gorseth. This is your opportunity to steal their spotlight. This is also your opportunity to get a college education and play the game on a much larger stage next fall." Mehrens paused. He rarely emphasized the individual nature of the game and felt a little uncomfortable doing so in this situation.

"But it's more than that," he continued. "It's also your responsibility—to the team and your family. Your mom and dad have made a lot of sacrifices to send you and your brother to Central. You can now repay them by performing to your potential and earning that scholarship. You can also help your teammates win this game—which might be the highlight of their football careers." And just in case Berry didn't pick up on the last point, Mehrens reminded him that he would go on to play college football and most of his teammates wouldn't.

Berry responded to Mehrens' talk. No one shone brighter under the spotlight that night than Wally Berry. He scored one touchdown, threw key blocks on two other scores, and played an outstanding defensive game—limiting Glenn Havskjold to a meager 24 yards.

Another letter from Al Zarowny to Miami followed, and soon after, Mehrens received a note from the University of Miami requesting game film of Wally Berry. Mehrens gladly obliged and sent the film of Berry's dominating performance in the season opener against Butte Central.

September 30, 1962

In Jackson, Mississippi, Governor Ross Barnett, who was opposing the Supreme Court's order to integrate the University of

Mississippi, gave a defiant speech before 40,000 of the Ole Miss faithful before the start of the game against Tulane.

On the following day, October 1, President John F. Kennedy appeared before a national audience to explain why James Meredith was going to be escorted onto the Ole Miss campus by federal marshals. Near the end of his remarks, he called upon the state of Mississippi to uphold its tradition of honor and demonstrate the courage the state had won "on the field of battle and on the gridiron."

Although the president had no way of knowing it at the time, that tradition was being tarnished as he spoke. More than 2,500 angry students and segregationists had stormed the campus in protest. The federal marshals fired tear gas, and in the ensuing melee, two people were killed. Later that evening, Kennedy called Barnett to get a read on the situation. Barnett pleaded with the president to withdraw the marshals, but Kennedy refused to back down from his responsibility to uphold the laws of the land and told the governor that Meredith was going to enroll at the University of Mississippi. He then ordered Barnett to go to Jackson and restore order.

On that Monday morning, James Meredith did just what Kennedy had said would happen when he walked across the still smoldering campus of Ole Miss and registered for classes. In so doing, he became the first black person to ever enroll at the University of Mississippi.

In Great Falls, Father Livix used the event in theology class to challenge his students to consider how they would have acted had they been in Kennedy's situation. The dilemma, however, was brought home in a much more personal way for Father Livix when he saw Valerie Dickerson crying in the hallway later that afternoon.

Father Livix did not see the incident. All he saw was a group of cheerleaders comforting Valerie Dickerson. The Mustangs' junior varsity team had just routed the Hardin team, and one of the

players from the opposing squad, as he was walking to the bus, bumped into Dickerson. Bitter from the 35–0 pasting his team had just taken, he said, "Get out of my way you stupid nigger— go back where you belong." It was not the first such comment Dickerson had heard since arriving in Montana, and she knew it wouldn't be the last. But her transition from living on a military base in Tokyo, Japan, to the lily-white state of Montana was proving to be a difficult one.

"What's wrong, Ms. Dickerson?" inquired Livix.

"Nothing," replied Dickerson. The other cheerleaders, however, told Livix what had happened. The priest put his arm around the girl and said, "Little people like to shoot at big targets."

"I know," she said, wiping back a tear. "It's just that I sometimes get tired of being the only black girl."

Livix empathized with her situation and knew that the epithet she had heard was not the first directed at her. He knew she had probably even heard a few from the student body at Central. "I tell you what. Why don't you come to my office tomorrow. I want to talk about an idea I have."

Livix's idea, as he explained to Dickerson the next day, was to have her give a speech to the entire student body before their first debate competition the following week. "I want you to address the issue of race relations in America—as well as here in Montana—head-on. It'll be good for our students to think about this issue. They need to understand that it's not just something happening down south in places like Mississippi."

October 2, 1962

Word of Berry's football ability wasn't limited to Miami. It reached in all directions across the nation. Recruiters soon began to litter the bleachers at Mustang games and hardly a day went by that Berry didn't receive at least one letter inviting him to visit a school's campus after the season was over.

The letters not only went to Berry's head, their influence soon began to appear on his biweekly report cards. At first, Mehrens let the "C"s pass, but as soon as the first "D" popped up, he acted.

The grade was a red flag to both Mehrens and Father Livix, who, as Dean of Studies, was responsible for rectifying the matter. Livix knew that Mehrens wanted—and expected—to be notified of any academic problems with his players. When he showed the coach the report card, Mehrens replied, "We need to nip this in the bud right now." Livix needed no convincing.

"Anyone else having problems?" asked Mehrens.

"Campbell," replied the priest. "He's barely keeping his head above water in chemistry. He got a C- on his last exam."

"I'll talk with both of them," said Mehrens.

"I'm also going to speak with them."

That afternoon, during his usual taping job, Mehrens spoke with his star fullback about his grades. "I just saw your biweekly report." Berry cringed. He knew what was coming next. "Your grade in Sister Mary Eleanore's English class is unacceptable. You're first and foremost a student, and as long as you're at this school, you will conduct yourself accordingly. If that D isn't gone from your next report card, you'll be suspended from the team until it is corrected. Do I make myself clear? It might not seem like it right now, but there is a lot more to life than football. You're in a unique situation. Football is your ticket to a free college education, but that education is a ticket to a more rewarding and meaningful life."

Berry lowered his head and, for one of the few times that season, sounded contrite. "Yes, sir."

That evening Mehrens also wrote a note to Berry's parents, alerting them to the situation. He knew they, along with Sister Mary Eleanore, would be his strongest allies.

Livix delivered the same message to Berry the next day when he called him into his office. After a stern lecture about the importance of academics, the priest quoted from the Bible. "This

comes from Timothy, chapter two, verse 5: *If any competes as an athlete, he does not receive the victor's crown unless he competes according to the rules."* He stopped and let Berry reflect on the passage for a moment. "Do you know what that means?"

"Yeah," replied Berry with an edge of disrespect. He never showed much affection toward any of the school's priests.

"No, you don't," shot back Livix. "And you probably won't for years to come. The rules have little to do with sports and everything about preparing you for life." Livix would have added that the rules were really meant to prepare him for eternal life, but with students such as Berry he knew he could only press religion so far.

Livix also had a talk with Bruce Campbell, but the conversation had a different tone. He knew that Campbell's situation was very different from Berry's. Campbell's mother died when he was three. His father had left the family when he was four, which was why he was raised by his grandmother and an elderly aunt. Together, the three lived off the aunt's modest pension from her service as a nurse in World War I.

Livix knew the struggles his aunt and grandmother made to send Campbell to Great Falls Central, and he wanted the boy to understand that as well. Having just recited a passage from Timothy to Berry, the priest reverted to it again. "Let me read you a passage, Mr. Campbell. It comes from the book of Timothy. *'If a widow has children or grandchildren, they should learn first of all to put their religion into practice by caring for their own family and so repaying their parents and grandparents, for this is pleasing to God.'*

"Do you know that means?" Campbell remained silent. "I'll tell you what it means. It means that your grandmother and aunt have fulfilled their obligation to give you a good education, and it means you have to apply yourself to your studies so you can do the same for your children some day." Livix could see he was getting beyond the boy, so he brought the conversation back to something more tangible. "But if God's Word isn't enough motivation for you,

I have spoken with *Coach Mehrens*—and you'll be off the team if your performance doesn't improve on the next chemistry test."

October 5, 1962, 2:45 p.m.

The class bell rang at 2:30. The energy in the school was already at fever pitch. Pep rallies at Central were a big deal, and the school day had been shortened by a full hour to accommodate the event. It didn't matter if you were a boy or a girl, athlete or nonathlete, outgoing or introverted; all the students were engaged in the rally, and they did it willingly. They had real pride in their school.

That pride was everywhere. The Mustang Activity Club had decked out the entire school with posters and banners. The Letterman Club had repainted the large golden Mustang statute in the foyer, and the Key Club had combed the campus grounds for every stray piece of litter.

The energy was even more evident today because it was homecoming. At the request of the five senior cheerleaders—Patty O'Loughlin, Susie Beaulaurier, Marian McKay, Barbie Theisen, and Chari Pat Dale—Father Reitz had agreed that they could conduct the pep rally from the roof of the school. The cheerleaders pleaded to have the venue changed from the gymnasium, arguing that the warm weather and fall foliage were ideal for an outdoor rally. Plus, they argued their "elevated" presence was in keeping with the homecoming week's theme which—in response to President Kennedy's recent call to land a man on the moon—had been dubbed "Stairway to the Stars."

As the band played the school rouser, the entire school body, aided by the pep club—whose sole job was to cheer more loudly than the average fan—joined with the cheerleaders. "Give me an M," Cheer Queen Patty O'Loughlin yelled as she led them in the opening cheer. "What does it spell?" she asked after she had spelled out the entire word. Over 800 students thundered in unison, "Mustangs!"

As the students had their eyes directed toward the roof and were screaming from the tops of their lungs, five players, dressed in cheerleader outfits and wearing wigs over their crew cuts, took their place in front of the assembly. The husky frames of Greg Mills, Jerry Kuntz, Byron Weber, Ed Flaherty, and Bob Kunz filled the tight sweaters, and their thick, muscular, hairy legs jutted out from under short, pleated skirts. Even Mehrens and McMahon, who both disliked all the distracting activities that surrounded homecoming week, smiled at the hideous contrast the players made to their real cheerleader counterparts on the roof.

Once the pep rally broke up, the coaches' patience for all things not related to the game evaporated. Mehrens did not allow his players to participate in the homecoming parade. Instead, he ordered them to go home or to a friend's home and have an early dinner and a nap before returning to the school later to get ready for the game.

Meanwhile, the rest of the student body made its way downtown to watch the parade. The citizens of Great Falls also came out in droves for the annual fall ritual and were treated to an impressive parade. It easily bested the public school's homecoming parade held the week before and reflected the Great Falls Central's tremendous spirit, as well as the pride it felt in its football program.

A banner reading "A Fantasy in Space" marked the start of the parade. This was followed by the freshman and sophomore class floats, entitled, "Let's Orbit the Bulldogs" and "We're Out to Launch...the Bulldogs." The Latin Club, the Gray Ladies (an organization dedicated to training future nurses), and a host of other school clubs also had a presence. The parade made its way down Central Avenue, past the Elmore Hotel, the Mint Bar, Woolworth's, the Liberty Theater, and the host of other small businesses that lined the avenue before ending at the Civic Center where the homecoming court was crowned.

October 5, 1962, 6:30 p.m.

Although the Mustangs had easily defeated the defending state champions the previous week, Mehrens was concerned about another Glasgow-like letdown against Hardin. Therefore, that whole week before each practice as he taped up Berry—who had been beaten up pretty badly by Havre—Mehrens took the opportunity to remind Berry again of his responsibilities.

On the day before the Hardin game, Berry came down with a serious flu virus and missed practice. As was his policy, Mehrens listed his star running back as questionable for the game.

The next day, he was relieved to see Berry in school but decided to take a wait and see approach on the issue of whether he would even suit up. Only at 6 o'clock, when Berry arrived in the locker room, did Mehrens give him permission to get dressed.

As he gingerly taped around his shoulder, Mehrens asked his fullback how he was feeling. "Felt better, Coach," responded Berry stoically. Mehrens could see that he was hurting. "Well, let's just play it by ear. If we play to our capability, we should be able to get by without you." Berry's competitive instinct caused him to recoil at the comment, and Mehrens could sense he had struck a raw nerve.

"At least let me play defense, Coach," pleaded Berry, in a tone that came as close to begging as he would ever allow himself.

"We'll see," replied Mehrens, who was nervous about every opponent regardless of their record. He was more nervous than usual because the Hardin game was the start of divisional play, which, in turn, would determine who represented the Western Division in the state championship game. "There are going to be times this season when you'll have to carry this team on your back. If this is one of them, I'll let you know."

Across the locker room, John McMahon was taping up Bruce Campbell, a big rawboned kid with a rough edge to him.

Although 5'11" and 160 pounds, Campbell had a lean, strong frame, befitting a kid who spent two summers lifting heavy parts in a junkyard and another two summers baling hay under the hot Montana sun on a wheat farm.

Campbell was nowhere near as talented as Berry, but he still had skills. And it was McMahon—the guy Campbell had come recently to call "Bug Eyes" and "Zipperhead" behind his back—who first recognized it. McMahon could be hard on his linemen, and he was especially hard on Campbell, but it was only because he saw in him the kind of intense mental toughness that, if properly channeled, could overpower the skills of more natural athletes. McMahon thrived on the challenge of getting the most out of kids such as Campbell, in part, because they were so much like himself.

The pair's relationship started the first day of practice. In fact, Campbell had the dubious distinction of being the first player to draw the wrath of McMahon. Campbell was late for the first practice of the season, and by the time he was fully dressed he was in the unfortunate position of having to walk out of the locker room behind both Mehrens and McMahon. As he plotted his course around the pair in order to get in position before calisthenics began, Campbell heard McMahon grumble, as he looked over his new prospects, "This is what I've got to work with?" The contempt was evident in his voice.

Hearing enough, Campbell strapped on his helmet and made his move. As he darted past the coaches, he was just beginning to think he was safe when he heard McMahon yell, "Hey, you!" Campbell stopped in his tracks and turned around. McMahon motioned for him to come closer and, when he was within reach, grabbed him by his face mask. "What's your name?"

"Campbell," replied the scared teenager.

"Well, Campbell, it's a minute after seven. Why are you late?" Campbell began to offer an explanation, but McMahon shut him down. "Wrong! You don't have an excuse," he replied, still gripping

Campbell's face mask. "Unless you have a family emergency, your first responsibility for the next three months is to this football team. If you don't have enough respect for Coach Mehrens, myself, or your teammates to get here on time, then you don't belong out here. Practice begins promptly at seven." After a pause, McMahon pushed Campbell away and said, "Now give me three laps." Dazed by the rude awakening, Campbell set off, wondering what he and his teammates had in store for themselves this season.

McMahon continued to ride Campbell throughout the two-a-day sessions. But it wasn't until the second week that the assistant coach began to coax Campbell's full potential out of him. As he had already done with a few other players, McMahon taught Campbell to properly tackle. He did it by focusing on technique. McMahon constantly admonished his charges to square up to the runner, keep their head to the side, wrap their arms around the runner, and keep their legs pumping until "he is on his back!" During one particular "meat grinder" drill, Campbell followed the rules to perfection and leveled Wally Berry. The hit felt so good to Campbell that from that point forward, he was a hitting machine. Over the course of the season, McMahon learned how to fan Campbell's newfound passion for hitting people. Often an encouraging pat on the head was all that was needed. It was like throwing a piece of raw meat to a hungry lion—it only stoked more aggressive behavior in Campbell.

The next step in Campbell's development occurred after the Glasgow game—during the notorious Hell Week. No one on defense the previous week, including Campbell, had played aggressively enough for McMahon. He was bound and determined to rectify the issue. So when he wasn't punishing his linemen with sprints or laps or working them on the blocking sled, McMahon used the remaining time to work with his linemen on technique. In addition to fine-tuning Campbell's stance, he taught him how to employ the forearm shiver—a hit that in 1962 was legal, within limits.

During the Havre game, Campbell showed his coach that he had been an attentive student by dropping Havre's star running back Glenn Havskjold early in the first quarter with a wicked forearm shiver. The hit not only nearly decapitated the Havre star, it sent chills down McMahon's spine. He always loved a good hit, and 40-plus years later he would still recall Campbell's hit as one of the most bone-rattling in all his years of coaching football at either the high school or college level.

But as McMahon was taping up Campbell before the Hardin game, all of that past performance was forgotten. The assistant coach was focused on the present. "I don't want another embarrassing home performance like we had against Glasgow," McMahon said in his gravelly voice. "We should be able to crush these guys. Just remember to stay focused and fire off the ball. Your job is to contain the end run. If they try it, deliver that forearm shiver of yours. I guarantee that they won't come around your way again. What they will try is either a screen play or maybe a short pass to the flat. Your job is to stay home. If you stay home and do your job, everything is going to be okay. Got it?" Campbell nodded. "Good. Now go out there and knock some heads."

October 5, 1962, 8:45 p.m.

The homecoming game against Hardin started poorly. On the second play of the game, Gary Wolf pitched the ball past the outstretched hands of Jerry Kuntz, who was sweeping left. It bounced right into the arms of a Hardin defender who raced it back 60 yards for the game's opening score. (The newspaper the next day erroneously reported that Kuntz had fumbled the ball. He never touched the ball.)

Determined to make up for his mistake, Wolf efficiently led his team down the field on its next possession, and the Mustangs tied the score when Voyd Richtscheid, on his still sore ankle, pushed it across from the four-yard line. Later in the first half, after a series of costly mistakes had stalled two promising drives, Kuntz caught a 12-yard pass from Gary Wolf to give the Mustangs a modest 14–7 halftime lead.

The go-ahead score did little to appease Mehrens' fury. He collected his thoughts as he walked to the warming hut at the far end of the field where his team always gathered for halftime. As he entered the small shack, he slammed the door shut so hard that it nearly came unhinged. He had everyone's attention.

"Didn't you learn anything from the Glasgow game!" he bellowed. He was beside himself. "Hardin is 0–4 and clearly the worst team in the Western Conference. They shouldn't even be in this game with us—but they are. And why are they? I'll tell you why—because no one is focusing. If you were, you wouldn't be making the stupid mistakes we've been making. And I'm not just talking about the fumble," said Mehrens, looking past Wolf. "It's all the other little mistakes. We have had four penalties for 40 yards this half. Those penalties killed two drives! We should be ahead by three or four scores.

"I really thought that after the Havre game that this team had turned the corner. Apparently not. Apparently, we need to push you every week like we did after the Glasgow game. Is that what you want?" he asked rhetorically. The team members all sat quietly. "Because, if it is, Coach McMahon and I *will give it you.*

"I can't begin to tell you how much it disappoints me that I have to yell and scream at you in an effort to get you motivated. Especially this week of all weeks. It's homecoming! The bleachers are packed with former students and players, and this is the best that you can do to honor them—by giving them a 14–7 lead over the worst team in the conference? You need to have some pride in your performance! And if some of you don't find some soon, you're going to find yourself riding the bench." He directed the last comment at Bruce Campbell who had two of the four penalties. "I saw how well the scout team practiced this week, and I am

not going to hesitate to put them in. In fact, if I don't see a marked improvement on the first series, you can expect to see some changes.

"And this doesn't just go for this game. It goes for the remainder of the season. Coach McMahon and I are tired of having to kick you guys in the butt! If you don't want to win a championship, then we'll find some guys who do. And I know we will too, because there are some very capable guys sitting on our bench right now just dying to get into the game! So I suggest that those of you who are more focused on the homecoming dance than the homecoming football game get your heads screwed back on right now!"

Mehrens had made his point. Although he was still seething with anger, he cooled down enough to turn his attention to the chalkboard in the corner of the room. Methodically, he dissected the Bulldogs' defense and pointed out a series of vulnerabilities he had spotted during the first half and which he now expected his team to exploit. Play by play, he diagrammed the opening drive of the second half.

After lecturing for a few more minutes, Mehrens sent everyone out to the field to warm up for the second half except Berry and Campbell.

"How do you feel, Berry?" asked Mehrens. His star player had seen limited action in the first half, but Mehrens knew that he needed him now. "I'm going to start you in the second half." Berry got up to go, but Mehrens pulled him back. "Remember earlier this season when I said there would be times when you're going to have to carry this team?" Berry nodded. "Well, this is one of those times. I know you're hurting, but we need you. You're the captain of this team, and now is the time to let your play do your talking for you. This is a responsibility that can't be delegated."

Across the locker room, McMahon was retaping Campbell's ankle—which he had twisted that week in practice—and was giving him a similar lecture. "You've played a good first half,

Campbell, but you've got to step it up a notch. Continue to watch for the short pass. Hardin is going to try to take advantage of your aggressiveness, but you've got to stay home. If the quarterback drops back to make that short pass, get your arms up in the air and just knock it down."

"Got it," replied Campbell. "Stay home."

The second half started with Hardin receiving the opening kickoff. The Mustangs' aggressive kick coverage team pinned them down at the 15-yard line. And after two futile runs that yielded no yards, the Bulldogs attempted a screen pass out to the flat just as McMahon had predicted. Campbell spotted it immediately, and as the Hardin offensive end released his block and slid out to the flat, Campbell stayed put and kept his eye on the quarterback. Never very adept at catching the ball—which is why he played only defensive end and not offensive end—his first reaction was to swat down the soft pass that the quarterback tried to float over his head. But as the ball lingered in the air, Campbell decided to make a play for it. To almost everyone's surprise—especially McMahon, who often chided Campbell for his "lobster-like" hands—he caught it.

No one was more surprised than Campbell himself, and he momentarily paused like a deer caught in the headlights before advancing the ball. It was unfortunate because there was nothing but green grass in front him, and he could have scored a touchdown had his reaction been quicker. As it was, he returned the ball to the Hardin seven-yard line before being hauled down.

As he came off the field, McMahon gave him a pat on the helmet and screamed "Attaboy! I told you good things would happen if you just stayed home."

On the ensuing play, Berry, still feeling weak from the stomach virus, mustered enough energy to burst through the line for the Mustangs' third score.

After another three-and-out, Hardin lined up to punt. Campbell, still riding high from McMahon's pat on the head, burst in from his left end position and blocked the punt. On the very next play, Berry followed the blocks of Dick Kuntz and Ed Flaherty and sprinted 38 yards straight up the middle to blow the game open. Three minutes into the second half, Great Falls led 28–7.

McMahon turned to Mehrens on the sideline and said with a laugh, "Maybe we should hold more of those one-on-one talks at halftime." A 43-yard screen pass from Wolf to Richtscheid in the fourth quarter rounded out the scoring of the Mustangs' 35–7 victory.

October 12, 1962

The following week, the Mustangs made the long trip to Billings to battle their other Catholic rival—the Billings Central Rams. A victory over the Rams would not only give the Mustangs a sweep over both their Catholic rivals for the year, it would also put them up 2–0 in divisional play.

Both Berry and Campbell continued to perform as quiet leaders and let their play on the field speak for itself. Berry began the game by demonstrating that he was as effective on defense as he was on offense. The Billings' coach would later say that Berry's performance from his linebacker position was one of the most dominating defensive performances he had ever witnessed by an individual player in his coaching career.

Berry was also a force on the other side of the ball. He scored Great Fall's second touchdown of the game on a 10-yard run and finished the game with 150 yards on 11 carries.

Bruce Campbell continued his stellar play, but in the middle of the second quarter, after the Rams had run three consecutive end arounds to his side, he began to get a little angry. In his exuberance to end such nonsense, he employed his newly honed skill and delivered one of his patented forearm shivers. Instead of hitting Billings' star running back across the chest, he caught him up around the chin and almost took off his head. The hit drew a

15-yard penalty and got Campbell thrown out of the game. Outraged at the referee's overreaction to what he thought was a legitimate hit, Campbell stormed off the field and threw his helmet at the team bench.

McMahon rushed over to him and yanked him hard by the shoulder pads. "Don't you ever pull a stunt like that again," he screamed in his face. "You might disagree with the call, but you handle it like a man. Throwing helmets is for losers. Now go pick it up and calmly walk to the locker room. I'm not through with you."

The truth was that McMahon *was* finished talking with him. He thought that Campbell's hit was fair and had come to appreciate Campbell's raw emotions. Deep down he also knew that he'd have done the same thing at his age.

Coach Mehrens, however, was another story. He pulled Campbell aside first thing after he entered the locker room for halftime. "That was unacceptable, Mr. Campbell. I know you disagreed with the call, and I'll even grant you that the decision may have been wrong, but as a member of the Great Falls Mustangs, you will *always* act as a gentleman. If I have to remind you of that fact again, you'll be off the team." There was no emotion in Mehrens' voice. It was simply a fact, *Great Falls Central players acted like gentlemen on and off the field.* Livix reiterated the message when he caught up with Campbell sitting on the sideline during the second half. "Everyone who competes for the prize exercises self-control in all things."

May 1963

By the spring of 1963, most of the seniors of Great Falls Central had things other than school on their mind. Bruce Campbell was no exception. One warm evening, he, along with some other seniors, including John O'Rourke, Fred Zadich, and Gary Wolf, went cruising downtown. And as teenage boys sometimes do, they started drinking beer. With spring in the air, some

good music on the radio, and the end of their high school careers clearly on the horizon, the seniors easily polished off a case of Rainer Beer. One thing led to another, and soon they were cited for disorderly conduct outside the Burger Master and given citations for underage drinking.

After considering that it was a first-time offense for all involved, Father Reitz decided to allow the students to participate in the upcoming graduation ceremony. He also recognized it would have been somewhat embarrassing for the school to dismiss its top students. Zadich was the class valedictorian, and Gary Wolf was the class salutorian. John O'Rourke was also a model student. Moreover, all three were headed to college.

Bruce Campbell was not. As a result, some school officials weren't as concerned about him because he was the kind of kid for whom high school was the end of his formal education. But they felt to deny him the opportunity to graduate from high school—especially after his aunt and grandmother had sacrificed so much to send him to Catholic school—seemed unnecessarily harsh. Plus, they couldn't really penalize Campbell and not the others. (Father Reitz allowed the four to participate in the graduation ceremony, but they were handed empty diplomas. They only received their official certificates after they performed 20 hours of manual labor cleaning up the school after the school year was over.)

John McMahon had a different take on the situation. One day shortly after the incident he grabbed Campbell by the collar in the hallway between classes. "What you guys got caught doing the other night was pretty stupid," he said.

"I know," mumbled Campbell meekly, avoiding eye contact.

"Look at me, Campbell," snapped McMahon. "Zadich, Wolf, and O'Rourke—those guys are book smart. That's why they're all going to college. You're smart too, but guys like you—and by that I mean the guys who work in the smelters and the factories—don't usually get the same breaks. More often than not, guys like you get nailed. You got a second chance on this one, and you should count your blessings. You're lucky you weren't thrown out of school." Campbell made a modest move to escape McMahon's hold but it only caused the assistant coach to tighten his grip. "Listen to me, Campbell. Life isn't always going to throw you second chances. After you get your diploma, you can do as you please. But if you mess up, the responsibility is yours. Just remember this: After you leave here, it's not life circumstances that will make you a winner or a loser; it's how you react to those events after they have happened that will define you.

"You're going to make some mistakes and have some setbacks. But you can either learn from them and admit your part in them— as you did after that time you acted like an idiot at Billings Central— or you can continue to make the problem worse by failing to own up to it and taking responsibility. The choice is yours." McMahon finished by looking him in the eye and saying, "Okay?"

"Yes, sir."

McMahon released his grip and walked away with a smile on his face. Campbell was the kind of kid that made coaching worthwhile for McMahon, and he was glad he had the chance to give him one more coaching lesson.

During this same period in the spring of 1963, Wally Berry was also involved in the same type of extracurricular activities as his classmates, although he was more preoccupied. Since the end of the football season the previous fall, he had received no less than 26 scholarship offers to play college football. Offers poured in from Iowa, Minnesota, Wyoming, Washington, Colorado, as well as all of the smaller regional schools, including Montana, Montana State, and South and North Dakota. Most impressive, at least to the Catholics of Great Falls, was the letter he received from Notre Dame, inviting him to come to South Bend on a half football scholarship. It was an attractive deal, but the cost was still beyond the financial means of Berry's family.

The sheer number of offers was gratifying, but it was also overwhelming. In his heart, Berry wanted to play at Montana State at Bozeman, where his best friend, Jerry Kuntz, had decided to go. But the pressure from friends and family alike to go to a major Division I football program and play on the big stage was immense.

That spring he traveled to Iowa City and visited the University of Iowa. He came away impressed, and it wasn't simply because they feted him with lobster—a delicacy that he had never before sampled. The University of Iowa was also home to Great Falls Central's only other Division I star, Bill Restelli. Restelli had graduated the previous spring and would later go on to become a two-year, All-Big Ten defensive tackle with the Hawkeyes. Berry figured it would be comforting to know at least one person at college. Plus, having grown up listening to many of the teams play on the radio, he relished the idea of playing football in the Big Ten.

He delayed making a decision, however. Partly, he was unsure which school was best for him. And part of it stemmed from the fact that Berry loved the attention and opportunities that the scholarship offers provided. There was hardly a day his mom or dad wasn't stopped on the streets and asked about his latest scholarship offer. Moreover, the recruitment process provided him some pretty exotic opportunities, such as the chance to visit the University of Miami.

The flight alone was almost enough to convince Berry to attend Miami. He had never been on a commercial airliner, and when he arrived on campus he was put in his very own room at the Holiday Inn near campus and told he could make unlimited long distance calls from the phone. For a kid from Great Falls, the flight, the Holiday Inn, and the free long distance phone calls were the epitome of high living. He was nearly ready to sign on the spot.

It only got better, though. His first evening he was wined and dined at the prestigious Bonfire restaurant in downtown Miami. It was here that Berry sampled his first Singapore Sling cocktail and had the opportunity to rub elbows with Miami's Heisman candidate, George Mira—the same guy he had watched lead Miami to an impressive victory over Pittsburgh on national television the previous fall.

The only black mark of the evening occurred when Berry was asked how he wanted his steak done. His honest response to the waiter was "Cooked." His comment elicited laughs from the coaches, players, and even the other recruits. Berry playfully laughed along. The only problem was that he had no idea what the waiter's question implied. He rarely had steak, and when he did, his father simply barbecued it on a grill in the backyard.

Berry asked the waiter what his choices were. "Rare, medium rare, medium, or well done," he was told. The latter sounded like the best and most sensible option, so he responded accordingly.

The waiter gave him a mortified look and condescendingly said, "Sir, the Bonfire does not cook steaks well done!" Berry turned 82 shades of red and wanted to hide under the table. He spent the rest of the evening trying to downplay the incident.

The experience reminded him that at heart he was still just a kid from Montana, and, in spite of Miami's warm weather and the university's growing reputation as a rising football powerhouse, he was a fish out of water.

On the return flight, he decided to attend the University of Iowa. The following day, with no guidance from either Coach Mehrens or his father, Berry wrote the other 25 universities and informed them of his decision.

There was only one problem. Since dining on lobster in Iowa City, Berry hadn't bothered to tell anyone at the University of Iowa of his continued interest in playing for their program. As a result, Iowa had distributed all of its remaining scholarships.

When he finally got around to telling them that he had accepted their offer, he was stunned to learn it no longer existed.

Berry panicked. He felt he had messed up a no-lose situation. In desperation, he turned to his coach. He told Mehrens what happened, and his coach offered him some simple advice.

"You made a mistake. The best thing to do is accept responsibility and call the coach at the college of your next choice and ask him if he'll still have you." Berry pondered telling Mehrens that his next choice was Bozeman but felt—perhaps justifiably so—that his decision would not be well received. When Mehrens pressed him about his next choice, he told him it was Miami. "Well, get on the phone and call the coach." Berry paused. "If you can't afford the call," continued Mehrens, "you can come over to my house this evening and use my phone."

Berry begged off on the offer, but later that evening placed an apologetic call to Miami's coach. To his great relief, he was told that Miami was still interested in him. When he received the scholarship paperwork in the mail three days later, he signed the letter of commitment on the spot and sent it back to the University of Miami. It was a fateful decision.

Fall 1963

Berry enrolled at Miami in mid August 1963. When he arrived, he was startled to learn that eight other freshmen fullbacks had also received full-ride scholarships. After the first day of three-a-days—the Miami Hurricanes then practiced from 7 to 9 a.m., 1 to 2:30 p.m., and again from 6 to 7:30 p.m. (with chalk talks between)—Berry crawled back to his spacious dorm room that he shared with four other freshman football players. He was so exhausted that he just wanted to sleep, but he couldn't get out of his mind the fact that there were eight other players all vying for the same job. And to compound matters this was just the freshman team.

Finally, he asked one of his roommates, who also happened to have been a star fullback on his high school team in Pennsylvania, what was going on.

"You must not have done your homework, Berry," he said laughing. "Didn't you know that Miami recruits fullbacks with the intention of converting them into pulling guards." Berry was speechless. He was a fullback, not a guard. For the next few weeks, he cursed the circumstances that had compelled him to select Miami in such haste.

Over the first month, he narrowly avoided being converted into a guard and moved his way up the depth chart to become the number three fullback on the freshman squad. Then the number two fullback, recognizing that the varsity team already had two underclassman fullbacks, saw the writing on the wall and left Miami to return home. Shortly thereafter, just before the big freshman game between the University of Miami and Florida State, the starting freshman fullback got hurt. Berry was now at the top of the list. The swagger in his step was back, and he was beginning to think that things would turn out all right.

The freshmen game against Florida State was played in the Orange Bowl, and it was the pinnacle of their season (in 1963 freshmen were not allowed to play varsity football). Some 28,000 Florida football enthusiasts showed up to catch a first glimpse of their respective team's future varsity starters.

Berry had a solid, if unspectacular, game. It was clear, though, that his 190-pound frame didn't carry the same clout in Division I football as it did on the high school gridirons of Montana.

He vowed to rectify the matter by lifting weights and eating more in the off-season, but when the football season ended, those responsibilities clashed with the responsibility of maintaining a solid 2.0 grade point average—which the university required of all its athletes in order to remain on scholarship. Those responsibilities also collided with all the extracurricular activities the vibrant city of Miami offered a young, attractive college football player.

Perhaps not unsurprisingly, with no coach or priest overlooking his every report card, lifting weights and partying won out over studies. In late spring, the situation was compounded when Berry contracted mononucleosis and started missing classes. Soon after, his GPA dropped below the 2.0 threshold.

The situation only went from bad to worse when the head coach, who had recruited Berry, was fired after the George Mira-led Hurricanes posted a very disappointing 4–7 record in the 1963 season.

The new coach, Charlie Tate, came to Miami with radically different plans, and, unfortunately for Berry, they didn't call for keeping a lot of modest-sized fullbacks on scholarship in the expectation that they might some day beef up and be converted into pulling guards.

Berry knew he was on the hot seat. Tate wasn't going to strip him of his scholarship, but he was going to make life very difficult for him and all those other players who didn't fit into his scheme. He wanted to use his limited number of scholarships in a much different way.

The first sign of trouble came when Berry was transferred from his air-conditioned dorm room to the regular small, hot, cramped freshmen dorm across campus. Next, Tate placed those players he viewed as dispensable on the junior varsity squad, where they were considered fodder for the varsity.

More than anything else, it was those bruising practice sessions that caused Berry to recognize his days as a Miami Hurricane were over. It was a difficult and painful pill for him to swallow, but he decided not to go back to Miami for his sophomore year.

Upon returning to Montana, Berry felt as if he had not only let down his family and Coach Mehrens but also the greater Great Falls community that had been so proud that one of their own had received a full ride to the University of Miami and was going to perform on the national stage.

His disappointment was tempered by the belief that he could still play at Montana State. Berry had no way of knowing it at the time, but his football career was over the day he left Miami. He did attend Montana State University the following fall with his buddy Jerry Kuntz, but his low GPA average—which had transferred from Miami—prevented him from obtaining a scholarship. And instead of playing football, he had to work part-time to pay for his tuition. It was an unfortunate set of circumstances, because he likely would have excelled at the smaller school.

Upon returning to campus life, however, the freedom of being away from home once again caught up with him and Kuntz. By the spring of 1965, both of their grades were insufficient to warrant a 2S draft deferment.

With no real alternative, the pair headed to the local Air Force recruiter and turned themselves over to Uncle Sam. Kuntz was not accepted due to his heart condition, but Berry was, and that summer he enlisted in the Air Force. He served for the next four years as a personal finance clerk in a variety of locations, including Germany.

The transition from high school football superstar and Division I college player to anonymous Air Force clerk was not an easy one for Berry. For years he hid behind the typical "coulda, woulda, shoulda"s that so often litter the conversations of those who fail to live up to their potential. But toward the end of his time in the Air Force, Berry began to own up to the fact that he alone bore responsibility for his missed opportunity.

Partly, this acknowledgment was due to growing up. Part of it, though, was the recollection of Mehrens' constantly needling him to step-up and accept responsibility. "There are some responsibilities that can't be delegated," Mehrens had told him years before. He now realized that how he chose to live his life was one of those responsibilities.

With a renewed and more mature attitude, Berry returned to

Great Falls in the fall of 1969 and completed his degree in accounting at the College of Great Falls. In 1973, he married an old neighborhood friend from his school days in Havre. Together, they had one daughter. His first job out of college was working at the credit union, and by the late 1980s, Berry had risen to a vice-presidency at Wells Fargo. In 1990, he became the president of Montana Federal Credit Union, a position he still holds today.

1970

Just about the time Wally Berry was starting to pull his life together, Bruce Campbell's was falling apart. In the summer after his senior year, Campbell married his high school sweetheart. By February 1964, at the age of 19, the couple had their first child. Two more followed in quick succession.

By 1968, however, Campbell's marriage was in serious trouble. The main cause was their young age. But there were other problems as well. Often after his long days working at the Williston Oil Basin in western North Dakota, rather than going home to be with his family, Campbell would hit the local taverns instead. Finances were also an ever present concern. But constantly lingering just below the surface was another more serious problem. Bruce Campbell had never really learned how to be a father. Since his mother died when he was three, and his father left the family when he was just four, his aunt and his grandmother had always provided a roof over his head, three meals a day, and a solid, loving foundation. The one thing they couldn't do, though, was teach him how to be a father.

That was something he would have to learn on his own. And in 1969, his hand was forced. After meeting a member of a local rock-and-roll band, his wife moved out on him and deserted him and the children.

So it was in late 1969, with little warning, Campbell found himself caring for three children under the age of five. He either had to sink or swim. His first recourse was to sink, and he sought relief in alcohol. One morning, after he woke up with a severe hangover and three crying children demanding breakfast, Campbell realized that he had to come to terms with his own shortcomings as a father and to change his life. He recalled Livix's lecture years before and figured that now was the time to put his own faith into action by caring for his family.

With the same determination he demonstrated in becoming a formidable football player—in spite of not having natural physical talents—Campbell trained himself to become a good parent. And employing McMahon's philosophy of focusing on fundamentals first, he learned how to cook, clean, and meet the ever-changing needs of his growing children. More important, he learned how to love and spend time with his kids.

Campbell made a lot of mistakes. There were some times when it appeared he was relapsing into old ways, but he persevered. By 1973, he was living in Sidney, Montana, where the prospects of a man with three kids finding a new wife were about as promising as finding an untapped oil reserve. Luckily, fate intervened, and contrary to McMahon's warning that guys like him didn't usually get a second chance, Campbell met Brenda, his future wife. She had two young boys of her own, and the pair married in 1974. The following year, they had a daughter of their own, and their blended families became a sort of real-life version of the Brady Bunch—minus the fancy house and live-in maid.

The first few years weren't easy. As a railroad maintenance worker, Campbell sometimes struggled on his modest paycheck to pay the mortgage and put food on the table for his six growing kids. But he and his family managed. Through it all, he stayed active in his children's lives. Not surprisingly, he took a keen interest in his boys' football careers—three of whom went on to play for the Sidney Eagles, whose teams won the Montana State Class A championship for nine straight years in the late 1980s and early 1990s.

Today, all of the Campbell kids are doing well, and Campbell himself is working for two of his sons, who own a successful and growing plumbing business in Belgrade, Montana. To this day, he credits John McMahon with being the closest thing he had to a positive male role model in his life.

This Is Your Responsibility

COACHING FOR LIFE TIP #7:
Responsibility is the one thing
that cannot be delegated.

QUOTE TO REMEMBER:
*"Train a child in the way to go,
and when he is old he will not turn from it."*
—PROVERBS 22:6

KEY QUESTIONS TO ANSWER:
Does everyone in your organization have
a clear understanding of their responsibilities?
How do you hold individuals accountable if they don't
fulfill those responsibilities?

Learning This Is Your Responsibility

1. What was the logic behind Mehrens selecting certain players to the role of team captain?

2. To whom was the players' first responsibility?

3. How did the coaches approach to discipline work in partnership with their approach to instilling responsibility?

4. How did the theme of responsibility foster a greater sense of team?

5. How did the coaches and teachers use the ideas of team, community, and society to inculcate in their players a deeper understanding of responsibility?

CHAPTER 8

"Decisions determine destiny."

—JIM IRWIN, APOLLO 15

DIG DEEPER

Greg Steckler's and Mike Donovan's Stories

August 7, 1962

The "Nameless Ones" completed their last set of songs and began packing up their equipment from the small, smoky dance hall in Belt, Montana. After they were done, as was their custom, they gathered in the parking lot and downed a couple of bottles of Great Falls Select—the preferred beer of teenagers on a tight budget—with a few of the local girls who had stayed behind to flirt with the band members.

Greg Steckler, although only a senior in high school, was the lead singer and ring leader of the band. The other members—all of whom were young airmen at the Malmstrom Air Force Base—

had been personally selected by Steckler to be in his band. They were the only people in the greater Great Falls area who shared his appreciation of what was, in 1962 in Montana, commonly referred to as "Black Music"—R&B, jazz, and songs from artists such as Fats Domino, Little Richard, and Chuck Berry.

After unsuccessfully trying to pick up some of the girls, Steckler, who had also been tipping a few beers back between sets, got behind the wheel of his 1953 Chevy Coupe and started the half-hour drive back from Belt. Feeling pretty good, he kicked it up a notch and was traveling about 90 miles an hour when, just outside of Great Falls, he came upon a sharp curve. The alcohol had sufficiently dulled his reactions and caused him to lose control of the car. He slammed on the brakes, but it was too late. The momentum carried the car over, and it rolled a few times before coming to a stop. Miraculously, Steckler wasn't seriously hurt. Dazed and bleeding, but sporting only a bruised ego, he walked back to the road to flag down one of his fellow band members, whom he hoped might still be making their way back from Belt.

His hopes rose when a pair of headlights appeared on the horizon but quickly faded when he realized the headlights belonged to the local sheriff, John Krsul. It didn't take long for Krsul to ascertain that Steckler had been drinking. He escorted the boy home and presented him to his father at 2 a.m. along with a citation directing him to report to court the following day.

Dressed in his best Sunday suit, Steckler and his father arrived at the allotted hour. In the ornate Great Falls courthouse, Judge Bob Nelson presided over the hearing, and when he asked Steckler how he pleaded, the boy stuffed his hands in his pockets, looked at his feet, and mumbled softly, "Guilty."

"Come, again," said Nelson, cocking one ear toward Steckler.

"Guilty, your honor," replied Steckler in only a slightly louder voice.

"Get your hands out of your pockets and stand up straight!"

Nelson glowered at him for a moment and then asked Steckler a surprising question. "Do you play football, young man?"

"No, sir."

"Have you ever played football?"

"Yes, sir."

"And why don't you play anymore?"

"Other interests, I guess," replied Steckler, still looking at his feet.

"Other interests?" replied Nelson in an exaggerated tone. "Like playing rock-and-roll music and drinking beer?"

"Music, yes, sir," responded Steckler, smartly avoiding the second part of the question.

"I see," said Nelson. He rested his chin in his hand and stared at Steckler before asking his next question. "Where do you go to school, Mr. Steckler?"

"Great Falls Central."

Nelson then recessed the hearing and called Steckler's father into the side chamber. A short conversation ensued about the best way to get his son "on the right track."

When the two returned and Nelson took up his position behind the bench, the judge spoke. "Here are your two options, young man. You can either go to the workhouse," he said, pausing to allow enough time for that option to sink in—the workhouse in Miles City was eastern Montana's juvenile detention home, and the sentence carried with it a minimum detention period of three months—"or you can go out for the football team at Great Falls Central."

Steckler turned to his father with a surprised look. His father stared back at him with a look that seemed to say, *I know what I'd do if I were in your situation.*

"I'll go out for football, your honor."

"Smart move, young man. Now, if I hear that you have quit the team any time before the end of the season, the full penalty will be imposed. Do you understand?"

"Yes, your honor."

"Good. But just to make sure you know what you're missing, I'm sentencing you to one day in the workhouse." Nelson slammed down his gavel to signal that the hearing was over. Steckler left the warm courtroom, wondering what had just happened. He had no interest in playing football, and after a year of smoking and drinking, he knew he was in no physical condition to play.

August 31, 1962

It was the Friday afternoon practice at the end of the first week of the two-a-day preseason practices. McMahon had spent the better part of the week focusing on fundamentals. Today, he wanted to turn his attention to tackling, which at GFC meant one thing—the tackling dummy. The dummy was a square-shaped device stationed inconspicuously at the far end of the practice field. To the naked eye, it didn't look like much. It was simply a big canvas-coated two-legged bag, tethered by a thick rope to a block. To the players who had to tackle the dummy and drive it back until the 100-pound cement block couldn't be lifted any farther, it came more closely to resembling some type of crude medieval torture device. This was especially the case when it was being operated by Poncho McMahon, because rather than simply allow his players to approach the device in its stationary position, he would often heave it into the path of the oncoming player. It made for a more realistic scenario of what they might actually experience on the field, and if a player wasn't careful or positioned properly, it could hit with the force of a 200-pound fullback running at full speed and easily take the player off his feet.

"All right, Miss Steckler, let's go," said McMahon, motioning to Steckler that it was his turn to get his first taste of the tackling block. On McMahon's command, Steckler, who was the only player on the field whose hair was visible from beneath his helmet, hesitantly charged the dummy. Just as he approached it, McMahon pushed the bulky device squarely at Steckler. The moving bag slammed into Steckler's chest and knocked him flat.

As a few of the better players laughed and made disparaging remarks about the kid they had nicknamed "Hollywood"—because of his big pompadour and strange taste in music—McMahon screamed at him to get back up and do it again. "The bag isn't going to bite you, Steckler. I want you to attack it! Now, keep your head up and put your shoulder into it. When you hit it, wrap your arms around the thing and drive it back."

As he walked back to the starting position, Steckler questioned his decision to select a season of football over time at Miles City. The first week of practice and conditioning had left him sore and exhausted. He didn't know if he could take three months of it—especially now that he was getting bruised by both man and machine on a daily basis.

To Steckler, the very notion that someone would willingly run toward another moving person with the intention of tackling him was counterintuitive. It just didn't make sense. He disliked hitting people, and he liked getting hit even less. The ribbing he took at the hands of the "jocks" on the team didn't help matters either.

September 4, 1962

After 10 days of two-a-day practices, Mehrens and McMahon sat down together at the small kitchen table in Mehrens' house and reviewed the team roster. "Thirty-seven," Mehrens said, tallying up the number of players who survived the annual rite of two-a-days.

"Out of the 70 players who showed up on the first day, that isn't too bad," replied McMahon. "It's always a good sign when you have more players than you do jerseys."

The latter remark was a sore spot with Mehrens. "We should have enough game jerseys for everyone. I'm going to speak with the Roundtable. Maybe they can raise some money to buy a few more. I don't want anyone to feel as though he's not a full member of the team." Switching topics, Mehrens then asked, "Any of the players surprise you?"

"Yeah, there were a couple of guys I didn't think would make it."

"Like who?"

"I thought that Steckler kid would be gone after a day or two," said McMahon. "I still don't understand his motivation. What makes a senior go out for football when he knows he doesn't stand much of a chance to play?"

"I don't know," replied Mehrens. "I had the same thought. I'd have thought that if he really wanted to play he would have come out for the team last year."

"As long as he keeps showing up though," replied McMahon, "I'll put him to good use. I can use him on the scout team."

"I'm still concerned about his attitude. He strikes me as the kind of kid who could cause problems."

"You're just saying that because of his hair," said McMahon, laughing. "You don't like his big greased back pompadour." Getting more serious, he added, "Trust me. I'll whip him into shape. He hasn't turned the corner in terms of becoming a football player yet. He's still reluctant to get in there and put a hit on someone—even a dummy—but at least he's no longer sucking wind after each sprint."

"You really think he'll come around?" asked Mehrens.

"I think so. I've been pretty hard on him, and he keeps taking it...that's a good sign."

"Any other surprises?" asked Mehrens.

"I didn't think that that Donovan kid would make it either. He's got heart though. Heck, he's so big and slow that he isn't even halfway done with a wind sprint by the time the rest of the team is already lining up to run the next one...still he keeps plugging away."

"I know," said Mehrens. "I like his attitude. Let's make sure he sticks with it. I'd like to see him play in enough games to earn a letter. Also, I want him and his big body back next year. If he can improve enough, he just might be able to start. The same with Steckler. Any senior who is willing to take the kind of punishment he has taken in practice—and knows he's not going to play much—deserves some consideration. Provided, that is, he continues to contribute in practice and continues to get better. Let's just try and get both of them in a position where they can contribute."

"Easier said than done" was McMahon's laconic response.

October 1, 1962, 3:30 p.m.

The Great Fall Mustangs were riding high after their impressive victory over Billings Central the previous week, and the Monday practice promised to be far different from the first practice that followed the Glasgow game.

As the players came out onto the practice field, one of the fall season's first V-formations of ducks flew overhead as they headed south for the winter. The cooler fall weather had finally arrived, and everyone was in a good mood as Mehrens ordered the team to run two warm-up laps. After watching everyone get started, he then headed back into the locker room to check if McMahon needed any assistance taping up some of the players who were still sporting injuries from the Havre game.

As he went into the locker room, he crossed paths with Bob Murray who had just gotten taped by McMahon. "Anyone else still in there?"

"Yes, sir. Coach McMahon is still taping up Berry and Richtscheid."

"Thanks. How's your ankle?" Mehrens asked. Murray had twisted it against Billings Central.

"Fine, sir."

"Good. Then get running."

Murray did just that, and in spite of his delay and modest injury, he soon caught up to Mike Donovan. Usually, Donovan compensated for his lack of speed and endurance by getting out to the practice field early and getting a head start on running laps—a trick that often allowed him to finish at roughly the same time as the rest of the team. Today, however, he failed to get his customary jump, and Murray decided to have a little fun at his expense. Rather than just jogging by him, Murray, instead, dropped to his knees and began crawling alongside Donovan—whose pace was so anemic that Murray was able to equal it even on his knees. Father Livix saw the incident from his window in the rectory and would have normally stopped it but he was late for debate practice. He would deal with Murray later.

At first, Donovan tried to pretend that he didn't see Murray. Next, he tried to ignore him. But when Murray began to mimic a cow mooing, his antics prompted the laughter of some of the other players. Donovan did the only thing possible, and that was to join in the laughter.

Normally, Donovan was an easygoing kid with a big, slightly tilted grin who liked to laugh, but today his laughter was a self-defense mechanism. He had long been ashamed of his weight, and the fact that he couldn't even outrun someone crawling on his knees caused him to burn with humiliation.

McMahon and Mehrens finished their taping job and came out of the locker room just after Donovan and Murray had completed their laps. They didn't see what had transpired. If they had, a heavy price would have been paid—not only by Murray but by everyone. Mehrens and McMahon considered every player an important and equal member of the team, and they expected—and demanded—that their players do the same.

The remainder of the practice, the coaches conducted some light drills and began going over the scouting report for the Bozeman Hawks, their next opponent. McMahon spent an inordinate amount of time briefing the second team on their responsibilities as members of the scout team. It was their job to replicate the offensive and defensive arrangements the coaches expected the Hawks to employ against their team.

"Donovan and Steckler," said McMahon, "you guys will be lining up on the left side on defense this week. Bozeman has a couple of good players, but we think we can exploit their size and aggressiveness to our advantage."

Donovan figured it was just McMahon's polite way of saying that Bozeman had a fat kid whom he felt they could run at with great success. That was not how either Mehrens or McMahon saw the situation. Bozeman did have a couple of tough, athletic linemen who were good players and were likely to cause the Mustangs some problems. Donovan, however, had no way of knowing that and chose to absorb McMahon's comments not as a compliment but rather as another blow to his self-esteem.

Following the day's practice, Donovan received the third—and the most bitter—shot to his crumbling self-esteem. Since middle school, he had endured his share of the cruel teasing about his weight. As a result, he had come to dread the showers after practice. The thought of exposing his naked body to his peers almost made him physically ill. With great effort, he swallowed his pride and mustered the courage to go into the shower. Often though, he lingered in the locker room and waited until everyone else was done. He would then go in and shower as quickly as possible.

He had intended to follow the same strategy this day, but his routine was disrupted by Murray, who had been delayed because he had to have the tape removed from his ankle. As it happened, the two boys entered the shower at the same time, and Murray decided to carry forward his earlier analogy to a cow by saying just out of earshot of the coaches, "Come on in here, Donovan. I want to get a look at those big titties of yours."

The comment was too much for Donovan. His face grew flush

with embarrassment, and he pretended not to hear the comment. Instead, he returned to his locker and dressed without showering. He then walked out of the locker room without talking to anyone. The tears welling in his eyes only added to his embarrassment.

As Donovan rode home alone on his bike in the fading sunlight that night, he thought about little else than quitting.

October 2, 1962

Bob Murray was on his way to Sister Mary Christina's English class when Father Harvey Livix stepped out of his office, just down from the principal's office, and forcefully yanked him by his arm into an adjoining boiler room.

After he closed the door, Livix grabbed Murray by his shirt and forced him to face him directly. "You think you're tough, Murray," he said with a fiery determination worthy of his East European ancestry but not entirely in keeping with his ministry. Murray said nothing. "Huh?" replied Livix, whose solid, husky build, square jaw, and crew cut gave him a formidable appearance and accurately captured his personality. "I saw that stunt you pulled on Donovan yesterday. If you ever do something like that again, I'll personally have you thrown off the football team and out of this school."

Murray was speechless, but he knew exactly what Livix was referring to. He rightly figured that the priest must have seen him mocking Donovan from his office in the rectory. "Donovan's a teammate of yours, and I expect you to treat him accordingly. How would you like it if I ridiculed you about some of your personal shortcomings in front of the entire assembly this Friday?" Livix asked. It was a thinly veiled reference to Murray's drinking—which Livix was aware of and knew Murray only kept in check during football season.

"I know your type, Murray. I've known guys like you my whole life. Oh, you can pick on little guys, and you think it's funny to bully those who aren't as popular or as good at sports, but you don't have the guts to take on someone your own size. Because if you did, you know you'd lose." Murray squirmed in the face of this truth.

"What you did yesterday was the act of a little man—a coward. Ever since the first day of practice, Donovan has been busting his butt. And what does he get in return? He gets pounded on day in and day out by the likes of you, Weber, Campbell, and Flaherty. And then, as if that isn't enough, he has to take garbage from you. Still, he sticks it out—that's character. But what you displayed yesterday wasn't character; it was weakness. And I don't want weak people on either my football team or in my school." Looking Murray squarely in the eye, Livix concluded with a little lesson. "Just remember, Murray, it's not the amount of talent that God has given you that matters. It is what you do with the talent He has provided you. And right now, Donovan is doing more than you can ever imagine doing. Now, get out of here."

"Yes, Father," replied Murray in genuine humility.

Donovan, like everyone else at the school, was unaware of Livix's conversation with Murray. Even if he had been aware, though, it probably would have only served to embarrass him further. His long bike ride home the night before had resolved nothing. He disliked the idea of quitting, but it seemed preferable to the alternative—which was to continue to be ridiculed by his peers.

He decided that he needed more time to weigh his next move, so that afternoon he feigned sickness and skipped practice. The following morning, McMahon sought Donovan out. "How are you feeling?" he asked after he caught up with him by his locker between classes.

"Good enough to come to school," replied Donovan, adding, "I still feel a little sick." It was a lie.

"We could really use you at practice today," said McMahon. "We missed you yesterday. Our first team just isn't getting the practice it needs. They need to be sharp for Friday, and you're a big part of getting them ready."

"I don't know, Coach," replied Donovan, trying his best to sound tired—as if he were still sick.

"Just keep drinking fluids throughout the day." McMahon placed his hand on Donovan's shoulder and then said, "I'll check back with you this afternoon."

Later that morning, Mehrens sat down besides McMahon in the teachers' lounge. "How's Donovan doing?"

"He said he was feeling sick."

"You think that's the whole story?"

"I don't think so, but I don't know what's eating him. He's been making good progress in practice. Maybe he's frustrated at his lack of playing time, or maybe he's just tired of getting hammered on every day."

"Well, talk to him," replied Mehrens. "Give him some encouragement. I'd hate to have the kid give up on football now. I think he and a couple of other guys are probably in the same boat. Why don't you pull aside your guys and give 'em a little talk. Talk about the value of persistence. Don't direct your remarks at Donovan. Just let him and others—guys like Steckler and Roos— know that we need them on this team."

True to his word, McMahon did check back with Donovan later, and his attention was enough to get him out onto the practice field for at least another day. Per Mehrens' request, following the day's last wind sprints, McMahon ordered his linemen into the gymnasium and told them to sit on the bleachers.

"That was a good practice, you guys. You've come a long way in the last month. Some of you were so clueless at the first practice I'm not sure if you knew offense from defense." In the case of Dale Roos, this was a factual statement. "We're still not where we want to be, but we're on the verge of accomplishing big things. I know some of you are probably getting frustrated at your lack of playing time, but, trust me, it'll come. The better the scout team gets, the better the first team gets. And the better they get, the more playing time everyone will see because we'll start having games wrapped up by halftime.

"What I'm saying is that if everyone just sticks with it—if you just persist—good things will happen. Like the old saying goes, the harder you work, the luckier you'll become."

Donovan wasn't sure, but he figured McMahon's little pep talk was conducted for his benefit. Ironically, though, it was Steckler who most benefited from it. The constant pounding had been wearing on him, and in spite of the judge's warning that he would face some time in the workhouse, he had been contemplating quitting.

October 17, 1962, 2:45 p.m.

The school gymnasium was buzzing with energy. At most schools, this would have been highly unusual considering the circumstances. That is because the student congregation was gathered to provide a rousing send-off to the school's debate team for its first competition of the year. The boisterous atmosphere, however, reflected the extraordinary school spirit that existed at Great Falls Central at the time—even for nonathletic-related events.

It was only after much consideration that Father Livix had decided to allow Valerie Dickerson to speak. He knew what he was about to do could sap the energy from the room—and was therefore risky. But in the wake of the racial events of the past few weeks—both in Mississippi and in Great Falls—he also knew it was the right time to have the students hear Dickerson's message.

As head of the speech and drama clubs, Father Livix was himself a powerful public speaker, and he had a unique ability to not only spot good speakers but make them better. From Dickerson's first day, Livix knew she could be something special, and he wanted to instill the same confidence in her.

He tapped the microphone once to quiet the student body. He had everyone's attention. "Before we begin today's rally, I want to take a minute to introduce you to Ms. Valerie Dickerson. She is a recent transfer to Central and is now a member of the speech and debate club. In preparation for our first tournament tomorrow, I have asked her to give a short speech." He looked over at Dickerson and nodded.

She approached the microphone and stared out at the sea of white faces. They stared back at her. "Imagine I hold in my hand a pill," she began. "This pill can change the color of my skin." The crowd went silent, and for the next five minutes Dickerson held the entire student body's attention rapt as she explained what it was like to be the only black in a school, a city, a state. She concluded her speech with a simple, eloquent sentence. "If not for the color of my skin, there would be no need for such a pill—but even if there were, I still would not take the pill." Her message was clear. She was proud of who she was. The speech was so powerful that it prompted her fellow cheerleader, Patty O'Loughlin, to write a letter to the governor of Arkansas, Orval Faubus, that night. She asked him to end his continued support of segregation.

Dickerson went on to graduate from Central in 1964 and attended San Jose State. Shortly thereafter, she began her career in broadcasting. For years she hosted "Good Morning, San Francisco" and later anchored an evening news program in Los Angeles. Today, she has her own program on CNN and is a regular financial reporter for CNN Headline News.

October 18, 1962

The Bozeman Hawks were having an off year, and Mehrens' biggest concern, as he told a local reporter before the game, was preventing his kids from "getting a bunch of swelled heads" as a result of their impressive victories the past two weeks.

By late in the week, Mehrens and McMahon were confident

enough that that would not happen that they decided to devote some extra attention to the scout team. Both coaches subscribed to the belief that "a team is only as strong as its weakest member" and felt their efforts, in addition to bolstering the spirits of the second stringers, would also help push the first team to a higher level of performance.

McMahon turned more of his attention to those linemen on the scout team. "Let's go, girls," he said. "Our footwork needs to get better. Everyone line up for the agility drill."

The drill was designed to improve a player's foot speed, agility, and coordination. McMahon would stand in front of the linemen—who arranged themselves in three neat rows—and then, holding a football in one hand, would point it in one direction or another. The linemen would run sideways crossing their legs over each other, while keeping their hips, shoulders, and head facing the front. They would then reverse directions whenever McMahon switched the direction of the ball.

"Steckler, Donovan...you guys need to get faster," bellowed McMahon. "Keep your legs moving! I swear if it's the last thing I do, I'm going to make you guys faster!"

The drill was followed by "Ups and Downs" and then the "Monkey Drill"—a short, fast moving drill that required three players to lie next to one another in a prostrate position. The player on the far right would start by jumping up and diving in between the other two players. Then, as he rolled to the left, the player who had been lying on the left would get up and repeat the process in the opposite direction. The result was a synchronized weave.

"Let's go, Steckler. The guys playing ahead of you aren't any faster than you," he said. "They just think they are." He then added a phrase he had picked up from Mehrens, "And the key to getting faster is to *think* you're getting faster. Quickness and speed are as much a function of anticipation as they are talent."

After the agility drills, McMahon next went to work on the

proper spacing of his linemen. It was a source of great frustration to him that although they were over a month into the season he was still working on the fundamentals. In truth, he was a perfectionist—a trait that was in full display a few weeks earlier when he spent the better part of a full practice making his linemen rehearse how they lined up for huddles. McMahon demanded that his linemen be exactly seven yards from the ball in a perfectly straight line with their heads up and their hands on their knees. And when they broke from the huddle, they were to sprint up to the line together—as a team.

"Steckler," said McMahon, kicking Steckler's feet apart, "how many times do I have to tell you to keep your feet shoulders-width apart when you line up? If they're too close together, you're going to get knocked on your butt." He then added in a sarcastic tone, "Do you like getting knocked on your butt?" Steckler admitted that he didn't. "Then get set right!" Steckler snapped his feet into their proper position.

McMahon walked down the line and continued to evaluate the other players' positioning with the care of an expert jeweler. He stopped in front of Donovan. "Your feet are *too* far apart!" Donovan wisely closed the gap before McMahon could stomp down on his feet—something he often did when he wanted to deliver the lesson with a little more staying power. "You're not going to get off the ball as quickly as you can unless your balance is just right.

"You guys need to start sweating the details! All of these things should be second nature to you by now. *It's the attention to the small details that is going to make the big things happen,*" said McMahon, repeating another coaching philosophy that he had picked up from Mehrens.

The second half of the afternoon's practice was dedicated to going over the offense. This meant the scout team was relegated to playing defense. "Okay, guys, let's line up in a 6-2 defense," said McMahon, directing Donovan and Steckler to line up in the two defensive tackle positions. "I want you guys to knock some heads today. If you stay low and keep your feet moving, you can beat your guys. I really want you to push Kunz and Murray," continued McMahon. "And once you do, I want you to stick it to those cookie-and-cake guys"—a phrase McMahon used to derisively refer to the quarterbacks and running backs, whom he felt unjustifiably received the lion's share of the glory at the expense of the linemen who did the hard work. "I want you to put 'em on the grass!"

Poncho McMahon knew only one speed. Whether it was practice or the fourth quarter of a game that was already decided, he refused to let up. McMahon was of the philosophy that you couldn't tell a kid to be aggressive most of the time and then tell them in other situations it was okay to lighten up.

Mehrens had a slightly different approach. On occasion, he spared his players full contact in the belief that the real hitting was best left to the actual game. As a result, their coaching styles sometimes clashed. This was one such day. Mehrens was intending to go easy on his first team, many of whom were still recovering from the Billings Central game. McMahon had no such plans.

On the second play from the line of scrimmage, Donovan followed McMahon's advice and stunned Murray—the player who had embarrassed him earlier in the week—with a quick move. Then, employing the techniques learned on the tackling dummy, he nailed Voyd Richtscheid just as he received the handoff from Gary Wolf. In so doing, Donovan re-aggravated a sprain in Richtscheid's ankle.

"That's it, Donovan!" McMahon screamed. Mehrens was less pleased with the hit, especially after he saw Richtscheid get up limping. To prevent more injuries, Mehrens ordered the defense to play at half speed. Unfortunately, his directive wasn't heard by Steckler, who was being encouraged by McMahon to keep his head up and get off the ball quicker.

On the next play, Steckler blew past Bob Kunz, lowered his

shoulder, and drove Wally Berry right into the ground. The bone-rattling hit thrilled McMahon—and Steckler. In fact, it was a defining moment for Steckler. He had finally overcome his reticence to physical contact. He had turned the corner in terms of becoming a football player. Getting up from the hit, Steckler experienced a most unusual sensation—he wanted to hit someone again.

"You got that tingly feeling?" asked McMahon with a sense of satisfaction. Steckler nodded. "Good. That's how a hit is supposed to feel."

Mehrens was not nearly as enthusiastic about the hit. Normally calm and collected, the head coach couldn't contain his anger. "Steckler, what are *you* doing? I said half speed! If you pull a stunt like that again, you're going to be running—for a long time." But Mehrens' rebuke could not take the luster from what Steckler was feeling. His confidence was only exacerbated when he looked over at McMahon, who shrugged off Mehrens' harsh words. He gave Steckler a wink and a smile. The acknowledgment was all the approval the boy needed.

Mehrens shot McMahon an icy stare. It was his way of telling his assistant to cool it. Later, Mehrens would complain to McMahon that the scout team's aggressive behavior might have cost the team two starting running backs. McMahon replied that that might be true, but added in his defense that he had also created two new football players in Steckler and Donovan. Mehrens grudgingly acknowledged his point.

At the end of practice, McMahon called his linemen over for a little talk. "We made some real progress today. We still have work to do, but you guys are coming along nicely. I know the repetition of all the drills can be boring, and you're probably wondering why I am so obsessed with the little things like your stance; well, it's because these things matter. If you do the little things well, the big ones will naturally follow.

"My job is also to get you guys as prepared as I can—and that means getting all of you prepared." He was now looking at Donovan and Steckler. "And if we're not the best prepared team on the field on Friday night, then I've failed. And, if you haven't noticed by now, I don't like to fail." The last comment brought some smiles to his linemen's faces. "Now, get ready to do wind sprints."

After the team had concluded their sprints, McMahon sauntered up behind Donovan. "How are you feeling, Dobe?"

"Better," he replied, still trying to catch his breath.

"Good," said McMahon, "because you're coming along nicely." It was high praise from a man who didn't distribute a lot of it, and it was exactly what Donovan needed at the moment. The practice had been hard, and although he had played well, every practice ended on a down note because he always finished last in every sprint. As a result, he still was not fully convinced he would stick it out.

What McMahon said next changed that. "That move you made on Murray today proves that you have what it takes to be a starter next year." He then affectionately slapped Donovan on the helmet and said, "Just keep working...as long as you're working you're improving."

In the locker room, even Murray complimented him on his performance. Donovan had no way of knowing it at the time, but his days of being taunted and ridiculed were over. What Murray didn't know is, that as a result of his own poor performance, McMahon was preparing to have another scout team member, Gene Ouellette, who had shown considerable improvement over the past few weeks, challenge him for his starting position.

October 20, 1962

The headline in the sports section of the *Great Falls Tribune* said it all: "Mustangs Trample Hawks 40–6 to remain undefeated." What the article didn't note was the outstanding performance of a number of the substitutes.

Greg Steckler blocked Bozeman's first punt of the game and set up the Mustangs' first score. Following another two quick strikes by Central, Gene Ouellette, who had replaced Bob Murray on both offense and defense, recovered a fumble that set up the Mustangs' fourth touchdown of the first half.

In the second half, Mehrens began by replacing a number of starters on the line. Both Steckler and Donovan saw their first extended action of the season. More important, from the coaches' perspective, was the fact that the team suffered no drop in its performance level. On the first two drives of the second half, the Mustangs scored, including a 19-yard quarterback sneak that was keyed by Mike Donovan's block.

November 23, 1962

The school gymnasium was packed. The annual ritual of distributing the football letters to those who had played enough to earn the honor was a big deal. For some, such as Donovan, it was the pinnacle of their high school athletic career. For others, such as Steckler, it would serve as a tangible validation of his time, effort, and hard work.

The problem was that for those who most desired the award, their status as award winners remained unknown until Bill Mehrens called their name from the podium. The wait for these players was the male equivalent of the tension female beauty contestants endure while awaiting selection as a finalist. For those honored, it was a great moment. For the others, it could be a crushing disappointment. This was especially the case if the player hanging in suspense was a senior.

The ceremony proceeded along as expected. The captains all received their blue and gold "GFC" letters as did the rest of the starters. Mehrens then began reading off the names of some of the key scout team players: Dave Nash, Jim Neufeld, and Barry Newmack were easy choices. Things then began to get precarious, and no one would have been surprised if Mehrens simply concluded the ceremony after those names. Everyone knew Mehrens was not the kind of coach who doled out awards just to make a kid feel better about himself. Players had to earn the award. To do less, Mehrens felt, would diminish the accomplishments of those who had rightly earned the honor.

So it was with some surprise that he called off the name of Mike Donovan. No one was more surprised than Donovan himself when he heard his name called. As his fellow teammates slapped him on the back and shouted "Dobe," the big kid got up from his seat and lumbered to the podium to accept the award. He had a grin as large as his face.

1968

The GFC letter did, in fact, prove to be the pinnacle of Donovan's modest high school athletic career. He never got the opportunity to start the following year, because in the spring of 1963 he contracted *Myasthenia Gravis*—a rare muscular weakness disease that often left him breathless and with double vision. He was unable to perform any physical activities.

Over the ensuing years as the symptoms persisted, Donovan's weight increased, and the self-confidence he had gained from the 1962 experience dissipated inversely to each pound he added to his growing frame. Fortunately, with the help of medication, he eventually gained control over his disease toward the end of his senior year in college.

He decided then that it was time he did something about his weight. With some apprehension and feeling very conscious of his physical condition, he walked to the campus track field and started to jog. The first day he made it two laps—or a half mile—before succumbing to fatigue. The next day, he was tired and sore and contemplated skipping it—much as he had skipped that one practice six years earlier. Instead, he mustered his resolve and went back out to the track. As he struggled to make it around the track, it was McMahon's short lecture about persistence that rattled in his head. *As long as you're working—you're improving.* Again, he made it around the track twice.

Disappointed with the result, he vowed to return the next day. As he prepared, he searched for motivation. He again found it in the words of his line coach. He revised McMahon's mantra about "the key to getting faster is to think you're faster" and transformed it into *"the key to running longer is to run longer."* That day he ran three laps. Within a week, he was running a full mile without interruption, and a month later, he was running three miles.

Over time, Donovan worked his way up to running 5- and 10-kilometer races on a regular basis and, in the process, shredded over 70 pounds. His confidence soared, and after college, he took a job as a ski patrol at Big Sky—one of Montana's premier ski resorts. In time, he worked his way up to become the director of the ski patrol—a position that required both superior conditioning and great stamina. During his tenure at the resort, he also became the assistant chief of the fire department and instituted the town's first emergency medical program—a program since credited with saving the lives of a number of victims of severe skiing accidents.

Today, Donovan has retired from the slopes. He incurred a serious injury that made his job at Big Sky difficult and also ended his running career. He has, however, successfully kept off most of the weight by transferring his persistence to bike riding. He now regularly competes in "Centuries"—100-mile bike rides in the Pacific Northwest, where he now makes his home.

In the mid 1980s, Donovan also applied the lessons of persistence to his academic studies. He returned to college and earned a second degree in accounting. Today, he is a senior vice president of management information systems for Freightliner, Inc. in Portland, Oregon, North America's leading truck manufacturer and an employer of 14,000 people.

November 23, 1962

When Donovan received his letter, even Greg Steckler shared in the collective joy that the rest of his teammates felt. Steckler's joy, though, was somewhat muted by the belief that Donovan had to be the last member of the 1962 team to receive the award.

He masked his disappointment behind his cool guy demeanor and took some small comfort that his short football career, much to his own surprise, had still been a worthwhile endeavor. During the course of the season, he found that he had actually become a pretty good football player, and he enjoyed being in top physical condition. He also learned that the "jocks" on the team were pretty good guys themselves, even if they did prefer Perry Como to Chuck Berry.

But more satisfying than those things, Steckler came to appreciate that as a result of his participation on the team, some of the girls in school started to pay him a little more attention. As he was mentally calculating these benefits, he failed to notice that Mehrens was still standing at the podium. Eventually, the silence in the auditorium became palatable. Mehrens had everyone's attention. including Steckler's. It was precisely the effect the coach wanted.

"It isn't often that a person goes out for football his senior year," Mehrens said solemnly. "It is even rarer when that person sticks with it the whole season. And it is rarer still when he improves enough to become a valuable and necessary component of the team's success. But that is exactly what this year's last letter award winner did." Mehrens then paused again for dramatic effect. "It is, therefore, with great pleasure that I would like Greg Steckler to come up and receive his letter."

The auditorium erupted with applause, by far the loudest of the day. Like Mehrens, most of the team had, at the beginning of the year, questioned the motivation and commitment of the kid they had nicknamed "Hollywood," but in time, his persistence

had won them over. And although most still didn't understand—let alone appreciate—his taste in music, everyone had come to respect Greg Steckler.

July 1984

Following high school and after a stint in the Navy, Greg Steckler, the kid who "always had music bouncing around in his head," lived up to his nickname and made his way to Hollywood. Shortly after he arrived, he found an agent to represent him. Upon landing him his first interview with a recording studio, the agent told Steckler that most of the record executives in town were Jewish, so he would be wise to take a stage name that didn't sound German.

The agent gave this advice to Steckler only a few minutes before his scheduled interview, which didn't allow the budding musician much time to give his new name any great thought. On the spot, he selected "Brian Elliot"—the first two names that popped into his mind. And so was born the career of Brian Elliot.

For years, Steckler—now Elliot—labored in obscurity. He subsisted by writing commercial jingles and playing in bands while diligently trying to produce a commercial hit song. With the same discipline that he had learned on the GFC practice field, where he played against stronger and more talented players day in and day out, he kept grinding it out. For 12 years, Steckler persisted and even made some money investing in real estate.

But then the floor collapsed. His girlfriend left him, a real estate venture went south, and the commercial music business dried up. By the summer of 1984, his house was in foreclosure, his car had been repossessed, and he literally had nothing to his name.

As he walked along the streets of Los Angeles, he came to a bus stop. Standing next to him were two young girls. They were 16 or 17 years old. Steckler overheard one girl confide to the other, "My dad's going to kill me." From the remainder of the conversation, it was clear the girl was pregnant, and she dreaded telling her father the news. She was convinced he wouldn't understand.

By the time the girls got on the bus, Steckler knew that this was his break. As McMahon always told him, *If you persist, good things will happen.* He rushed home to his small unfurnished apartment that night and composed in a matter of hours the first draft of a song that would soon become "Papa Don't Preach." The following day, he gave a copy of it to his agent and told him that he had written it for a young woman named Christine Dent.

As luck would have it, Dent had a small contract with the same label that represented Madonna. After a record executive heard the song, he convinced Steckler that Madonna should be given an opportunity to sing it. The executive felt that it would be better suited for the former Catholic schoolgirl, who went by the name Madonna Louisa Veronica Ciccone, before she become the most successful female entertainer of the 1980s.

Upon reading the score, Madonna instantly fell in love with the song. And, in the course of just a few short weeks, she recorded "Papa Don't Preach"—a song about a young pregnant teenage girl struggling with her decision to keep her baby.

The song skyrocketed to #1 on Billboard's charts and stayed there for seven weeks. Since then, it has gone on to sell over 30 million copies and was re-released by Kelly Osborne in 2003.

The song's lyrics have also been hailed by right-to-life groups, adoption agencies, and parents for preventing thousands of young women from terminating their pregnancies. More significantly, the song has been praised by many women who were pregnant and credit the song with helping them through a difficult stage in their lives.

Steckler subsequently followed up his success with a number of other hits, including Chris Isaak's "You Can't Do a Thing." True to McMahon's word, *the harder he worked, the luckier he got.*

WEEK EIGHT GAME PLAN:
Dig Deeper

QUOTE TO REMEMBER:
"Luck is what happens when preparation meets opportunity."
—SENECA

KEY QUESTIONS TO ANSWER:
Do you understand the personal aspirations and motivations of all of the members of your organization? Do you understand why they are working for your organization and what they hope to achieve?

Learning to Dig Digger

1. How did the coaches make Donovan and Steckler feel like a part of the team?

2. How did the coaches utilize the scout team?

3. Why did Mehrens and McMahon work so hard to improve the performance of second and third teams?

4. What percentage of Donovan's and Steckler's performance do you think could be attributed to physical conditioning and what percentage to an improved mental attitude?

5. What classroom techniques did the coaches use to improve on-field performance?

6. What did the coaches feel was the key to continued improvement?

"Nothing in this world can take the place of persistence. Talent will not; nothing is more common than unsuccessful people with talent. Genius will not; unrewarded genius is almost a proverb. Education will not; the world is full of educated derelicts. Persistence and determination are alone omnipotent."

CHAPTER 9

—CALVIN COOLIDGE

EXTREME PERSEVERANCE

Dale Roos's and George Leffler's Stories

August 20, 1962

In appearance and upbringing, Dale Roos and George Leffler couldn't have been more different. Roos stood only 5'8" and weighed 125 pounds, while Leffler was a tall, gangly 6'4" and 190 pounds. Roos lived his whole life on a farm outside of Great Falls, while Leffler, the son an Air Force officer, had literally grown up around the world.

In spite of these differences, it was perhaps a bit surprising that the two became such good friends, especially since neither boy had a past history of forming any close or lasting friendships.

Both Roos and Leffler were relative loners—

albeit for different reasons. Roos wasn't naturally outgoing, and his father, a stoic German farmer, demanded that his son work on the farm whenever he wasn't in school. The combination left him little time or inclination to make friends.

Leffler was more isolated than a loner. His father's Air Force career required the family to move every two years, leaving him little opportunity to form any lasting friendships outside his family. This was never an issue for Leffler, because he never lacked for companionship. All seven of the Leffler children were born within a span of seven years, ensuring there was never a shortage of playmates.

The two boys' lives intersected on the practice field behind Great Falls Central High School in the summer of 1962 on the first day of football practice. Although both had played football the previous year, neither boy had done much to distinguish himself on the playing field. This was hardly surprising given that Roos had only gone out for football because his father had given him the choice of spending his time after school shoveling chicken manure on the family farm or playing football. Never fond of chicken duty, Roos didn't need any more incentive to give football a try.

Leffler, on the other hand, was only a few years removed from his grade school experience of once showing up for a football practice in dress shoes—a fact that not only highlighted his family's tight budget, but also underscored his lack of understanding of the finer points of the game.

Leffler had one big advantage over Roos going into the new season, and that was his size. On that first day of practice, though, this advantage mattered little to the new assistant coach, John McMahon. He was more interested in finding out who had the mental toughness to become a football player.

McMahon used that first practice to push the players to the brink of physical exhaustion in an effort to weed out those who weren't up for the task. With only a limited amount of time in every practice, McMahon's philosophy was simple. He didn't want to waste an iota of time or energy on any player who wasn't truly committed.

"All right, girls, line up again," he yelled to his charges, after granting the players a short rest at the end of their ninth 100-yard sprint. Roos and Leffler, along with the rest of the team, knelt over and gasped for air in a desperate attempt to suck up a sufficient amount of oxygen to allow them to complete the next sprint. "I'm either going to make men out of you or send you packing," McMahon said matter-of-factly. He then gave a long, hard blow on his whistle. The shrill sound sent the prospects huffing and puffing down the length of the field.

Roos's and Leffler's legs felt like lead, and their lungs burned. Still they pushed forward. McMahon's exhortation to "keep their knees pumping" echoed in their heads as they concentrated on reaching the goal line. "If I catch any of you loafing," McMahon barked, "everyone is going to run again. You guys are now part of a team, and you'd better start acting like it." The admonishment worked, and every player dug a little deeper.

When they finally reached the goal line, everyone doubled over again. Roos, who didn't have the opportunity to participate in the informal summer practices with many of the other players because of his responsibilities on the family farm, was more winded than most. Soon his body revolted against the flurry of physical exertion, and he vomited.

Leffler had the unfortunate luck of being the player closest to Roos, and upon hearing, seeing, and then smelling Roos's regurgitated breakfast, he lost his, too. The two boys would not be the last to fall prey to one of the more ignominious rites of two-a-day practices. Unfortunately, they were the first and, thus, caught the attention of McMahon.

Mehrens, always more sympathetic than McMahon, used the episode to draw an end to the season's first practice. He had urged everyone to come to practice in top physical condition and, to his way of thinking, running ten 100-yard dashes in the hot, humid summer heat until someone threw up was one way of assessing their general level of fitness.

"Go get some water," said Mehrens. But before the players could even begin moving in the direction of the water, McMahon added a refrain which would become all too familiar to his linemen for the rest of the season, "Linemen go last!"

Too afraid to mutter even a disparaging sigh out of fear that such an act would earn them another sprint, most of the linemen silently swore under their breaths at the indignity and injustice of the secondhand treatment.

McMahon sensed their frustration. "I know what some of you are thinking," he said before changing the tone of his voice to mimic the whiny voice of a young girl. "Why do the quarterbacks and running backs get water first?"

As his sarcastic question hung in the humid air, he grew serious again and returned to his regular gravelly voice. "It's because as linemen you have to be tougher than everyone else. And I intend to make you the toughest linemen in Montana. You guys aren't going to like it, but I can guarantee you this: By the fourth quarter of every game, we will have more energy and be better conditioned than any of our opponents. And by the end of the season, we're going to be pushing the other teams all over the field because of our superior conditioning." McMahon paused and looked at Roos and Leffler and said, "And that even goes for you two pukers over there...provided, that is, you decide to come back this afternoon."

After the running backs got their water, McMahon finally released the linemen—with the exception of Roos and Leffler, whom he physically held back. The two boys, still pale from their little episode, offered no resistance. "If you thought today's practice was hard, you ain't seen nothing yet. You guys have a decision to make right now. If you want to contribute to this team, you had better be willing to make some sacrifices. The first of which is to get your sorry butts in shape. The second is to make a commitment to this team. If you're not willing to do those two things, turn in your equipment right now. I only want guys on my line who will persist and give it everything they've got. Do you understand?"

"Yes, sir," both boys replied.

"Good. Now get out of here."

The two boys walked away and toward the water spigot. "I only puked because of you," said Leffler in an easygoing tone once he was out of earshot of McMahon, "so I should go before you."

"Seeing as how you didn't beat me in any of the sprints," replied Roos without missing a beat, "I think I should go first." In spite of their exhausted state, they were both still able to laugh.

The conversation then turned to the one area where they knew they shared common ground, and that was their mutual disdain for the new assistant coach. Commenting in hushed tones, both constantly looked over their shoulder to make sure their new nemesis wasn't around.

After the two showered, Roos, not really knowing any of the other players that well, asked Leffler what he was doing between practices. "Nothing," replied Leffler, who had just planned to find a shaded place to lie down and recover before the next practice began in a few hours.

"You want to go to Burger Master?" asked Roos. "They have some pretty big cartons of root beer. We could replenish some of the fluids we just lost."

"Sure," replied Leffler, trying to size up the little farm kid. "It'll probably just come back up after this afternoon's practice, but it can't be any worse than the aftertaste of whatever it was I just spit up a few minutes ago."

And so it was over root beer, a mutual dislike of John McMahon, and the shared shame of having thrown up on the first day of practice that Dale Roos and George Leffler began their friendship. It

was soon cemented because Roos, who lived out past Malmstrom Air Force Base where Leffler lived, would often give him a ride home after practice.

August 23, 1962

Of the 70 players who had begun two-a-days just two days earlier, 10 had already departed. Today was the first day of full contact. By the end of the day, McMahon figured the herd would be culled by an additional dozen, and by the end of the week, he surmised about half of the original 70 would still be in pads.

The morning session began just like the others with a relentless focus on conditioning. After the first hour, the linemen moved to working on technique. Having already mastered how they were to huddle and what a proper stance looked like, McMahon was determined to teach them how to stay low. Nothing made him angrier than seeing one of his linemen lose a battle on the line of scrimmage because he stood up too quick and too high.

No one was guiltier of this than George Leffler. His size and strength made him an obvious candidate for a starting position on the line, but he was constantly being outmaneuvered and pushed around by smaller and slower players because of his tendency to stand up too swiftly.

Like a cowboy determined to break a wild calf, McMahon intended to break Leffler of this tendency. He even intended to employ a rope to do it. After the coaches broke the team into separate groups, McMahon led the linemen down toward the goalpost at the far end of the field. No one noticed the thin, industrial strength rope tied waist high between the two legs of the H-shaped goalpost.

"Break into two groups," commanded McMahon. "I want the side closest to me to be on offense and the other on defense. You're to line up on either side of the rope. Imagine that the rope is the line of scrimmage. This drill will teach you to stay low."

In theory, it didn't appear to be that difficult of a drill, but

Leffler, as the first offensive player to go under the rope, learned that appearances can be deceiving. When McMahon blew the whistle, Leffler lunged forward to block the defensive player, but he stood up too soon and the tightly wound cord slashed the front of his neck, yanking him back and leaving a big, raw, red reminder of the danger of standing up too quickly. "You gotta stay low!" said McMahon.

Leffler felt he had learned his lesson as he switched over to the other side and awaited his turn on defense. But the next time he was pitted against "The Animal," Bob Murray. On the whistle, Leffler struck out low, but again popped up too soon, and Murray pushed him back against the taut rope. His back contorted at a wrenching angle, and he flipped over backward.

"It's not enough to strike out low. I'm telling you...you've gotta *stay* low. Now, we're not going anywhere until all of you—especially you, Leffler—learn this lesson." By the time they were done, there wasn't a lineman on the team without at least one red mark on his arm, back, or neck. They were, however, all staying noticeably lower.

McMahon's next herd-culling exercise took place at the end of the day's second practice. While he sent everyone for two laps around the field, he and Mehrens dragged two heavy canvas blocking bags to the middle of the field. "This is my favorite drill," said McMahon with boyish enthusiasm. "It's when I begin to separate the wheat from the chaff...it tells me who likes to hit."

"Me, too," replied Mehrens, "but I like it because it gives us the opportunity to convince some of these kids that they're a lot tougher than they think. I just never know which ones we'll reach...there always seem to be a few surprises each season."

As the last player straggled in from running laps, anyone with an ounce of football experience knew the coaches were preparing for the Meat Grinder. The drill, so named because players took a real beating during it, required two players to square off against each other. One was in an offensive blocking position and the other a defensive tackler. The offensive blocker was then told by one of the coaches which way to block the defender. A running back then ran the ball to that side. The defender's job was to tackle the running back.

McMahon ordered all of the linemen to break into two lines. The directive set off an intricate dance whereby the smaller players tried to maneuver themselves into a match with a player of similar size and talent on the opposite side. Inevitably, there were mismatches. As a policy, Mehrens would not allow severe mismatches—say between his biggest and most experienced lineman and a much smaller sophomore. But, at the same time, he wanted to force his players to challenge themselves and was not opposed to having a 180-pound player go up against a 140 pounder—which was Dale Roos's fate as he was pitted against George Leffler.

Roos tried to maneuver in line so he could go up against Joe Gilsoul, a junior who weighed only about 15 pounds more, but McMahon spotted him. "No moving in line, Roos," he yelled. "The only way you're going to get better is to pit yourself against bigger and better players. If you don't want to do that, I suggest you consider going out for Chess Club." Roos knew he'd been caught red-handed and was embarrassed.

He squared off against Leffler to predictable results. He was flattened. "Get up, Roos," McMahon barked. "And give me a lap for trying to change positions in line."

On his next turn, Roos was matched against Jim Goldsworthy, a 160-pound guard. Although he still gave up 20 pounds to Goldsworthy, Roos battled him to a standstill and was able to grab the runner's ankles and make the tackle.

"Better, Roos," replied McMahon. It was as close as either McMahon or Mehrens would come to a compliment during two-a-days, and the assistant coach's praise went a long way toward bolstering Roos's self-confidence.

October 21, 1962

The Mustangs were coming off their impressive 40–6 victory over the Bozeman Hawks and now had the Livingston Rangers squarely in their sights. In their last three games against Hardin, Billings Central, and Bozeman, Great Falls Central had outscored their opponents by a combined score of 109–13. Mehrens and McMahon were again worried that the team might suffer a letdown.

The coaches decided the best way to guard against such a possibility was to continue ratcheting up the scout team's performance in practice. And the best way to do that, they believed, was to engage in full contact scrimmaging.

After the usual warm-ups, Mehrens pulled together the first team offense and ran through a series of plays he felt would be effective against Livingston. On the opposite side, McMahon was motivating the scout team. "You guys have seen a lot of action the last few weeks," he said, "and I know you want to see more. Well, the best way to make that happen is to keep pushing the first team. And the better they play, the sooner all of you will get in the game. But the second—and far better way—to get into the game is to prove that you belong out on the field with the first team."

McMahon turned his attention to Leffler. "Because you're already a defensive starter, Leffler, I expect you to really push Mills." Mills was the first team offensive tackle lined up opposite Leffler. "I want you to push him back into the backfield. Make life difficult for the backfield. Jam up the middle and force them to go outside. Remember to stay low. If you keep popping up that large body of yours like a prairie dog, Mills is going to have no problem cutting you down to size. The way to win the battle is to stay low."

Play after play, McMahon concentrated on Leffler and critiqued his every move. During one break in the scrimmage, he

pulled the lanky kid aside. "I'm going to stay on your case, Leffler. I know you don't get the glory of being a two-way starter, but you're every bit as important to the offensive team as any of the starters. You're helping Mills sharpen his skills—and it is those skills that are going to help us win the war in the trenches against Livingston. Now keep after him."

Following McMahon's instructions, Leffler continued to improve and, eventually, closed down the inside run. On one play he drove past Mills and laid a devastating hit on Wally Berry. McMahon knew Mehrens would use the hit as an excuse to rest his ailing fullback and correctly surmised that Mehrens would try an outside run on the next play.

He turned his attention to Roos, who was playing linebacker. "All right, Roos, get ready. Now that Leffler has jammed up the middle, be on the lookout for an end run."

On the opposite side of the ball, Mehrens was instructing the first team offense to run a new, modified version of the sweep that he had installed that week specifically for Livingston. The play called for the burly Ed Flaherty to pull from his center position and become the lead blocker for Jerry Kuntz.

Wolf took the snap from Flaherty and faked a pitch to Berry, who plunged into the line. Leffler and most of the defense bought into the fake. Wolf then swiveled and tossed the ball to Kuntz, who was heading the other way with Flaherty in front of him.

With a full head of steam, Flaherty barreled down on the pint-sized Roos, who was the only player standing between the two oncoming offensive players and a sure score. After Roos had vomited at his first practice and was later caught trying to change positions in line during the Meat Grinder, he had vowed to meet McMahon's challenge to persist. With that in mind, he stood his ground and braced himself for the oncoming hit. Unfortunately for Roos, Flaherty got his shoulder even lower. The force of Flaherty's 60-pound weight advantage snapped Roos's head backward and propelled him into the air and straight backward. He landed with a sickening thud. He had hit his head so hard that he temporarily lost consciousness.

The next thing Roos saw was a blurry vision of John McMahon standing over him. If his vision had been clear, he would have seen genuine concern in the assistant coach's eyes. "I don't think he's getting up," McMahon said.

A singular thought sprung to Roos's mind upon hearing those words: *Get Up*. For two months now, through endless sprints, drills, and scrimmages, Roos had been working to erase the indignity of being the first player to puke. He felt he needed to regain McMahon's respect. And as he lay on the ground, he feared that whatever progress he had gained over the past few weeks was about to be lost.

Through sheer willpower, Roos pushed himself up. "You all right?" asked McMahon in near disbelief as Roos staggered up.

"I'm fine, Coach," lied Roos with great conviction. His head was still ringing; his vision still foggy, and it took every ounce of his energy to keep his legs from buckling. Still, he declined McMahon's invitation to take a short break and for the remainder of practice stayed on the field. To everyone's surprise, he even got in on a few more tackles, including one especially hard hit on Billy Sprinkle.

Mehrens turned to McMahon. "He's one tough son of a gun. The kid doesn't have an ounce of quit in him."

"You've got that right. I've been hard on him. A lesser kid would have quit...but, to his credit, he's stuck with it."

"Not only has he stuck with it," replied Mehrens, "he's gotten better."

"A lot better. I might even use him a little against Livingston."

That evening, as was their custom now, Roos offered Leffler a ride home. Usually Leffler, who wanted to practice his driving, had to plead with Roos to let him drive his souped-up 1955 Sierra Gold Chevy. But today he didn't even have to because Roos, still shaken from his earlier collision on the practice field, asked his friend to drive.

As they rode, the conversation turned to their post-high school plans. "What are you going to do?" asked Roos.

"Don't really know," replied Leffler. "My dad wants me to go to college. What about you?"

"I'm thinking of going into the Marine Corps," volunteered Roos.

"Man, you must have really taken a hit to your head," said Leffler with a laugh. "There are easier ways to get yourself killed."

"I'm serious," replied Roos.

Leffler reflected on his friend's plans for a moment. "No kidding? You sure you can handle it?"

"After this season, I think I can handle almost anything."

Leffler laughed again. "You're probably right. Plus, if you can withstand that hit you took today...you can withstand almost anything." Roos didn't say anything, but he was proud of his performance. In his mind he had crossed an important barrier. His response to the hit had helped convince him that he was capable of almost anything.

As they reached the outskirts of the base, the pair was met by an armed guard. "The base is in lockdown mode," said the young airman, who was barely a year older than Roos and Leffler.

The two looked at each other. "It must be Cuba," said Leffler after a moment.

He was right. Two thousand miles away President Kennedy, having confirmed that Soviet missiles were stationed just 90 miles from the U.S. mainland, had only hours earlier requested the Soviets to remove the missiles. He also put the U.S. military on high alert.

The Cuban Missile Crisis was now in full swing, and Great Falls, although physically far removed from the political tension, as home to the largest number of Minuteman Missiles in the continental United States, was squarely at the center of the first—and most serious—showdown of the new nuclear age. In the event of an attack, most experts expected that after Washington, D.C., Great Falls was next on the list of the Soviet's priority targets.

In fact, just a month earlier a nationally renowned nuclear physicist, traveling at the behest of the United States government, had visited Great Falls and informed the large audience of civic and town leaders who had gathered at city hall that the threat of a nuclear attack to the city was very real, and it would be a good idea for the citizens of Great Fall to "get used to the idea of living with radioactivity."

Such sobering thoughts were not on the minds of either Roos or Leffler when they said their good-byes to each other outside the Malmstrom Air Force Base gate that evening. The seriousness of the emerging crisis was soon, however, brought home to Leffler when he learned that his father—a lieutenant colonel and the missile control launch officer for the air base—was confined to his bedroom because a new high security phone had recently been installed in the room to assist him with his job. The phone, which had a direct line to the White House, had a singular purpose. It was to connect Lieutenant Colonel George Leffler with his Commander-in-Chief, President John F. Kennedy, in the event the president had to order a retaliatory nuclear strike against the heartland of the Soviet Union. If the call came, it was Leffler's father's responsibility to turn the key to launch the missiles that would rain down an unprecedented amount of destructive power on the Soviet Union's military and civilian centers.

October 22, 1962

The following morning Roos swung by the base to pick up Leffler but was told no one was being allowed either on or off the base. For security reasons, the guard said everyone at Malmstrom was confined to the airbase until the crisis had subsided.

Leffler, who had been brought up in a military environment, accepted his fate with no complaint. He was disappointed that he would miss the upcoming game against Livingston and asked his father if he could use the family's regular home phone to call Coach Mehrens and inform him of his predicament.

Mehrens took the call in his kitchen nook as he was reading about the crisis in the morning paper. "Coach Mehrens? This is George Leffler," he said. "I'm not sure if you'd heard, but the base is in lockdown mode. I'm confined to base. I won't be at school or practice today." He then added, "And my dad doesn't think the situation is likely to change by the time of Saturday's game. I'm sorry."

Mehrens pondered the news for a moment. "There's no need to apologize, Mr. Leffler. I've said it before, and I'll say it again now: Football is a passion of mine, but it's just a game. There are a lot of things far more important: God, country, family, school. At this particular time, it just happens to be our country before football. We look forward to having you back whenever that might be— which I pray, for all of us, is soon. In the meantime, rest easy knowing that you've helped us prepare for the Livingston game."

Mehrens then reminded Leffler that he was a member of the team regardless of where he was, and that as a senior he had a responsibility to ensure the other team members who were living on base—Jim Neufeld and Jim Goldsworthy—continued to exercise and study their playbook. He then concluded the conversation. "God bless you and your family."

Mehrens was thankful for the call in one way. The Cuban Missile Crisis was about the only topic serious enough to draw his attention away from football, and Leffler's confinement required him to begin plotting how to reconfigure the defense in his absence.

Global events did little to dampen Roos's newfound enthusiasm. When he arrived at school that morning, he had a new air of confidence about him. It was based on his gutsy performance the day before. He finally felt like a football player. Whether it was real or imagined, he also felt as if he was being accepted as a member of the team. Guys such as Bob Murray and Gary Wolf acknowledged him in the hallway. Even Wally Berry said "Hey" to him and asked him if he was okay after yesterday's hit.

By normal standards, it wasn't much to hang one's hat on, but for a kid who never received any acknowledgment at home for shoveling chicken manure, and who had never felt like he belonged to any group, it was special. He truly felt like a member of the 1962 Great Falls Central Mustangs, and it was a great feeling. Not even a civil defense warning—which reminded everyone of the global crisis playing out between the world's superpowers—could dampen his mood.

The real confirmation for Roos, though, came later that afternoon. He had dressed for practice and was heading out to the practice field when McMahon stopped him. "Hey, Roos," he shouted, motioning for the boy to come over.

"Yes, coach?"

McMahon looked him in the eye. "I just want you to know that without guys like you, we couldn't go where we're going." It was McMahon's way of telling Roos that his persistence and hard work were not only being noticed but had paid off. The comment brought chills to Roos's spine and cemented in him a lifelong feeling that if he put his mind to something, he could do anything.

October 26, 1962

The Cuban Missile Crisis or, more specifically, the lockdown at Malmstrom Airbase worked in Roos's favor because it required Mehrens to shift around his defense in a way that ultimately benefited Roos—the duty of bringing in plays fell to Roos, who was to be rotated in with Billy Sprinkle at defensive back.

On the long bus trip down to Livingston, Mehrens notified Roos of his plans to use him more. "I've got complete trust in you," he began. "You've proven to both me and Coach McMahon what you're capable of." Sensing Roos's anxiety, Mehrens sought to calm his nerves. "It's natural to be a little nervous. Just remember you've got a whole team out there with you, so don't think you have to do anything special. Play your game, and when things come your way, stick your nose in there. If you get knocked down, just pick yourself up like you did yesterday." Mehrens then placed his hand on Roos's shoulder and squeezed it and said with a smile, "You'll do great."

As the kickoff approached, Mehrens called his team to the sideline for some last minute words. "This is a big game for us. The winner will most likely represent the Western Division in the championship game. We've had a good week of practice, and if we play our game, Livingston can't beat us. Don't get me wrong, they're good," continued Mehrens, who never underestimated the strength of any opposing team, "but we're better. Since the beginning of this season, Coach McMahon and I have preached persistence, pride, and teamwork. Tonight, we'll need to call upon all of those things to defeat the Rangers—but let's really focus on teamwork.

"And that's because a few of our teammates can't be here tonight. As many of you know, George Leffler's father is the missile control officer out at Malmstrom. He's now in the thick of the crisis. Because of his service to our country, his son—our teammate—has been prevented from playing in this game. It might seem like a small sacrifice, but we should be thankful that families like the Lefflers, the Goldworthys, and the Neufelds are willing to make the sacrifices they do. It is the result of the courage of men such as Lieutenant Colonel Leffler that the United States is going to prevail in this battle of wills with the Soviet Union. It's in this spirit that I want to dedicate this game to Leffler and Neufeld and Goldworthy. They can't be here, but they're still a part of this team!" He paused to let his players reflect on their teammates' sacrifice. "Now," he continued with even more energy in his voice, "let's go out and win this game for Leffler and the others so they can be assured of the opportunity of playing for a state championship in a few weeks."

As the kicking team ran out to the field, McMahon called the defense together. "Tonight, I want 11 guys meeting at the ball carrier!" He then corralled both Mills and Roos. He spoke first to Mills. "You saw how Leffler manhandled you all week in practice. Now that you're replacing him, I expect you to show the same tenacity." He slapped him on the helmet and added, "Do it for Leffler."

Next, he then turned his attention to Roos. "This is it, Roos. Coach Mehrens is going to be calling your number tonight. I don't know when it might be, but you need to keep your head in the game. And when you get in there, just play your position. I don't want you to do anything stupid. If it's a pass, stay home and cover your area. If it's a run, come up and lay a hit on the guy. Got that?" Roos nodded. "You've proved to me and everyone else on this team that you've got what it takes."

The game didn't open well for the Mustangs. The weather was unseasonably warm for late October, and it seemed to make the team sluggish. To make matters worse, on his first run of the game, Wally Berry got spun around and was speared in the back. He was forced to leave the game with a severe contusion. The Rangers proceeded to stop the Mustangs' drive and, on its first possession, marched straight downfield to the three-yard line.

On first-and-goal, Great Falls Central held the Rangers for no gain. Fearing a sweep on the next play, Mehrens wanted a change in the defense and instructed McMahon to send Roos in with a new defensive alignment. McMahon snapped his fingers and motioned to the boy. Roos sprinted over in his clean uniform and listened intently to the assistant coach's instructions. He was about to run onto the field when McMahon pulled him back. "Aren't you forgetting something?" In his excitement, Roos had forgotten to put on his helmet. After he strapped it on, McMahon literally pushed him onto the field. "Keep your head in the game, and if they come your way, get the job done!"

The two sides lined up, and just as Mehrens suspected, the

Rangers ran a sweep left. The offensive end boxed in Bruce Campbell on the outside. The Ranger tackle, after delaying Greg Mills, released and trapped Ed Flaherty, who was playing inside linebacker. The only thing that stood between the Livingston running back and the end zone was Dale Roos.

Unlike he did earlier that week in practice, Roos didn't wait for the runner to come to him. He moved in the direction of the much larger ball carrier and lowered his shoulder just before the two collided and hammered the Ranger running back right on the thigh. But Roos knew he couldn't stop. He kept his legs churning, wrapped his arms around the runner, and drove him into the ground for a one-yard loss. The play didn't look like much, but the Mustangs' season could have easily turned on it.

On the sidelines, McMahon was ecstatic. "Attaboy, Roos! Attaboy!" He sent Sprinkle back into the game and slapped Roos on the helmet as he came off the field. "You done good, Roos."

On third down, Central's good fortunes continued. Greg Mills, filling in for Leffler, expertly maneuvered around his blocker and laid his shoulder right into the torso of the fullback and jarred the ball lose. Gary Wolf, coming up from his safety position, recovered the fumble on the three-yard line. The team's most serious crisis in weeks had been averted.

The Mustangs then executed their most impressive drive of the season. They ran the ball 14 straight times, used up more than 10 minutes on the clock, and covered 97 yards before Wally Berry, playing in considerable pain because of the bruise on his back, took it in for the game's first score. The two teams pounded each other for the next three quarters. Neither team had much success moving the ball. Only in the game's final seconds did Great Falls Central add another touchdown. The final score was 12–0, and the Mustangs headed back home for their last regular season game with a record of 6–0–1.

September 1963

High school ended on a sour note for Dale Roos. Whereas the priests and nuns were willing to overlook the drinking exploits of Wolf, Zadich, O'Rourke, and even Campbell, they took a decidedly less favorable view of students who struck teachers with metal folding chairs.

In late May, a few weeks before the end of school, Roos was in the school cafeteria when Leffler asked him if he could borrow a quarter. Roos didn't hesitate to oblige his friend and stepped in line to pass him the money.

From his position as cafeteria monitor, Ray Mehrens, the cousin of Bill Mehrens and also a teacher at the school, yelled, "No cutting in line, Roos!"

Stunned at the unfair accusation, Roos tried to reply, "I was just—"

"I know what you were doing," interrupted Mehrens, who unlike his older cousin had a hot temper. "Now get to the back of the line." He then grabbed Roos, lifted him by the arm, and pushed him toward the end of the line. "I said, get back."

Humiliated at the false accusation and, worse, the childlike treatment, Roos struck back. Without thinking, he picked up a folding chair and in one smooth motion flattened it and smacked Ray Mehrens squarely across the back.

Surprised at his own actions, Roos instantly recognized the foolishness of his ways and sprinted straight up to the principal's office. "I think I'm in trouble," said Roos in an understatement of epic proportions to Father Reitz.

Upon learning of Roos's infraction, Reitz had no choice but to suspend him from school and bar him from attending the graduation ceremony. As Roos was clearing out his locker later that afternoon, McMahon spotted him. "I hear you're planning on joining the Marine Corps."

"Yep," said Roos sheepishly, feeling as though he had let down his coach.

"Well, you're certainly tough enough, and based on that stunt you pulled this afternoon, it seems you've got the aggressive attitude the Marines are looking for." The two laughed at the comment.

McMahon then got serious. "You've got to learn to control your emotions, though. I don't care if you're playing football or fighting for the Marines, your teammates need you, and you can't afford to be doing stupid things. And what you did today was stupid. It's not enough to be tough. You've got to be smart, too. If you put the two together, no one can stop you. No one," he repeated. McMahon then patted him on the shoulder and said, "Do us proud."

That summer—on his eighteenth birthday—Roos traveled to Camp Pendleton, California, to begin boot camp. But before he even had his head shaved, Roos was initiated into the ways of the Marine Corps. He arrived at the bus station outside Camp Pendleton at 2 a.m. and, after being picked up by an irate staff sergeant who didn't like being awakened from his sleep to collect lowly recruits at a deserted bus depot, was detailed by the sergeant to picking up cigarette butts outside the base until sunrise because he caught Roos flicking a cigarette butt on the floor of the bus station.

The following day things didn't get much better, and, ironically, his predicament bore a striking similarity to his run-in in the student cafeteria just months earlier. Only instead of hitting a superior, this time he struck a fellow recruit.

In typical Marine Corps fashion, Roos and the rest of his platoon had been ordered to stand at attention for the better part of two hours at the end of an already long and grueling day. The indignity was made worse because they were forced to do it naked. When their drill sergeant finally told the recruits they could take a seat, Roos and a fellow Marine dove for the same chair. They both reached it at the same time, and neither was about to let go of it. A fight between the two unclothed Marines ensued, and Roos, in spite of his smaller size, gained the advantage. The only problem was that he ended up using a chair as a weapon to beat down his opponent.

The performance earned him the night in his wall locker and an admonishment from his drill instructor. "Roos, you've never met anyone tougher than me. You're going to wish you'd kept your scrawny little butt back in cowboy land."

For the next 16 weeks the drill instructor did his best to get Roos to quit. But just as Roos had done the previous football season, he persisted. *Heck*, he thought to himself that first night in the wall locker, *if I can handle McMahon, I can handle this.* As he sat cramped in the locker, he also reflected on McMahon's other words about being tough and smart. He vowed to do a better job of applying that advice in the future.

At roughly the same time Roos was being indoctrinated into the harsh realities of the United States Marine Corps, George Leffler was getting off a train on the outskirts of Platteville, Wisconsin. As he stood at the base of the hill and looked toward the campus, he felt supremely confident that his football experience at Great Falls Central had prepared him well for college and, more important, Division III football.

April 1964

After successfully completing boot camp, Dale Roos was dispatched on temporary duty to the *USS Constellation*, where he served as an admiral's orderly for a few months before being transferred to Vietnam to serve in a reconnaissance and air delivery unit in April 1964.

In September, Roos's platoon was ordered to conduct reconnaissance and gather some intelligence on a group of Vietcong insurgents, who were disrupting the U.S. military's supply lines by staging a series of successful hit-and-run attacks.

Before the Marines could drop enough men and supplies to the secure region, the area first had to be surveyed. And before the area could be surveyed, one man had to be parachuted into the region as a "wind dummy."

The role of the wind dummy was simple. A Marine, typically a private, was tossed out of the plane for the sole purpose of assessing direction and velocity of the wind. Depending on the conditions, a more senior officer would then determine if it was safe enough for the rest of the platoon to be dropped into the area. The job was so simple—and yet so dangerous—that the Marine Corps later used monkeys for the job. Unfortunately for Roos, as of 1964, the Marine Corps had yet to reach such an enlightened policy. And as the most junior enlisted man, the dangerous job fell to him.

So it was on October 6, 1964, just after dawn, Private Dale Roos steeled his body against the cold hard frame of the lumbering C-130 and waited for the signal from the jump sergeant to hurl himself out over a strange country. As he waited, his thoughts flickered back to the courage he demonstrated in facing up to Ed Flaherty as he barreled down on him, and he reminded himself that it was his performance after he was hit that was what really mattered.

The jump sergeant then called, "Go!" and without thinking, Roos flung himself out. Because he was jumping from a relatively low altitude, his chute deployed immediately. He fell fast from 4,000 feet and landed hard. After shaking off the force of the impact, he sought protective cover in a nearby rice paddy.

As he waited, he was comforted by the fact that he would soon be joined by his fellow platoon members—most of whom had considerably more experience in jungle warfare. Unbeknownst to Roos, however, that small consolation was taken away from him before he even reached the ground. The wind had taken him farther than expected, and his superiors decided it was too risky to drop the other men into the area.

Private Roos was now on his own, although he wouldn't reach that conclusion until hours later. He had been told by his sergeant that such a scenario was a possibility, but in typical Marine fashion the risk had been downplayed.

The first day was a blur. Hoping against hope, Roos remained hidden in the rice paddy and prayed that his platoon would soon be joining him. He vainly searched the sky for hours, looking for any sign that more troops were on the way or, at a minimum, at least they were looking for him. They weren't.

With only a limited amount of food and water, Roos came to the conclusion he had to act. With only a compass, he began moving that night in the direction of his base camp—or what he thought was the direction of his camp. As he moved silently across the darkened fields, he cursed himself for not asking more questions of his platoon leader in the event of just such a contingency. He had no idea how far away he was from camp. He wasn't even sure he was headed in the right direction.

Through the darkened night, Roos continued to move. Progress was slow because, fearing the Vietcong, he stopped at the slightest sound. He had a great many thoughts that evening, but he kept coming back to the theme of persistence. *Just keep moving,* he thought to himself.

At daybreak, he found a thick patch of grass and rested. He tried to get some sleep in spite of his exhausted condition, but the bugs and insects made it nearly impossible. By the end of his second night, he had run out of water. By his calculation, he figured he had walked more than 10 miles and should be seeing signs of camp. He even thought that he might be able to reach the home base that evening. Vietcong were in the area, and he wisely decided against it. *Better to be smart than tough,* he thought, recalling McMahon's advice, as he quit at the first sign of morning light.

At the start of his third day in the field, as he lay down in the bamboo field under the rising morning sun, Roos tried to get some sleep but couldn't. He thought he could hear a stream close by, and being very thirsty, the sound was driving him mad. He searched in desperation for the source. Soon, he came to the conclusion that the sound wasn't a stream of water at all; it was water coursing through the bamboo stems.

Frustrated, he likened his situation to having to watch the quarterbacks and running backs get water at the end of a long hard practice while he and the other linemen were told to wait behind. *Makes you tougher*, McMahon always said.

As he continued to suffer under the hot afternoon sun, he also came to the depressing conclusion that he must have been moving in the wrong direction for the past few days. If that weren't the case, he figured he would have seen at least some sign of U.S. troops. He decided to reverse his course.

Hungry, dirty, thirsty, and frustrated, he eventually fell into a light restless sleep in the hot humid conditions. The bamboo forest provided a little relief from heat, and the slightest sound sent a shot of adrenaline coursing through his blood, making meaningful rest virtually impossible.

As he contemplated his fate, his mind sometimes drifted away. During one episode, he recalled the words of his drill instructor at Pendleton who told him Marines never despaired. He reflected on how similar the advice was to that which McMahon and Mehrens had instilled in him only two years earlier. The sense of accomplishment he felt at finishing both boot camp and enduring the 1962 season strengthened his resolve.

With renewed spirit, he waited for the sun to set on his third full day in the jungle before moving out. He made better ground on his return trip because not only was he familiar with the terrain but also because of man's innate ability to adapt to their surroundings when the core issue of survival is at stake. Roos's steps got lighter and faster, and his hearing more acute.

About an hour before dusk, Roos reached the outskirts of a

small village. He knew it was too dangerous to try to go around it in the remaining hour, so he surveyed the field for a hiding place and spotted a pig sty. Figuring that Vietnamese farmers probably despised the smell of farm animals as much as he did, he concluded the sty offered not only some water but also the best possible protection from enemy detection.

He crept into the sty, lay down in the cleanest spot he could find, and waited out his fourth day. As he rested, his mind again drifted in and out of sleep. He sometimes found himself thinking about his family. At other times, he wondered what his old teammates were doing. *Were they having fun at college? Were they hanging out with their girlfriends? Were they cruising the strip in their hot rods as he and Leffler used to do on Saturday nights?*

The one thing that he didn't contemplate was not making it back. He knew that the area was littered with Vietcong who wouldn't hesitate to kill him if they found him, so he resolved in his mind that failure was simply not an option. He figured his positive, can-do attitude had worked for him on the football field, and he was confident that it would work for him in this situation.

Late on his fifth day in the jungle, his confidence in himself was borne out. He spotted some friendly troops traveling on a road and flagged them down. They provided him with some water and food and directed him safely back to the base. His long ordeal was over.

October 29, 1962

On the Monday following the Livingston game, George Leffler was back in school. The base lockdown was lifted the day after the Soviet Premier, Nikita Khrushchev, announced on Radio Moscow that he agreed to remove all nuclear missiles from Cuba. President Kennedy still had to verify that the missiles were removed, but for all practical purposes, the world's most serious confrontation involving nuclear weapons had been peacefully resolved.

Father Livix, while the event was still painfully fresh in everyone's minds, seized upon the crisis to further hone his students' ethics-based reasoning skills. "Here in Great Falls," he said, "a few of the better-off families have installed fallout shelters in their backyards, and I know that Malmstrom has bunkers that are hardened to withstand a nuclear blast.

"Let's imagine that each facility can hold six people for a week. Now, let's further imagine that you are the only person on your block to have such a facility. You and your neighbors have just learned a missile is headed toward Great Falls. After you get your family of six tucked safely inside the shelter, suddenly six more of your neighbors come pounding on the door pleading to get in. What do you do?" Livix looked directly at Leffler. "Mr. Leffler," he continued, pounding on his desk to mimic the panicked knocks of a neighbor facing certain death, "you have less than a minute to decide. What do you do? Do you let them in and, in the process, put your own family at risk by depleting your food supplies early; or do you allow them to perish?" Leffler looked back at Livix and felt the eyes of his classmates upon him. "I need an answer, Mr. Leffler. The bomb is coming."

"I'd...I'd let them in," he said.

But Livix was not about to let him off so easy. "Why? Because of your decision, you and your family—as well as your neighbors—may have to leave the shelter earlier than is considered safe because all the food and water has run out. Now *all* of you could die because of your decision."

Leffler pondered his response. He still wasn't sure himself why he had answered the way he did. "I guess I feel it's better to take a chance on saving 12 lives," he said tentatively.

His response sparked a vigorous discussion, but as the debate went on, Leffler became surer of his answer. He figured it would have had been hard living with himself if he didn't at least try. The conversation was forever cemented in Leffler's mind when, later that afternoon, a loose wire inadvertently triggered the warning siren that sat atop Ursaline Academy, which was adjacent to the high school. For a few tense minutes, students and faculty alike thought the agreement between America and the Soviet Union had broken apart and that the unthinkable was about to happen.

October 1966

At about the same time Dale Roos was finishing his second tour of duty in Vietnam, his old friend George Leffler was living large at the University of Wisconsin at Platteville. His decision to attend Platteville was pretty simple. The town was near where his parents grew up, and the school was where his father had attended but not graduated from college. Equally important from Leffler's perspective was the fact that Platteville was a small enough school that a player of his skill could still play football.

Leffler started as a freshman, and by his junior year he had earned all-conference honors as a defensive tackle. During those first few years, with football as his primary focus, he matured into a far more solid and agile defender than he was in high school. Gone was the lanky, awkward appearance. He had also forever rid himself of his penchant for standing up too fast.

When he wasn't playing football, he was either spending time with his girlfriend, Jane—whom he had met his freshman year— or hanging out with his buddies. But by the start of his junior year, larger world events began to encroach on Leffler's idyllic world. The Platteville student body, feeding off the massive anti-war demonstrations at the University of Wisconsin at Madison, started to hold rallies protesting the war in Vietnam.

One blustery fall afternoon, shortly after his third season had ended, Leffler was sitting around drinking beer with some of his fellow football players, when the conversation veered off to a discussion about the war. After a few dismissive comments about the demonstrators' long hair and scraggly appearances and their radical politics, Leffler was taken aback by the remarks of one of his good friends.

"I don't know why we should have to go to the war," the player said. "After all, there are a lot of bums out there who aren't doing anything. They're the ones who should go. At least we're trying to get a college education."

The comment struck a raw nerve in Leffler. He knew that most of his college buddies, including the one who made the comment, were no more occupied with their academic studies than he was. Football was their primary focus, and it was disingenuous to assume they were somehow adding more value to society than their peers who were not attending college.

Leffler thought about his friend Dale Roos, whom he knew was still in the Marine Corps, and all the other guys just like him. He was about to interrupt and counter his friend's statement when he was thrown for another loop. One-by-one, all of the other guys in the room sided with his friend. He was shocked at their attitude. Coming from a military family, Leffler knew he had a stronger opinion of the military than most, but the righteous tone of privilege among his friends stunned him.

"Are you guys serious?" he asked. "Do you really think that we don't have a responsibility to serve?"

Leffler listened as his friends gave a series of weak, convoluted, or incoherent arguments, but finally he grew agitated. "I can understand people who are opposed to the war on religious or philosophical grounds—like the hippies protesting the war. But that's not what you guys are doing. It sounds to me like you're okay with the war—you just don't want to be the ones who have to fight it."

One of his more flippant friends replied, "By George, I think you've got it." The others laughed, and the conversation was adroitly steered away to the safer topic of the upcoming Green Bay Packers' game that weekend.

But Leffler couldn't move on from the conversation. His mind raced, and he tried to make some sense of the situation. At some point, he was reminded of Mehrens' words, *Country before football.* Suddenly, he knew what he had to do. He excused himself from his friends and walked straight down to the Marine Corps recruiting office.

The lucky recruiter on duty never had an easier sell. The staff sergeant informed Leffler that he only had an opening for a four-year enlistment. Naively, Leffler thought to himself that since high school was only four years and that seemed to go by pretty fast, his four years in the Marine Corps would go by just as fast. He signed on the dotted line and officially became the property of the U.S. Marine Corps.

Little did Leffler imagine the problems that would follow. He first told his father—a former Army infantry man in World War II and now a full colonel in the U.S. Air Force—that he had enlisted. His father went completely ballistic. His reaction had nothing to do with the nobility of his son's desire to serve, which he was proud of, and everything to do with his decision not to finish college.

Leffler's father knew that his own ability to be promoted beyond colonel had been thwarted by his lack of a college degree, and he desperately wanted his son to have the opportunity he never had. "The military needs better officers, George, not just more warm bodies," he said with genuine anguish. "I wish you would have consulted with me *before* you made this decision." He tried to control his fury. "You'll find out soon enough that war isn't anything like the John Wayne movies. Vietnam is a nasty, ugly war, George."

Over time, his father came to forgive Leffler for his youthful and patriotic exuberance. His girlfriend, however, was another story.

The previous fall, Jane had dropped out of college to become a flight attendant for Northwest Airlines. She was stationed in New York City. Leffler, having now dropped out of college to join the Marine Corps, traveled east to tell her the news. Before he did, however, he thought he'd grease the skids by proposing marriage to her. Prior to arriving at her apartment in Queens, Leffler went to the diamond district in Manhattan and bought the largest diamond he could afford.

His ploy worked well at first. He then took her to dinner and popped the question. She enthusiastically accepted after he dropped to his knee to ask for her hand. Only as the night concluded did he muster the courage to share his other bit of news with her. When he told her that he had joined the Marines and had to leave for Camp Pendleton in the morning, her face went slack. At first she thought he was joking. When she realized he wasn't, she was beside herself. "Does your father know?" Jane screamed. She knew how important college was to him. Leffler stayed silent. "Because if he doesn't kill you, I'm going to!"

He eventually got his fiancée to calm down, but after hearing that his commitment was for four years, she became unglued again. He received an early indication of what actual combat might be like when she took off the engagement ring and hurled it with all her might at his head. As he went to retrieve the ring, she steamed out of the bar.

He attempted to patch things the following morning before he left, but Jane wouldn't hear anything of it. She drove him to the airport, and when he asked her to keep the engagement ring, she reluctantly agreed. The two, though, would not see or hear from each other for another 15 years.

1969

Leffler joined the Marine Corps in November 1966. While studying photo intelligence at the Fleet Intelligence School in Jacksonville, Florida, he met a female reservist from Madison, Wisconsin, and, having lost contact with Jane, married her.

After a series of stateside postings, Leffler received orders to Vietnam in December 1969 and was assigned to serve in the area of reconnaissance planning and mission support for the 1st Marine Division. At the time, the unit was severely understaffed, and for the bulk of his nine months in Vietnam he lived and worked in a small hut. Often his only sleep came on an inflatable air mattress that was kept in the office.

During one particularly brutal three-day stretch, Leffler got no sleep at all. He was given the responsibility for finding a location from which to safely extract an elite Marine Corps hunter-killer team. The team consisted of four men whose mission it was to infiltrate North Vietnamese strongholds and assassinate their leaders. As a way to leverage the psychological damage they inflicted on the enemy, the team, after slitting their enemies' throats, would often mark the job by leaving an ace of spades on the head of the victims. It was their unique calling card.

As a result of this practice, the group's notoriety spread, and they became a top priority for the Vietcong. After one particularly harrowing mission, the unit was being savagely pursued by the Vietcong, who even used dogs to hunt the men down.

For three straight days, the unit was kept on the run. Whenever a brief window of opportunity would present itself, the team would frantically radio into headquarters for help. It fell to Leffler to find a spot from which to safely extract them—a nearly impossible job. Not only did Leffler never know from one hour to the next where the Marines might be, but the satellite photos of the area were grainy, out of date, and incomplete at best. And even when both the location was known and photos of the area existed, often the terrain was ill-suited to a helicopter landing.

Knowing that the lives of four Marines hung in the balance, Leffler worked around the clock to find a suitable spot. If he ever needed an adrenaline jolt, he usually got one whenever he heard the sheer distress in the voice of his fellow Marines as they were pleading to be rescued.

Eventually, Leffler's hard work combined with some luck. The

Marines radioed in that they had backtracked to a large grove of trees where they had hidden the day before. Leffler was familiar with the spot because he had previously gathered photo intelligence of the area. He figured that the land must be pretty solid if it could support trees, and he pointed out to his commanding officer that a possible landing area could be manufactured by simply bombing away the trees.

The officer was skeptical, but Leffler reminded him that this could be their last best chance for saving the unit. The officer agreed and called in an F-4 Phantom to clear the location. Shortly thereafter, another F-4 laid down a line of fire to give the team some separation from their pursuers and dogs. A Huey helicopter then followed close-in behind and landed in the designated spot. In less than 30 seconds all four soldiers were hustled aboard and whisked away to safety.

Before he faded off to his first sleep in 72 hours, Leffler briefly thought back to his football days. His decision to leave Platteville had been the right one. As Coach Mehrens always said, football was important...but not that important. He had just helped save four men's lives. And even though he was not directly involved in the physical extraction, the satisfaction of being a member of the team and doing the right thing reminded him of his days at Great Falls Central. Individual glory was secondary to the success of the team, and a man had to do his part.

March 1982

Leffler's first marriage ended in 1980. On a return trip to Platteville to visit his parents, who had retired there the following year, he made some discreet inquiries about his old flame. Word eventually reached Jane that he was asking about her. Recently divorced herself, she mustered the courage to send him a postcard in San Diego, where he was living at the time. and suggested that they rendezvous in Denver.

Leffler agreed, and in spite of the 15-year layoff, the two quickly rekindled their romance. Less than a year later, they married. They liked to joke that since they never officially ended their engagement on that fateful night in New York City in 1966, it was only a matter of time before they were reunited.

With their blended families—Leffler had two daughters and Jane had three children—they agreed to settle in San Diego. For the past 22 years, the pair has remained happily married, and Leffler now works as a successful real estate agent in San Diego.

2000

After his Vietnam experience, Roos quietly returned to Montana and has become a solid, productive citizen. He and his wife have been married since 1967 and have three children. In addition to running a successful insurance adjusting business, Roos also moonlights as a custom furniture maker and home remodeler.

In 2000, a client, who was impressed with his custom work, asked Roos if he would consider building him a million-dollar home. Although he had never undertaken such a job, Roos's long held belief that he could do anything gave him the confidence to accept the job. Today, many million-dollar-plus homes later, Roos's new business is going strong and growing. He, like George Leffler, credits both Bill Mehrens and John McMahon with instilling in him the belief that everyone has a job to do, and success is more a result of perseverance, hard work, self-confidence, and initiative than raw talent.

Extreme Perseverance

Commitment is the only foundation upon which
perseverance can be built.

QUOTE TO REMEMBER:
"Nothing in this world can take the place of persistence."
—CALVIN COOLIDGE

KEY QUESTIONS TO ANSWER:
Is everyone in your organization committed to
the organization's goals? Are they also committed
to one another as well as their own
personal improvement?

Learning Extreme Perseverance

1. How did John McMahon first test his players' commitment?

2. What were the coaches' motivations in driving their players so hard during the season's first practices? What effect did that have on the players?

3. What strategies did the coaches employ to convince their players of the value of perseverance?

4. What techniques did they employ to test their perseverance?

5. How integral was perseverance to creating and sustaining a strong team?

6. Where did the principle of perseverance yield the most value to the players?

CHAPTER 10

"The first step to leadership

is servanthood."

—JOHN MAXWELL

PASSING THE TORCH

The Scouting Team's Stories

The Livingston game had extracted a serious toll from the Great Falls Central Mustangs. Wally Berry's back was badly bruised; Ed Flaherty's ankle was swollen to the size of an apple, and Bruce Campbell's wrist was severely sprained. All three were listed as questionable for the upcoming game against the Laurel Locomotives. Also sporting less serious injuries were Bob Kunz, the starting left tackle, and Voyd Richtscheid, who started at halfback.

When asked about his team's prospects early in the week by the local sports writer, Mehrens replied, "Our second unit has a big responsibility in this game." What he didn't say publicly was that he had a growing amount of confidence in his

second unit. In fact, Mehrens or McMahon no longer even considered players in terms of their status as starters or substitutes—they were simply members of the team. From their perspective, all of the players had endured the two-a-day practices, survived Hell Week, and, in the past month, performed admirably in the team's decisive victories over Hardin, Billings Central, Bozeman, and Livingston. The two coaches felt confident interchanging almost everyone on the squad. This was not always the case.

August 20, 1962

Fred Zadich arrived at the first practice of the season for one reason. He was a wrestler and had decided to go out for football to get in better shape for the upcoming wrestling season. He had played football in grade school but hadn't donned a uniform in almost four years.

Considering that he was a senior and of relatively modest size—he weighed only 140 pounds—his decision raised a few eyebrows among his teammates. Few doubted his toughness or quickness. What they did doubt was his knowledge of football.

On the first day of practice, McMahon ordered him to get into a three-point stance. Zadich awkwardly stuck out his leg. It scarcely resembled anything that one would normally see on a football field. McMahon grabbed Zadich by the face mask and pulled him close. For one of the few times in his life, the scrappy Zadich was intimidated.

"What's your name?" McMahon growled.

"Z-Z-Zadich."

"What kind of n-n-name is that?" asked McMahon in a mocking tone. Zadich said nothing. He couldn't take his eyes off of McMahon's imposing scar. It was growing redder by the second, and it paralyzed the boy into complete silence.

"Well, if you're not going to answer me, give me five," he yelled. Zadich remained frozen. "That means five laps! Get running!"

Zadich did as instructed and returned about 10 minutes later. McMahon was still instructing his lineman on the finer techniques of a proper stance. "Okay, Vladich," he said, unwittingly mispronouncing his name, "get in a three-point stance." Zadich again butchered his assignment. His left leg was so far out that his knee was almost touching the ground.

"What is that?" McMahon asked, shaking his head in disgust. He then studied Zadich's stance for a moment longer before proclaiming that it more closely resembled a dog that needed to go to the bathroom than a stance befitting a human. He went on to offer that his grandmother could get into a better position. Zadich bore the muffled laughs of his teammates and silently cursed his decision to go out for football.

"Vladich, you've got to be one of the dimmer guys out here," continued McMahon, who intended the statement less as an insult and more as a means to test the boy's resolve. "I'm going to show you once what a proper football stance looks like. Now pay attention and learn." Just then McMahon heard a player laugh behind him and wheeled around to see who it was. "Why are you laughing?" he barked in an irritated tone at Bob Kunz, another senior.

"Uh," mumbled Kunz, who was now being stared down by McMahon. "It's, uh, it's just that Zadich will probably be our class valedictorian."

McMahon turned back toward Zadich and said with a tone of amazement, "You're a senior?"

"Yes, sir."

"And you don't know how to get into the proper stance? Have you ever played football?"

"In grade school," replied Zadich.

McMahon was dumbfounded. "That was the last year you played? In grade school?" He then muttered the word "unbelievable" under his breath. "You mean to tell me that this is your first year of high school football?" Zadich nodded his head. "And what made you decide to go out for football now?"

"I want to get in shape for wrestling."

McMahon's eyes bugged out, and the scar on his face flared up again. "Wrestling!" he screamed. Although he had also been hired to coach wrestling, McMahon considered the sport inferior to football and didn't know what to make of Zadich's confession. Only moments earlier he had been instructing Steckler—another senior who didn't know the first thing about football. *For crying out loud,* he thought to himself, *I'm coaching seniors who don't even know how to get in a stance.*

"Well, Vladich," he said after regaining his composure, "I've got news for you. Football ain't wrestling. First off, it's a team sport. All 11 guys on the field need to work together. So if you're not willing to work with your teammates, I suggest that you think long and hard before returning this afternoon. Second, football requires a lot more technique and hard work than most people think. It's not just a bunch of big, dumb guys hitting one another.

"To begin with, you need to know how to get into a proper stance. So I'm now going to show you how to do it. You think you can handle that, Mr. Valedictorian?" said McMahon, looking at Zadich. He then demonstrated the proper technique, careful to show Zadich precisely how he wanted his head up, his legs shoulders-width apart, his left elbow resting on his left leg, and his right hand down on the ground in front of him, resting between his two legs so as to properly balance his weight. He then told him how he wanted him to stay on the balls of his feet so he could "explode off the ball." He then looked around at everyone before settling his gaze back on Zadich. "Got it?"

"Yes, sir."

"Well, then show me!"

Zadich jumped into the position. "Praise be to heaven," said McMahon. "There's hope for you after all. Now, since you want to get in shape for wrestling season, why don't you give me another five laps." He then looked over to Bob Kunz. "That goes for you, too. If you have enough energy to laugh, you have enough energy to run a mile."

After the first practice was over, McMahon pulled Zadich aside. "Listen, Vladich," he said, still mispronouncing his name, "I don't have anything against you wanting to get in better shape for wrestling, but I'm a football coach. My job is to get this team to perform at its highest level. I don't have time to babysit you. You have to ask yourself whether your heart is really in this game. If it's not, don't come back this afternoon, because I need to concentrate on those players who are committed to helping this team win...not just in improving themselves. If you're willing to do that, I'll treat you just like everyone else, but I'll only guarantee you the following: one, you *will* get in better shape; two, you *will* become a better football player; three, you *will* learn what it's like to play a real team sport; and, four, you *will* learn that hard work and effort are their own rewards. Beyond that, what you'll get out of this season is up to you."

Zadich pondered McMahon's words that afternoon before the start of the second practice and for a brief period seriously considered "bagging it." He figured that he could get in just as good of shape on his own—with much less hassle. But, in spite of the new assistant coach butchering his last name, questioning his intellect, and comparing him to a dog taking care of his business, the assistant coach's words about teamwork struck a cord with him. Zadich realized that he always had been more interested in doing his own thing than being a member of a team. He wasn't sure if McMahon was right about everything that he would get out of the season, but he decided to take him at his word.

September 1, 3:00 p.m.

Mehrens and McMahon were nearly ready to begin the last

two-a-day practice when the conversation turned to the status of the line. "When you told me they were green, I didn't think they'd be this green. Heck, they're even greener than Butte on St. Paddy's Day," said McMahon, referring to the strong Irish influence of Mehrens' hometown. "Why, I've got a couple of seniors who haven't played football in years and a few underclassmen who are big and strong but are so rough around the edges that it'll be October before they can contribute."

"I never said it was going to be easy, John," replied Mehrens, "but you've got to admit one thing. They might all be a little rough but most of 'em are as tough as leather. Take Zadich for instance. You didn't think he'd come back after the first practice. The kid might have a shot to win the state wrestling championship this year if he can improve his work ethic. Plus, if you can channel his energy and enthusiasm into becoming a better football player, we might just have a real player on our hands by the end of the year. The same goes for Neufeld, Newmack, and Nash."

"Which one is Neufeld?" asked McMahon, still struggling with the names of the three junior linemen whose names all began with the letter "N."

"He's the big kid from the Air Force base."

"The backup center?"

"Yeah. He clearly knows the game; he just doesn't know how to play it yet. With a little work, we might just have ourselves another solid addition to our team. Same goes for Nash and Newmack."

Laughing, McMahon said, "Is Nash the kid who showed up for the first team meeting in his Eagle Scout uniform?"

"That's the one," replied Mehrens.

"I didn't know whether to laugh or cry when I saw that. I thought he'd be just a big pansy, but I think you're right. The kid's got some potential. If I do my job right, by the end of the season Nash will be able to whip anyone on this team."

"I sure hope so, because we may very well need his help by the end of the season."

Afternoon practices were now reserved primarily for blocking and tackling drills and live scrimmages. With the season opener now a week away, the competition for the starting spots was heated. The blocks were being sustained longer, and the hits were becoming progressively more savage.

Jim Neufeld, who nearly matched Ed Flaherty in weight, often lined up opposite him in the scrimmages. The first few days had been really rough on the junior lineman as Flaherty schooled him in almost every way. Under McMahon's patient, albeit often caustic, guidance, Neufeld slowly improved his game. Barry Newmack and Dave Nash did the same.

During the day's final scrimmage, Neufeld was playing middle linebacker and was lined up in front of Flaherty. "I want you to plug up the middle, Neufeld," said McMahon. "If Flaherty comes out, I want you to stay low and drive him back into the ball carrier. Keep your legs driving at all times. He's not that much stronger than you; he's just using better technique. Now get in there and start making some tackles."

On the first play, Mehrens called a quarterback sneak. The two starting guards got on the inside of their defenders and created a hole for John O'Rourke to run through. The only guy standing in the way of a sizeable gain was Jim Neufeld, but Flaherty had him squarely in his sights.

Having just been admonished by McMahon, Neufeld knew his performance was being closely monitored. As soon as he saw Flaherty come out with O'Rourke right behind him, he knew it was up to him to make the tackle. He charged forward and lowered his head. He didn't get low enough, and Flaherty straightened him up with a powerful shot to the shoulders.

"Way to stick your nose in there," said McMahon, putting his best on the situation. "But you've got to hit harder and get lower.

No one should be able to do that to you. The only difference between you and Flaherty is the size of your hearts. Right now, his is bigger. He simply wants it more than you do."

Neufeld picked himself off the ground, and, as he did, he put his hand inside his face mask to see if he was bleeding. McMahon spotted the gesture immediately. "You ain't bleeding, Neufeld, so you're not hurt. Now get your head back in the game and start hitting like I know you can. And if you don't, I'll find someone else, like Nash, who does. Are you ready to start hitting?"

"Yes, sir."

"Good. Then show me. I'm not always going to be around to push and prod you. Only you can determine how badly you want to play." McMahon moved a little closer to Neufeld and out of earshot of the other players to say, "The only thing limiting you is your heart. I know you can play football. But there's a big difference between being coached in the technique of the game and actually becoming a football player. I'm responsible for the first. Only you can take care of the second." That afternoon he gave similar talks to Nash and Newmack.

Monday, October 28, 1962

Shirley Mehrens cooked a breakfast of fried eggs, bacon, and toast for her husband and John McMahon, their year-long boarder. She then poured a cup of black coffee and left the pair to discuss their all-consuming passion—football.

"It's time we have another talk with our captains," said Mehrens.

"About what?"

"Their responsibilities," replied Mehrens, who was fond of using the art of conversation to mentor his young assistant. "I think you and I have taken these guys about as far as we can. The only ones who'll be able to get them to the next level are...themselves. That means that Wolf, Berry, Flaherty, and some of the other seniors are going to have to start asserting their leadership. They're going to have to push the underclassmen to the next level. I'll talk with Berry, Kuntz, and Wolf, but why don't you speak with the senior linemen. I want them to understand the performance of the offensive and defensive lines now rests on their shoulders. They've got to get the most out of the juniors. If we win the state championship, I think there's a good chance we'll move up to Double A next year. And if that happens, our underclassmen—Sprinkle, Kochivar, Dick Kuntz, Richtscheid, Ouellette, Neufeld, Newmack, and Nash—are going to have to carry us. I want those guys to learn from this year's seniors.

"I'll get Berry to work with Kochivar, and Jerry Kuntz to work with Sprinkle and Richtscheid. I'll also get Wolf to help Strizich. I need you to get Flaherty, Weber, and Campbell to instill their work ethics, their passion, and their understanding of technique into the underclassmen linemen." Continuing, he said, "We won't necessarily have the time next week—so this is the time to do it. Plus, we're pretty banged up, and I want to rest some of our starters to keep 'em healthy for the championship game. I also want everyone on this team feeling as though they have contributed to our success going into the championship game. If we beat Laurel like I know we can, we'll be able to carry that momentum into the championship game."

"Aren't you getting a little ahead of yourself, Mr. Confident?" said McMahon with a wink. He knew the point Mehrens was trying to make.

"No. I'm not underestimating Laurel," responded Mehrens defensively, "and neither will our team. I'm just looking out for our best interests—for both this season and next. In both instances we'll benefit if we can up the level of our underclassmen's play."

Before practice that day, Mehrens called two sophomores, Clark Kochivar and Tom Strizich, into his office. After directing them to take a seat, he got straight to business. "Neither of you will be suiting up for the final junior varsity game of the year," he said, pausing to gauge their reaction, "because we need you this week on varsity." When he saw Kochivar flash a smile, Mehrens was quick to react. "I don't want this promotion to go to your heads. I'm moving both of you up because I think you have the skills to help us beat Laurel on Friday. I'm also moving you up because I want you to gain some more experience in the event we need you in the championship game." He looked both boys in the eye. "Take this opportunity to learn from the seniors. Kochivar, watch everything Berry does. Strizich, do the same with Wolf. You guys have the chance to learn from the best, so make the most of it." He then dismissed the two. Mehrens gave a modified version of the same speech to his junior running backs, Billy Sprinkle and Voyd Richtscheid. "Watch how Kuntz protects the ball by switching it into the other hand after he gets past the line of scrimmage. It's why he hasn't fumbled once this year."

Across the locker room, McMahon was lecturing his juniors, "the three Ns"—Nash, Newmack, and Neufeld. He was preparing them for the possibility that they would see considerable action against Laurel.

Following their discussions, the two coaches turned their attention to two of the senior captains—Berry and Flaherty. Mehrens knew he'd have plenty of time to talk with Wolf later. As was customary, they did most of their coaching while taping them up before practice. Mehrens took Berry, while McMahon sat down with Flaherty.

"How's the back, Berry?" asked Mehrens, tenderly placing a donut-shaped pad around the bruise he suffered against Livingston. Its vivid purple color had faded over the weekend to a mellower but still sickly looking hue of purple.

Berry flinched when Mehrens pressed against the bruise but said, "Nothing that'll stop me from playing, Coach."

"That's what I like to hear. Still, I expect to use Kochivar a lot this week. I want to keep you healthy for the championship game." Mehrens could see that Berry, who hated to come out of any game, was preparing to register a protest. "Don't worry. I'll keep you in until the game is well in hand." He added that he figured that this would be by the end of the first half. Berry concurred with his coach's assessment.

"This week I really want you to focus on helping Kochivar do the little things right. Help him with his footwork and his timing. He needs to do a better job of meeting the quarterback at the right spot at the right time. Also, make sure he keeps his elbow up on handoffs so that he can do a better job of selling the fake on the Belly Series."

On the training table opposite Berry, McMahon was doing a "figure eight" tape job around Flaherty's swollen left ankle. "We're going to work on Nash's and Neufeld's technique this week. They've both come a long way this year, but there's still a lot of room for improvement."

Always more intense than the others, Flaherty bounced his leg as McMahon tried to tape it and said, "We've got to keep this going. If we beat Laurel, we'll be playing for the state championship." The excitement was evident in his eyes.

"That's right," replied McMahon, sensing an opportunity to stoke his enthusiasm even more. "And that means you've got to get Nash, Newmack, and Neufeld up to your level. There's no reason those guys can't have as big a presence on the field as you. Neufeld might not have your quickness, but he's got the size. And Nash, he's about 20 pounds heavier than you and just as mean— if not meaner." McMahon purposely dropped in the last sentence because he knew it'd get Flaherty's competitive juices flowing. It worked.

When the tape job was complete, McMahon slapped Flaherty on the shoulder pad and sent him out onto the field with a

reminder that his injury was "a long way from his heart." Mehrens and Berry followed shortly behind, and once out on the field the head coach told his team to gather around him. The 37 players hustled over. "Take a knee," he said.

Mehrens began by reminding them that since the Glasgow game they had allowed only four touchdowns, and only one of them had occurred while the outcome of the game was still in doubt. Because of these dominating performances, he said he was now past warning them of the dangers of a Glasgow-like melt-down. Instead, he took the opposite approach and reinforced the message that he and McMahon *expected* them to defeat their opponents in a similar, businesslike fashion. He added that the past four games were worthy of the Great Falls Central Mustangs' tradition.

"With our victory over Livingston," he continued, "we have now clinched at least a tie for the division title. As I have said all season long, no one can beat us. Only we can defeat ourselves. It's your job to make sure that doesn't happen—especially you seniors. You know what this game means. You shouldn't need any extra motivation. If we lose, it could well be your last game—because there's no guarantee we'll win the tiebreaker. If we win, we control our own destiny. Not only will we have won the Western Division championship outright, it means the championship game will be played right here in Great Falls." He then looked around at the players as they rested on one knee. "We're a week away from achieving the goal you seniors set almost a year ago. I know I don't need to say anything more, so I won't. The theme this week is a simple one: Take care of business. We're a better team than Laurel, and I expect us to prove that this Saturday." He paused and looked at his seniors. "Seniors, the responsibility is yours. If you want to keep this season going, you have to meet the challenge." He was done, but he let the players reflect on his words.

"Let's start with five!" yelled McMahon, jolting everyone back to the task at hand—practice. The players strapped on their helmets and took off for the obligatory laps around the field. The improvement in the team's level of conditioning from just 10 weeks ago was evident. Mike Donovan was still the slowest on the field, but even his time had improved considerably. What was really different, though, was the players who went back to jog with Donovan as he finished his laps. It was no longer just the captains. Bob Kunz, John O'Rourke, and Fred Zadich also joined in. As they finished, Zadich, who was normally standoffish from underclassmen, turned to Donovan and said, "You should really think about going out for wrestling after the football season is over. You're in good shape, and you've proven you got what it takes." Kunz and O'Rourke, both also wrestlers, concurred.

Donovan's humble "thank you" masked the pride he felt at the acknowledgment. It was another sign that he had been accepted as a member of the team. It was also a sign that some of the other seniors were now emerging as leaders in their own right.

From the opening set of jumping jacks, it was clear that other seniors had also taken up Mehrens' challenge. "Twenty-five push-ups," barked Wolf to the squad. "Walsh and Strizich," he added, looking at the two underclassmen quarterbacks, "let's make 'em fingertip push-ups...it'll strengthen your hands and help prevent jams."

Berry followed Wolf's lead and on the next drill of "Up-Downs"—the exercise that required players to pump their legs and hit the ground and then get up as quickly as possible—he focused on Kochivar. After spitting out a "hit it"—the signal for everyone to drop to the ground—Berry yelled at his likely replacement for next year, "You need to get up quicker, Kochivar!"

"Hit it," he repeated. "Faster, Kochivar! You need to get up faster. You might still make another block if you can get up quicker."

He called out "Hit it" a number of other times. When he finally saw that his protégé was hustling, he tossed him a rare compliment. "That's it, Koch! Now you're starting to look like a fullback."

Following calisthenics, Mehrens took the backfield to work on their drills, and McMahon took the linemen. Per Mehrens' instructions, Berry tutored Kochivar on the finer techniques of how to pull off a good fake handoff, and Jerry Kuntz worked with Richtscheid on protecting the ball.

After working on their respective techniques and a few select plays for another half hour, it was time for the live scrimmage. The first team played for a few minutes, and then the coaches began substituting those players they intended to give considerable playing time against Laurel.

On defense, Nash and Zadich were inserted, and on offense, Kochivar replaced Berry at fullback, Neufeld was put in at center, and Newmack at guard. Berry, Kunz, and Flaherty were ordered to the sidelines to nurse their nagging injuries.

From the first snap, it was evident that Neufeld still hadn't mastered the finer techniques of snapping, but his less than stellar performance was masked by Nash's equally shoddy play on the opposite side of the ball.

"Nash," screamed McMahon, "how many times do I have to tell you...your first move has got to be *out* and not up! Neufeld was able to knock you back because you exposed your legs. Once you do that, the offensive guy has the advantage. Don't give him the opportunity!"

On the other side of the ball, Flaherty rushed over to Neufeld and pointed out his mistake. "Focus on moving your lead foot forward in conjunction with the snap," he said. "Your foot should hit the ground at the same time the ball reaches the quarterback's hand. As center, you're going to be a half step behind the rest of the line because of your responsibility snapping the ball. You can minimize that disadvantage by moving your lead foot out in conjunction with the snap. You'll have better balance, and you'll be better positioned to block your guy."

Flaherty could see Neufeld was getting a little discouraged, so he offered some encouragement. "It'll just take some work, Neufy. I've been working on it since my freshman year. Keep concentrating and practicing until it becomes second nature." He then added one small piece of advice. "Remember, this is a game of inches, and if you can gain even a small advantage on your opponent, it could be the difference between a small gain and a huge one." He patted Neufeld on the helmet. "Now focus."

On the next play, Nash and Neufeld both took their respective lessons to heart and made the corrections that McMahon and Flaherty suggested. The only problem was that new mistakes were made. Nash failed to utilize the forearm shiver, and Newmack didn't properly position his feet on his block.

Two other seniors now jumped in to rectify the problems. Bob Kunz directed his attention at Newmack. "Newmack," he said, "you're going to be our starting tackle next year. And if we're playing in Double A, you're going to be one of the smaller tackles in the division. That means you really need to pay attention to the small things. You need your first step out to be placed right in the middle of the defensive guard. That's where you have the best leverage. If you're too far one way or another, you can easily be pushed aside." Kunz then got down into a stance and showed him how it should be done.

And as Kunz was helping Newmack, Bruce Campbell stepped in to help Nash. "Nash," he said, "I've heard you pop the dummy in practices with your forearm shiver. You've got to use that same strength now. The center has a slight advantage on you because he knows the count. You can neutralize that advantage by hammering him with your forearm shiver...throw him back on his butt." His enthusiasm was evident. "At a minimum, you'll get him into a Mexican standoff, and then you can read which way the runner is going. If you can start using your strength to your advantage, you're going to be unstoppable next year."

The practice ended where it normally did—on the blocking

sled. McMahon ordered the first team to line up. On his command, the seven boys, in unison, hammered the cast-iron sled. The force of their collective power nearly bucked off McMahon, and he held on tightly until they had driven him back 10 yards. Once he regained his balance, McMahon directed the next team to line up. Neufeld, Nash, and Newmack took their positions at the center and guard spots. The result was the same. The scout team nearly jarred McMahon's hands loose from the sled when they hit it, and they too proceeded to give him a very unpleasant ride downfield.

For his own safety, McMahon forsook riding the sled the rest of the season. He was convinced his linemen knew how to hit and sustain their blocks.

March 30, 1963

From the opening wrestling match of the season against Cut Bank, it was clear the physical conditioning Mehrens and McMahon had demanded of their football players would also pay early dividends on the wrestling mat. The Mustangs won their match against Cut Bank 36–16. John O'Rourke took his match at 127 pounds. Zadich followed with a victory at 138 pounds, and Bob Kunz won at 180 pounds. One of the two setbacks was a pin on Jim Neufeld, who was wrestling at 165 pounds.

Much as they had done during the football season, the seniors continued to demonstrate their leadership skills. Zadich began to view wrestling less as an individual sport and more as a team sport. He also worked hard to make sure everyone on the team sustained his conditioning and ensured that a number of under-classmen were schooled on the sport's more intricate techniques.

Bob Kunz did much the same. He worked extensively with Neufeld and much as he had helped him hone his blocking techniques on the gridiron, did the same on the wrestling mat. After the opening match, Neufeld lost only one other match the remainder of the season.

The wrestling Mustangs never gave up more than 13 points to an opponent in any match and cruised to a perfect 9–0 record during the regular season. Although the team fell to a much larger school in the state tournament, Bob Kunz captured the divisional championship in his weight class, and Zadich came in second after losing 1–0 in overtime at the finals.

Friday, November 2, 1962

As was their weekly routine, Mehrens had the three captains over to his house the evening before the game. Custom also dictated that Shirley Mehrens—per her husband's instructions—feed the boys cookies and ice cream. Mehrens didn't consider them treats as much as he did "carbohydrates"—something he was constantly imploring his players to load up on the day before a game.

After the small formality, Mehrens got down to the purpose of the meeting and went over the game plan one last time with his captains. He wanted to make sure they were "on the same page."

Mehrens started by outlining his team's strengths and how he intended to take advantage of the opportunities those strengths presented. Next, he delved into the opponent's weaknesses and dissected them one-by-one. The purpose of this two-pronged approach was to build confidence in his captains.

Next, he offered a realistic assessment of the opponent's strengths and his own team's weaknesses. He made it a point not to dwell on the latter, instead emphasizing how they had corrected those shortcomings over the past week of practice.

Once he was done with this analysis, he opened up the discussion. Typically, due to his thoroughness, the captains had few questions. This week was no exception, so Mehrens turned his attention to his captains' impression of their substitutes and underclassmen. He wanted to see if their impressions matched his own.

"Do you think Kochivar is ready to fill in for you on Saturday?" he asked Berry.

"I do. I don't think I could have said that at the beginning of the year. In fact, I know I couldn't. I don't even think I could have said that a few weeks ago. But now, I really think he's got it down. He's been working on his blocking and his fake handoffs."

"I agree," volunteered Wolf. "He's been getting his arms up high enough to receive the ball, and he's gotten much better at meeting me at the right spot, with the right foot, and following through on the fake. No offense," he continued, looking at Berry, "but he's just as good as Wally now...maybe even better." Everyone laughed except Berry.

"Good," replied Mehrens. "Keep building his confidence." He then asked Wolf for a progress report on his replacement, Tom Strizich, and received a similar response. Mehrens next queried Flaherty about Nash, Newmack, and Neufeld.

"They're ready, Coach. Neufeld seems to have mastered everything but the long snap, and Nash is definitely ready to go on defense. He still stands up a little too quick, but Weber and Campbell are staying after him pretty good."

Next, Mehrens asked the question that he really wanted to know the answer to. "If any of these guys have to go in the game early, do any of you have any concerns?" The three captains briefly looked at one another and then responded in the negative. "Are you sure?" asked Mehrens. "I want—and expect—your honest opinion. If someone needs work or isn't ready, you're not doing them or the team any favor."

"Coach," replied Flaherty, "if for some reason we need to replace anyone on the line, I'd recommend that we put in either Nash or Newmack ahead of either Murray or Fish." He then paused before adding, "I know they are seniors, but—"

Mehrens cut him off. "I understand. And I agree." He then looked at his captains and asked, "Anything else?" They all shook their heads.

"Good. I'm really proud of all of you. You guys have stayed

after your teammates all season and it shows. I know it hasn't always been easy, but you've made this team much better than it otherwise would have been. You've also taught the underclassmen what it means to be winners...and leaders." He thanked them for their leadership and excused Berry and Flaherty.

Keeping Wolf behind was not unexpected. Mehrens always spent more time with his quarterback than any other player. It was because although he expected the other captains to think like him on the field, he *demanded* the quarterback to do so.

For the next half hour, he ran Wolf through a series of game-day scenarios and quizzed him on what he would do in each situation. The two covered everything from what Wolf would do if it were fourth-and-one on the goal line in the first half, to third-and-long from the 50-yard line with less than a minute to go in the game. Often he would ask a follow-up question and have Wolf tell him what the other players were supposed to do on the play. The cerebral Wolf rattled off the right answer without blinking an eye.

After he was done, Mehrens escorted Wolf to the door, and Shirley Mehrens offered him an extra cookie for the walk home. The head coach then went to bed confident of his team's prospects the following night.

November 3, 1962

Saturday was a classic Indian summer day in Great Falls. Most of the town's residents used the day to rake up leaves from their postage stamp-sized lawns. A few spent the day canvassing for their favorite politician in anticipation of next Tuesday's elections. Most, however, spent the day discussing football. If one were a fan of the city's public high school, the focus was on the school's victory in the Double A championship game the previous night. If one was a fan of Great Falls Central, the topic of the day was that evening's game against Laurel.

About an hour before game time the temperature hovered

near 65°F, but as the sun set, a slight chill started to creep in. To stay warm, the student body held a bonfire just outside the school gymnasium.

Inside the school, the players had donned their white home uniforms and were making their way up to the small chapel, which adjoined the gym, to go through their rite of saying a pregame prayer. Knowing that Mehrens had been stressing the issue of senior leadership this week, Father Livix posted a quote from the Bible to reinforce the message. On the outside of the door, it read: *"As iron sharpens iron, so one man sharpens another."*

After everyone said their prayers, Mehrens and McMahon gathered the team in the gymnasium and put them through their paces. The coaches quizzed everyone about their assignments—including those players from the junior varsity—because he expected everyone to play in the game.

Just before the players were to depart and join the student body at the bonfire for a rendition of the school rouser before taking the bus for the short ride to Memorial Stadium, Mehrens gathered the team together for a pep talk. "This is a great night to be playing football," he said. "At the beginning of the season, when I looked at our schedule and how inexperienced many of you were, I honestly thought I'd be giving you guys a much different talk tonight. I thought this game would be the end of the line for you seniors, because our season would be over after tonight. I thought I'd be telling you how proud I was of all of you and telling you to go out and enjoy the last game on our home field." He paused and a smile formed across his face. "Obviously, I am not going to give that speech, because I expect us to be back here next week for the championship game.

"The reason I am so confident is because of the commitment all of you have demonstrated not just this past week but all year. Everyone in this room has contributed to making this team better, and all of you are going to get the opportunity tonight to show to your families and our fans what outstanding football players you have become."

Mehrens then turned to face many of the seniors who had made so many contributions in practice. "Zadich," he said, "at the beginning of the season I had my doubts as to whether we could convert you into a football player. Today, I know the answer—you are. Coach McMahon and I would like to think we had something to do with it, but, at the end of the day, it was you who turned yourself into a football player.

"The same goes for you, Steckler. If Kunz would have gotten hurt early in the season, I would have been concerned...very concerned." There was some light laughter in the room. "But tonight, you're going to see plenty of action because you have proven that you've got what it takes." Kunz reached over to Steckler and tussled his pompadour. No one noticed but Steckler's face became a little flushed at the attention and the compliment. Mehrens then went around the rest of the room and singled out his seniors—Jerry Kuntz, John O'Rourke, Bruce Campbell, Byron Weber, Dale Roos, and others—and explained not only how each had improved, but how each had contributed to the Mustangs' championship run.

Next, he spoke to the juniors and the other underclassmen. "I hope you underclassmen realize how lucky you are to have had the opportunity to practice and play with this group of seniors this year. They're a special group. I encourage all of you to pay special attention tonight, because they're going to give you at least one more lesson in how to play this game—and what it means to be a Mustang! Take their lessons to heart, because we're going to need to call upon all of them next season.

"I've heard through the grapevine that there is an excellent chance that our petition to move up to Double A will be accepted." A loud cheer went up. Great Falls Central was tired of being thought of as a second class team compared to the town's larger public school, Great Falls High, and they desperately wanted the chance to prove they could compete against the bigger public school. Mehrens quickly brought everyone back down and refocused them to the task at hand—beating Laurel.

"But whether you are a senior, junior, or sophomore, when you step onto that field tonight, you're all members of one team. There are no seniors or underclassmen. There are no starters or substitutes. There are no stars or special team players. There is only one team, and playing together as one team, we're going to take care of business."

The intensity exploded when Bruce Campbell jumped up from his seat, slapped his hand across his helmet, and yelled, "Now, let's go out and show Laurel what Mustang football is all about!" Normally, Mehrens would have reprimanded Campbell, but it was useless because the emotional kid was already headed out the door along with the rest of the team. The team was so excited that they stormed right past the bonfire and the awaiting student body and jumped on the bus. Mehrens had promised the cheerleading captain, Patty O'Loughlin, that they would stop by the bonfire for a proper send off, but when he got on the bus and saw the passion in his players' eyes, he couldn't bring himself to ask them to get off the bus. He feared it would zap their highly charged emotional state.

He was right. The Mustangs' energy never dissipated. They received the opening kickoff and proceeded to stuff the ball down Laurel's throat. Following behind two well executed blocks from Bob Kunz and Clark Kochivar, Billy Sprinkle scored from four yards out just minutes into the game.

The defense held the Locomotives to a three-and-out on its first series, and the Mustangs got the ball back. On the first play from the line of scrimmage, Gary Wolf, seeing the defense had changed positions, audibled for the 90 Belly Series.

On the hut of two, Flaherty snapped the ball, and Wolf, just as he had demonstrated to Strizich all week, stepped first with his right foot and moved at a 45° angle toward the fullback. Berry met him at the prescribed spot just inside the right tackle and proceeded to ride Wolf's fake perfectly. The defensive line and the linebackers all surged in the direction of Berry. After following Berry for a step, Wolf stealthily pulled the ball out and kept it hidden on his hip for a moment. He then pitched it out to Jerry Kuntz, who, having gotten outside of the defensive end pinned inside by Byron Weber, had nothing but a field of green in front of him all the way to the end zone.

Alas, Wolf and Berry performed the fake too well. Even the referee was duped by the effectiveness of the play and blew it dead when Berry was smothered by four Laurel defenders. Kuntz, already 10 yards downfield with the ball clearly in his hand, was so dismayed that he continued to run all the way to the end zone in the hopes that the horrible call would somehow be overturned.

On the sideline, the normally stoic Mehrens threw his hat to the ground and tried to bite his tongue. But he just couldn't hold back and blurted out to the referee, whom he knew by name, "Tom, I told you to watch for that play. I told you we run it well." He then picked up his hat and, in a calmer voice, reminded the referee that he had just cost his team a touchdown. True to form, Mehrens regained his composure and quickly moved on. He ordered Wolf to keep running the 90 Belly Series until they scored. To all the underclassmen on the sidelines, he said, "Watch this drive carefully. It'll be textbook." He was correct. Five plays later—after runs of 8, 9, 10, 8, and 11 yards all by Berry—the star fullback punched the ball across the goal line for the Mustangs' second score.

Following another touchdown by Jerry Kuntz on the next series, Mehrens began freely substituting his players. By halftime, the Mustangs led 21–0.

To start the second half, Dave Nash and Fred Zadich opened on defense. They held the Locomotives to another three-and-out. On fourth down, Nash blasted the Laurel center back on his rear with a punishing forearm shiver and proceeded to drive straight up the middle and block the punt. Zadich, who had fired out from his position, was only a step behind and easily recovered the loose ball. John O'Rourke replaced Wolf at quarterback, and another Mustang score soon followed. After a second fumble recovery, Jerry Kuntz added a fifth score behind the blocking of Neufeld and Newmack. The icing on the cake came in the fourth quarter when Clark Kochivar added the Mustangs' sixth and final touchdown. The game ended with the score 41–0, and everyone on the team played at least a full quarter of football.

May 18, 1963

The annual letterman initiation began innocently enough. All the boys who had earned their first letter in a sport over the course of the past year were lined up in the school gymnasium and informed by the current lettermen that before they could actually wear the coveted "GFC" letter, they first had to prove their mettle by successfully completing a series of "simple" tasks.

The first required that they be blindfolded. They were then unceremoniously marched into the locker room and escorted into the bathroom stalls, where they were ordered to kneel before the toilet. They were then told to reach into the cold toilet water and fish out the bowl's contents. Having accomplished the task, they were ordered to squeeze the soft item. Naturally, most of the boys recoiled at the directive, but did as they were instructed. Often an anguished scream accompanied the unpleasant chore. The truth, as they would later learn, was much more humane. They were just squeezing an overripe banana.

While still blindfolded, they endured a number of other small indignities, including swallowing a dozen or so oysters and then washing them down with a pungent concoction of foul smelling liquids.

The initiation ended with four laps around the practice field. The task was complicated by the fact that they also had to chew on a clove of garlic the entire time. To add insult to injury, those being initiated were also subjected to an untold number of "paddy whackings" by those who had already earned their letter.

As Dave Nash neared the halfway mark of his garlic run, John O'Rourke took his measure and prepared to swing his paddle at Nash's sizeable rear end. Nash saw what was coming and reached back with his hand to protect his exposed flank. O'Rourke's paddle caught him flush on the wrist. It immediately began to turn purple, and by the time he had finished his run, his wrist had tripled in size. The next day it would be revealed Nash had suffered a hairline fracture.

It was the beginning of the end of the letterman initiation—a ritual Mehrens had inherited years before when he took over as coach. He had never seen much harm in the tradition, but the more he thought about it, the more he realized it was counterproductive to his core message. As he told Father Livix when he made his decision to ban the ritual, "Sports at Great Falls Central is about building our kids up and learning to play together as a team. The lettermen initiation is not in keeping with that mission."

Fall 1963

On September 26, 1963, President John F. Kennedy visited Great Falls at the behest of the city's most famous resident, Senate Majority Leader Mike Mansfield. To the residents of Great Falls, it was an honor to host the President of the United States. To the Catholics of the town, it was an even greater honor, because, as the first Catholic president, they considered Kennedy one of their own.

As momentous as the event was, Coach Mehrens was only momentarily distracted by the historic visit. After listening to the president's speech at Memorial Stadium, Mehrens promptly returned to his office and got back to the business of the season— coaching football.

Due to the 1962 team's success, the school's petition to the

Montana High School Athletic Association to move Great Falls Central up to the Double A division had been approved by a razor-thin margin. The dissenters were concerned about the Mustangs' ability to compete against the larger schools.

Following early season victories over two of the smaller non-conference teams, the 1963 Mustangs traveled to play Billings West—their first Double A opponent. The game had Mehrens popping Tums again.

The student population at Billings West was 2,000—nearly triple that of Great Falls Central—and the size of its band alone seemed to have intimidated his players before the game had even started. During warm-ups, Mehrens watched as his players' eyes grew larger with every chorus the band played. By the time he got to the locker room, he knew he had to calm his team down and make them believe they could win. On the fly, he opted to latch on to the president's recent visit to Great Falls.

"Most of the fans out there," began Mehrens, motioning his head toward the door that led to the stadium field, "don't think we belong on the same field as Billings West. They say we're too small and that we lack the size and strength to be competitive. Well, you know what, they're wrong!" The confident tone in his voice seemed to have a stiffening effect on his players' spines, and they began to sit a little taller.

"A couple of years ago, people were saying John F. Kennedy didn't have what it took to be president. They were saying he was too young...too inexperienced. They were even saying he didn't belong in the White House because he was Catholic. Well, you know what, they were wrong! And just like all those folks were wrong about President Kennedy, everyone outside this locker room is wrong about us! We're the Great Falls Central Mustangs, and I'm telling you that just as sure as President Kennedy belongs in the White House, we belong out there on the same field with Billings West...or any other Double A school for that matter!

"The responsibility of carrying the Great Falls Central tradition—our torch," continued Mehrens, "has now been passed on to you. I just received a letter from Ed Flaherty the other day. He knew this game was coming up, and he knows how much it means to this school. I could feel from the tone of his letter that he wished more than anything in the world that he could be playing in this game tonight. He asked me to tell you guys to live up to the Mustang tradition and make him and all the other past graduates, who wanted this opportunity but never got it, proud."

As the fired-up Mustangs stormed onto the field, McMahon pulled Neufeld aside. "Flaherty asked me how you were doing. I intend to give him a report after tonight's game." McMahon's implicit message was very clear: *Don't let him down.* The 1963 team didn't and whipped the Billings West 33–20. The only setback was a broken collarbone suffered by Neufeld, but nobody knew about it because he refused to come out of the game. In fact, it was only later in the season that the coaches learned of it, and when they asked Neufeld why he kept it quiet, he replied, "Because I know that's what Flaherty would have done." McMahon simply smiled at the response. Neufeld had become a football player.

The following week the team traveled to Kalispell to meet the undefeated Braves. The previous week, the talk among the state's football prognosticators was that the Great Falls Central victory over Billings West was a fluke, and they were unprepared to deal with the size and strength of Kalispell. The Braves boasted two guards who weighed 240 and 270 pounds respectively, along with a tackle weighing over 300 pounds. The largest player on the 1963 Mustangs was Dave Nash, who had bulked up to 215 pounds since his junior year. No other player topped the scales at more than 200 pounds.

The Mustangs scored early on a long run by Sprinkle that was sprung by two perfectly executed blocks by Newmack and Dick Kuntz. The Braves then used their imposing size to equal the score at 6–6.

To contain Sprinkle, who had grown considerably faster since his junior year, Kalispell shifted to a 5-4 defense. The change confused Great Falls and took away the advantage of Sprinkle's speed. The Mustangs' defense, however, also calmed down behind the ferocious play of Dave Nash, who terrorized the Kalispell offense the remainder of the game. The contest then settled into a grudge match with neither team able to effectively move the ball.

At halftime, Mehrens was confident his defense was quick enough to prevent another score, but he was worried that Kalispell's defense was going to be equally effective at stopping Sprinkle and his offense. He knew he had one opportunity to exploit the defense, but that he had to strike early in the second half.

Mehrens also knew that everyone had to pull off his blocking assignments flawlessly. He diagramed the play—a variation of the 90 Belly Series—down to the smallest detail. McMahon even reminded Neufeld how to position his feet on his block.

On the first offensive play of the second half, Tom Strizich took the snap and executed a textbook maneuver in the direction of Clark Kochivar. Kochivar, in turn, performed a perfect fake. The nose guard and both inside linebackers moved left in response. The entire line exploded off the snap and surged forward. Neufeld took care of the 240-pound nose guard, and Dick Kuntz stood up the 270-pound guard who was filling the gap on his right. Nash did the same thing to the 300 pounder on his outside shoulder, and Kochivar slammed into the first linebacker. After he knocked him down, Kochivar heeded Berry's advice and got back up to look for someone else to hit.

Following the fake, Strizich wheeled and handed off to Sprinkle, who had feigned going outside before slashing back toward the middle. He then squirted through the small hole and ran toward daylight. He only had to get past a defensive back, who was picked up by Kochivar. Sprinkle easily outran the lone defender. Seventy-five yards later he was in the end zone.

The touchdown made it 12–6, which is how the game ended. With the victory, the Great Falls Central Mustangs put to rest once and for all any more public discussion of whether they belonged in Double A ball. The 1963 team added an exclamation point a few weeks later with their victory over Butte Public. Down 21–20 with less than 25 seconds to go, Mehrens considered sending out Mike Walsh to kick the winning field goal but instead opted to take a risk on a play to Clark Kochivar.

Knowing that all eyes would be on Billy Sprinkle because he had already scored Great Falls Central's first three scores—on a long run, an interception, and a punt return—Mehrens called for Strizich to run the 90 Belly Series. But instead of pitching to Sprinkle, as everyone in the stadium anticipated, Mehrens directed his quarterback to go with the first option and handoff to Kochivar.

Kochivar took the ball and ran straight off tackle for a 25-yard touchdown. When he came off the field, Mehrens said, "Wally Berry couldn't have done it better." And in the locker room afterward, he told his seniors that they had demonstrated outstanding leadership and played like a real team. He then paid the 1963 team its greatest compliment: "The 1962 team couldn't have done it better."

Passing the Torch

COACHING FOR LIFE TIP #10:
Great leaders create other great leaders.

QUOTE TO REMEMBER:
"The first step to leadership is servanthood."
—JOHN MAXWELL

KEY QUESTIONS TO ANSWER:
Are you creating followers or leaders?

Learning to Pass the Torch

1. How was the coaches' philosophy toward developing leadership integral to the team's success?

2. How did the coaches reinforce the concept of leadership throughout the season?

3. How did the coaches leverage the seniors' leadership?

4. What were the ancillary benefits to getting the seniors to think of themselves as "coaches on the field"?

5. What role did the *expectation* of leadership play in players assuming increasingly higher levels of responsibility?

6. What more could the coaches have done to develop strong leaders?

CHAPTER II

"Character is the firm foundation
upon which one must
build to win respect.
Just as no worthy building
can be erected on a weak foundation,
so no lasting reputation can be
built on a weak character."

—R. C. SAMSEL

REINFORCING THE FOUNDATION

Glenn Fish's Story

Sunday, November 4, 1962

Bill Mehrens sat with his wife and two young daughters and listened to Father Livix preside over the early morning Mass. Seated next to him was John McMahon. Both men had a hard time concentrating on the service. Part of this was due to the fact that it was said in Latin, and neither man, in spite of years of formal schooling in the ancient language, had a good command of it. They also had problems concentrating because their minds were already focused on the upcoming championship game. Their opponent, Havre, had defeated Glendive the previous night, and Mehrens and McMahon were anxious to sit down with Jim Trudnowski, who had scouted the game, so they could begin preparing their game plan.

As the pair made their way out of the church, they were stopped by a number of well wishers. When they reached the back of the long narrow church, near the confessionals, they bumped into Livix, who was greeting his parishioners in the foyer.

"Top of the morning," said Livix with a sheepish grin. He then looked at McMahon and, glancing over at the confessionals, said, "If there's anything you wish to unburden onto the Lord, John, we can just step inside and take care of it."

"That's an excellent idea, Father," added Mehrens. "I don't want anything cluttering his thoughts as we prepare for Havre this week." McMahon turned a slight shade of red but managed to laugh along with the pair. Mehrens and Livix often poked fun at their younger colleague.

Livix had more people to greet, so in a more serious tone, he added, "As you prepare for the game this week, just keep in mind what has gotten us this far this season. I don't know how good your Latin is, but one of today's readings was from the book of Corinthians. Translated, it said this: *If any man builds on this foundation using gold, silver, costly stones, wood, hay, or straw, his work will be shown for what it is, because the day will bring it to light. It will be revealed with fire, and fire will test the quality of each man's work. If what he has built survives, he will receive his reward."* Livix paused and then added, "I think the scripture has great relevance to your work. You've already done a lot with our boys this season, but what you need is to continue strengthening the team this week. Stay focused on what has gotten us to this point: high expectations, discipline, hard work, and teamwork. If you do that, I'm confident you'll have built something that survives long past Friday night's championship game...and there can be no greater reward than that."

Mehrens and McMahon thanked Livix for his personalized

sermon and headed straight home to begin putting together their game plan for winning the state championship. They knew the game would test the quality of their work.

Monday, November 5, 1962

Mehrens and McMahon had spent the better part of the previous day grilling Trudnowski about Havre's offensive formations and defensive alignments and their tendencies. He wanted to know what the distance to the first down marker was on every play. He even wanted to know how long it took their center to snap the ball to the punter. No detail was too small to be overlooked by Bill Mehrens. By the time the freshman coach was finally allowed to go home, he was mentally exhausted.

After they were through squeezing every ounce of information out of Trudnowski, the pair poured over the film of their earlier game with Havre. They also wanted to watch the game film of their tie with Glasgow but couldn't. Mehrens, in a sportsman-like gesture, had sent the film to Havre's head coach, Ralph Frank, in early October. At the time, Mehrens thought nothing of the gesture. He was more than happy to help out an opponent he had already defeated. After his repeated calls to Frank, asking him to return the film, went unheeded, he began to grow suspicious. Now, with just four days to go before the championship game, Mehrens was downright paranoid. He knew Frank was breaking down every aspect of their game. "Frank is using *our* film to prepare against *us*," he said with disgust.

The two coaches were still talking about it the next morning as they drove to school. "I never would have given it to him in the first place," said McMahon. "Frank is a good coach, but he's not above pushing the boundaries—on and off the field." He was about to add something derogatory about the Havre coach but remembered Mehrens' five-year old daughter was in the backseat. They had to drop her off at kindergarten before they went to work.

"It's all about character," replied Mehrens calmly. "It's a bush-league move, and it just motivates me to work that much harder this week. I don't intend to take any prisoners this Friday."

The two men then became so engrossed in trying to figure out how Frank might exploit the mistakes that they made at Glasgow that they completely forgot about Mehrens' daughter in the backseat until she piped up and said, "Daddy, we just drove by my school!" It was a tangible reminder that this week every-thing—including his own daughter—would take a backseat to preparing his football team for victory.

During their lunch break, the two coaches holed themselves up in Mehrens' classroom and poured over old films. Today, they were studying the Mustangs' 1959 matchup against Havre. Mehrens knew the players were all different, but he was looking for any-thing—however small—that would give his team an edge. Finally, he found what he was looking for on the seventh viewing of the film. "There it is," he said, stopping the projector. He ran the film backward and played it again for McMahon. His assistant still didn't see it. "It's right there," replied Mehrens. "Every time they run their screen pass to the flat, the halfback sets up a step deeper than usual. McMahon strained his eyes and finally saw it. He knew he could have watched the film a hundred times and never picked it up, but now that it was pointed out to him, it was obvious.

"Go get Flaherty and Berry," replied Mehrens. Moments later, after pulling the two co-captains and starting linebackers from their seats in the school cafeteria, McMahon had them perched in front of the screen. Mehrens ran the play over and over again until he was sure both players had picked up on the key. "Now, I expect you guys to adjust accordingly whenever you see Havre's halfback set up like that. And when he does, I expect you to go for an interception. In fact, one of your defensive goals for this game is going to be for both of you to get an interception."

At the end of the session Mehrens excused Berry and kept

Flaherty for a moment longer. He wanted to devote some extra attention on the senior center, because of the team's three captains, Mehrens knew Flaherty's tough and workmanlike mentality most closely resembled the team's personality—and soul—and he wanted him to keep after his teammates this week in practice.

"This is your moment of truth," said Mehrens. "I told you at the start of the season that you would play like you practiced. I couldn't have asked more from you for the past 10 weeks, but now, I need you to redouble your efforts this week. Your teammates are going to key off of you. You have to continue to demonstrate your character—the character of this team—through your actions. Your goal of winning a championship is within reach."

Summer 2002

With over three dozen different companies and 6,000 employees operating under his holding company, Ed Flaherty no longer had the time or the inclination to involve himself in all the day-to-day personnel issues of those entities. By nature, he selected good people, trained them, and then delegated as much authority as he thought each manager could reasonably handle.

Still, on a monthly basis as part of his mentoring, he made time to meet with each of his managers to both bring himself up to speed on any issues that were of pressing concern to his business and to assist the managers with any problems they might be encountering.

For a number of months, one particular manager had been struggling with an entry level factory worker, who had both attendance and performance issues. In his earlier visits, Flaherty encouraged the manager to lay out his expectations for the employee and asked that he also provide her with the necessary training to do the job. Failing that, Flaherty suggested the woman should be given a fair warning that if her performance didn't improve, the company would have no choice but to let her go.

Flaherty, who made it a point to know as many of his employees as possible, knew this particular employee by name and sight, but otherwise had little interaction with her. The first time he became acquainted with her was at an employee appreciation event he held annually for his workers and their families. As soon as he met the woman's family, it was clear that her productivity and absentee problems stemmed from something more than just a lackadaisical work ethic. To begin with, her son was severely mentally handicapped and lacked the ability to work outside the home. In the course of his conversation with her, Flaherty also learned that the woman's husband had a serious work-related disability. It was obvious she was the family's sole breadwinner.

In the months that followed, the woman's work didn't improve, and the manager informed Flaherty that if she didn't heed his final warning he intended to fire her. Flaherty used the opportunity to explain the woman's family situation to his manager and advised him to do some additional coaching. If that still failed, he said, he would leave the decision of the woman's future with the company to the manager.

The woman's performance didn't improve, but the day before the manager was set to fire her, she informed him that she had been diagnosed with cancer. The manager called Flaherty and explained the situation.

"What are you going to do?" asked Flaherty.

"I'm going to let her go today," replied the manager without hesitation. There was silence at the other end of the line. The manager justified his decision by saying that he had made the decision before he had learned of the diagnosis. "Plus," he added, "it's going to kill our health insurance rates."

"You'd better think about this real hard," Flaherty advised. "You have 100 other people working at your plant, and they're all watching how we're going to handle this situation. This is our moment of truth. They want to know if they get diagnosed with cancer...are we going to throw them out in the cold?" The manager listened. "I don't think we want a culture that says, 'We're going to throw you to the winds the minute something bad happens to you.' This isn't about job performance or economics any longer...it's about values. Specifically, it is about *our* values, and we now need to demonstrate our values through our actions.

"This is how we're going to deal with this," continued Flaherty. "We know two things. First, we know her family relies on her. Second, we know she needs to get healthy. What we're going to do is grant her a three-months' leave of absence—with pay. That way she can focus on her treatment without having to be concerned about also meeting her family's needs."

After informing the woman of the decision, the manager and Flaherty immediately saw a different side to the woman. Although she wasn't required to come in to work, whenever her health permitted, she showed up. Overall, plant productivity also crept up in the months that followed. The reason was simple. The company had not just demonstrated its compassion to one employee, it had communicated its values to the facility's other employees.

Tuesday, November 6, 1962

Election day politics dominated the outside world. By the day's end, 30-year-old Edward Kennedy would be Massachusetts' junior U.S. senator-elect, and former vice president Richard Nixon would be griping to the press that they wouldn't have him "to kick around anymore" after he was defeated in his bid to become California's governor. Nonetheless, football permeated every aspect of school life at Great Falls Central. The first banners began to appear on the school's otherwise stark white hallway walls. Typically, the walls were adorned with nothing more than a few pictures of a stern-looking Pope John XXIII and a smiling President John Kennedy, along with a few visibly placed crucifixes oddly juxtaposed next to yellow and black fallout shelter signs.

Father Livix was as caught up in the excitement of the upcoming championship game as his students, but he wasn't about to let election day pass without using the day's current events to instruct the pupils in his theology class about the kind of moral issues they would soon be facing in the real world. This was especially true for the group of seniors sitting in his first hour class.

Livix spotted student body president Byron Weber in the first row and used him to begin his lesson. "Mr. Weber," he began, "this past August you attended Boys State. In the course of that convention, you and your colleagues did something historic. Why don't you tell the class about it?"

Weber looked tentatively at Livix. He was fairly sure he knew what Livix was getting at, but he was still hesitant for fear he'd give the wrong answer and embarrass himself. "We, aah, elected a black governor," he said softly.

"That's right," replied Livix forcefully to both emphasize his response and give Weber more confidence to engage in the conversation. Weber took the bait.

"Now tell me," continued Livix, "if you were a citizen in Mississippi today and able to vote for Governor Barnett—the man who tried unsuccessfully last month to bar James Meredith and the other black students from entering the University of Mississippi— what do you think you'd do?" Weber responded that he would have voted against him.

"Why"

"Because it's the right thing to do. Meredith is a U.S. citizen and served in the Air Force. Plus, the Supreme Court ordered the university to accept him. Everyone has to obey the law—even the governor."

Livix, although he agreed with Weber and his rationale, wasn't about to let him or the rest of his class off so easy. For the next 20 minutes, he challenged them with a series of confrontational questions. "What if you agreed with all of Barnett's other policies except for his position on racial issues? Would you still vote against him? What if you were a poor white parent and feared that blacks would take away your child's chance at a college education?"

In each case, Livix pushed his students to consider the issues. "Is the parent selfish to want the best for his son or daughter? Or is a person wrong to vote for Governor Barnett if he or she sincerely believes that his economic policies will do more to help blacks more than his opponent?"

During the second half of the class, Livix turned his attention to something a little closer to home and something that had been weighing heavily on his own mind. For the past few months, he had begun to wonder if the priesthood was really the right place for him. "So tell me, Mr. Weber, now that you have voted against Governor Barnett, is your job done? Have you done your part as a citizen? Are you now free to wash your hands of the issue and just get back to your own life?"

Weber didn't relish being put on the spot, but he was smart enough to know that Livix was throwing him a leading question for the sake of generating a discussion. He played along. "No," he responded, "I think we all have a responsibility to help integrate society." His comment spurred another round of lively and thoughtful discussion among the students. A minute before the bell was to ring, Livix brought the discussion back to the point he had wanted to make.

"Whether you know it or not, all of you in this room are privileged. By virtue of your race, educational status, and income, you have been given a distinct advantage over many of the other citizens of this country. I know that Mother Maryrose in her French class is always reminding you of what the French say, *noblesse oblige*. President Kennedy is fond of saying, *'Of whomsoever much has been given, of him shall much be required; and to whom men have committed much, of him they will ask even more.'* Both are wonderful philosophies, and the latter happens to have been lifted directly

from the Bible, Luke chapter 12, verse 48. What the president and the Bible are reminding us of is that those of us who are entrusted with leadership responsibilities have an obligation to live up to those responsibilities." Livix was looking at Weber as the bell rang. "Class dismissed."

Although the class was over, the lesson Livix was trying to implant in Weber was reinforced later in the day by Mehrens and then McMahon. At lunchtime, it was Weber's turn to be called into Mehrens' classroom. He was subjected to almost the identical treatment Flaherty and Berry had received the previous day. "Look at how Havre's defensive end and outside linebacker are lined up," said Mehrens as he showed Weber some film from their earlier game with Havre. The defensive end was lined up on the inside of Weber's shoulder, and the linebacker was directly in front of him. "If you see this particular alignment, or if you notice that Havskjold is cheating up to the line of scrimmage to prevent the run, I want you to report it to Wolf and tell him to throw you the ball. If he balks, I expect you to insist on it. I know he's the quarterback, and one of the team's captains, but you need to push him. You're just as much of a leader on this team, and I expect you to act like it." Mehrens went on to describe how he wanted Weber to exploit the opportunity. "It's the perfect opportunity to run the '93 Pass.' Just do a quick slant in—like you're going inside—and once you're past the linebacker, cut back to the outside. There'll be no one within seven yards of you. The play is good for at least 20 yards...maybe even a touchdown."

Later that afternoon McMahon picked up on the theme as he worked his linemen on the blocking sled. From the intensity of the drill, it was evident that the assistant coach was not concerned about overexerting his team. The drill was just as grueling as it had been the week after the Glasgow game. "I don't want anyone to let up this Friday," said McMahon after his boys had pushed the sled up and down the length of the field. Since being bucked off the sled a few weeks earlier, he no longer rode on it. "I want each and every one of you to sustain your blocks until the whistle has blown." He then looked at Weber and added, "I don't want a repeat of what happened against Glasgow. This game is for keeps, and you've got to play like it."

2001

After a good deal of soul-searching, reflecting, and therapy—much of it personally painful—Byron Weber came to terms with his experiences in Vietnam. He would be the first to tell anyone that he never expects to fully "get over it," and that the best he can do is accept it as a big part of his life and deal with it accordingly.

In the spring of 2001, with the support and blessing of his wife, Byron Weber took it upon himself to begin locating the family members of the seven men who were killed under his command in August 1967. Deep inside himself, a thought kept nagging at him, and he knew he had to do something more before he could fully come to terms with his traumatic experience in the jungles of Vietnam.

Weber came to appreciate that he was still those men's commanding officer and that his job was not yet done. The counseling had brought him to this point, but so too had Livix's words: *To whom men have committed much, of him they will ask more.* As did McMahon's old lesson: *Sustain your block until the whistle is blown.* He realized that the whistle had not yet blown on his experiences in Vietnam and that he wasn't yet free to release his block.

Over the ensuing years, Weber established contact with a great many family members of his fallen comrades and told them, in person, what their fathers, husbands, and sons were like, and how they had spent their final days, hours, and minutes on this earth. In his own way, Weber had once again accepted—and responded to—the challenge.

Wednesday, November 7, 1962

Billy Sprinkle was not looking forward to his visit to Mehrens' classroom. He knew what was coming. Mehrens had made him watch the play a couple of times after their first game with Havre, and he knew enough about Mehrens' personality that his coach would make him watch it a few more times this week.

Although the Mustangs had beaten Havre 28–13 in their first meeting, and Sprinkle had scored a 70-yard touchdown on a perfectly executed counter play, the team had also given up two late touchdowns, including a 54-yard strike to Havre's fleet offensive end Harry Lippy, who had somehow managed to get behind Sprinkle on the play. "We both know that you made a mistake on this play," said Mehrens after he ran a clip of the play. "We all make mistakes. What I want you to do is learn from the mistake and use it to get better. It matters less that you get knocked down on the football field...and more that you get back up. Now, I want you to key in on Lippy the whole game. I'm confident that our linemen and linebackers are going to shut down Havre's running game. What I'm worried about is their passing game, and Lippy is a big part of their attack. I expect you to help shut down that aspect of their game. I want two of your goals for this game to be to get an interception *and* to hold Lippy to no catches."

October 19, 1968

The Washington Huskies were coming off two close losses to Oregon and Oregon State when they traveled to Los Angeles to play the top-ranked team in the country at the time, the USC Trojans, who were led by Heisman candidate, O. J. Simpson.

The Huskies starting cornerback and punt returner was Billy Sprinkle. A week earlier he had severely bruised his hand, but he refused to allow it to keep him from playing. When asked by his coach how it felt before the game, he said simply, "It's a long way from my heart."

In attendance at the game was Bill Mehrens, who, after 12 seasons of coaching, had decided in 1967 to pursue his other lifelong ambition and become an agent for the FBI. By that fall, he had completed his training at the FBI training facilities in Quantico, Virginia, and had been stationed at the FBI branch office in Phoenix.

The game was knotted at 7–7 early in the second half when Sprinkle went back to field a Trojan punt. The kick was a high tight spiral. It was the type of punt the fleet and sure-handed Sprinkle would normally catch with ease—even with 100,000 sets of eyes watching him. But the ball got caught by a gust of wind and angled sharply to the left. As he moved in reaction, Sprinkle was momentarily blinded by the sun. It was enough to cause him to lose his focus for a split second. The situation wasn't improved by two 200-plus pound Trojans barreling down on him. The ball hit his injured hand and squirted through his arms. As he reached out for the ball, he was hammered by the first Trojan. The second jumped on the ball. A deafening roar went up from the Trojan faithful. USC went on to convert the muff into a touchdown and escaped with a 14–7 victory and its number one ranking intact.

Sprinkle was inconsolable after the game. A victory over the Trojans would have kept the Huskies in contention to win the Pac-10 and kept alive their hopes of playing in the "Granddaddy of bowl games"—the Rose Bowl. He had agreed before the game to meet with his old high school coach after the game, and although he didn't feel like talking with anyone, Sprinkle honored his commitment.

When the pair connected outside the locker room, Mehrens knew enough not to bring up the topic of the fumble. He knew the boy, whom he had mentored since his father had died almost six years earlier—ironically, just two weeks before he had planned to take his son to see the University of Washington play in the 1961 Rose Bowl—would talk about it when he was ready.

By the end of the conversation, it was clear that Sprinkle's mind

was somewhere else and that he wasn't going to talk about the fumble. Mehrens, although no longer a coach, couldn't help but offer the kid who was most like a son to him one parting piece of advice. "Remember how you responded in the championship game to the one mistake you made in the 1962 season?" Sprinkle cracked a small smile as he recalled his performance in the championship game. "I said back then what matters most is how we respond *after* a mistake. You've had a great three and a half seasons at Washington, and you still have another half season to show the fans of Washington your incredible talents...and your character."

Sprinkle did exactly that the next five games. The following week, the Huskies thrashed Idaho 37–7 and then held eighth-ranked California to a tie and defeated UCLA 6–0. Furthermore, Sprinkle was an integral component of the defensive backfield that intercepted a record 36 passes—a record that still stands. (His teammate and fellow cornerback, Al Worley, holds the NCAA individual record for interceptions in a season with 14. And, as Sprinkle likes to joke, his teammate set the record only because opposing quarterbacks were afraid to throw the ball to his side.)

Thursday, November 8, 1962

As far as quizzes went at Great Falls Central, it wasn't particularly taxing. But for the 37 players who had the paper in front of them, the quiz was as nerve-racking as a pass/fail final exam. Bill Mehrens was administering his weekly quiz on player assignments for the upcoming championship game. Everyone knew that it did not matter to either Mehrens or McMahon that this was the championship game. A single wrong answer would result in a player—even a star player—being replaced for the first quarter of the game. Even for the members of the scout team, the quiz was important because it could well be the difference between them getting into the game in the fourth quarter and not playing at all.

Greg Steckler studied the sheet of paper before him. It had only the Xs and Os to designate offensive and defensive alignments. There were no other lines. He was to diagram whom he was supposed to block and in which direction on the play Mehrens stipulated. Although Steckler had twice missed questions on quizzes earlier in the season—one of which had caused him to miss an opportunity to play in the game against Bozeman—he marked off his answers with the confidence of a four-year starter. He knew his position inside and out, and he was not about to miss his chance to play in the championship game.

Every other player on the team did the same. When they were done, each boy placed his quiz on Mehrens' desk and went to dress for practice. Mehrens would grade the quizzes at home that evening. Those who had incorrect answers would be informed of their transgressions in the morning. But this time there would be none.

As the players filed out, McMahon, who was standing near the door, said, "I want everyone in full pads." The announcement came as a surprise. Most of the players had expected their last practice to be a light walk-through. The two coaches, however, had something else in mind. They knew that for most of the seniors today would be the last football practice of their lives. And, depending on the outcome of the game tomorrow—especially if it was close—it might well be some of the scout team players' last chance to put a hit or block on someone in full pads.

After Mehrens and McMahon had taped up the injured players, they walked onto the practice field and called everyone over. "We're going to run through our key plays once and then do the same thing on defense," said Mehrens. "We're then going to work on our kicking and punting game. After that, we'll finish up with one final drill." He didn't elaborate on what that drill might be. "Let's get started with two laps."

The practice went according to schedule. Based on everyone's performance, it was clear they had all aced their earlier quiz. Every player knew his assignment, and the linemen were firing off the line, staying low, and sustaining their blocks. The backfield was operating with similar precision. To an outside observer, it was virtually impossible to tell the first team from the scout team. John O'Rourke and Bob Bailey played their roles of mimicking the Havre quarterback and fullback to perfection. On the line, Fred Zadich and Greg Steckler battled the starters—Greg Mills and Bruce Campbell—to a standstill. Mehrens ended the scrimmaging after Mike Walsh had nailed three consecutive extra points. They were ready.

He then turned to McMahon with a smile. "Okay, girls," said McMahon, "I thought about bringing out the rope one last time and tying it to the goalpost...to help you guys remember to stay low. But I think we've cured everyone of that problem." He looked at George Leffler. "Instead, I thought we'd do the meat grinder one last time."

At the beginning of the season the drill elicited spasms of fear in many of the smaller and more inexperienced players, as evidenced by their switching positions in line. Today, there was still some jockeying in line, but it was for a far different reason. A number of players were anxious to prove to both themselves and their coaches that they were ready to hit and to play.

Steckler was one such player. He spotted Ed Flaherty in the opposite line and put himself in the final position so he could go up against him. Steckler watched with growing anticipation as Mike Donovan slammed into his onetime tormentor, Bob Murray, and Glenn Fish went head-to-head with starting right end, Bruce Campbell. He cheered as Dale Roos, the scrappy second stringer, who gave up nearly 50 pounds to Bob Kunz, gallantly battled the team's starting right tackle.

The drill continued one by one until Pete Rice, in a repeat of the year's only challenge, asked to go up against Bryon Weber for the right to start in the final game. Weber again won the best two of three matches, and again showed why he deserved to be the team's starting left end. As the others watched the battle between Weber and Rice, Steckler ran through a mental list of things to do: stay low, fire out, keep the legs driving, and use the forearm shiver.

When Weber and Rice were through, McMahon signaled for Flaherty and Steckler to line up for the last meat grinder of the year. Steckler twisted his neck around and slapped his helmet. He was surprised with himself. There was no fear—only the strange sensation of anticipation. He couldn't wait to hit somebody. He could care less that the player in front of him would soon be named to Montana's all-state team as center and later receive a full scholarship to play football at the University of Wyoming. Steckler knew that just like the others, he was ready for action.

The two boys collided into each other, and with McMahon cheering in the background, it was clear that Steckler was a fully functioning member of the 1962 Great Falls Central Mustangs.

Mehrens complimented Steckler on his performance and called everyone to gather around him and take off their helmets. "Today wasn't just a great practice," he said, "it was a great demonstration of team football. If you guys play tomorrow as you practiced today—as you are playing for one another—there is no stopping us. Football is a team sport and, no matter what the scoreboard says at the end of the game tomorrow, if we play together as a team, we will have achieved victory."

August 29, 1968

On August 27, 1968, just one month into his first tour of duty in Vietnam, Sergeant Glenn Charles Fish of Charlie Company, 2nd Battalion, 9th Infantry Division, was dispatched to Lon An, a province 25 miles south of Saigon. The flooded rice paddies were known to be a stronghold of Vietnamese guerillas. It was here that Glenn Fish, the easygoing reserve lineman for the 1962 Great Falls Central Mustangs, was killed by small-arms fire. Little else is known regarding the circumstances of his death.

A few days later, Fish's body was unceremoniously dumped

on the sweltering tarmac of the airfield at Cam Ranh Bay to be processed for return to the United States. The task of identifying the dead soldiers—known as "bagging and tagging"—fell to a small cadre of freshly minted Marine Corps recruits. It was the type of temporary duty typically given to a new Marine as a way of introducing him to the grim realities that awaited him in Vietnam.

On the second day of his 30-day assignment, Private Dale Roos approached the day's work with steely determination. Dozens of dead soldiers had been carted onto the tarmac and awaited proper identification. Roos apprehensively worked his way down the line, recording the particulars of each soldier. Less than an hour into the work and still visibly uncomfortable with the job, Roos came to an unrecognizable body. The soldier's face was horribly disfigured from his wound. Turning his head away from the listless body, Roos groped for the dead man's dog tags.

He pulled them up and was stunned by what he saw. The tags read: "Glenn Charles Fish, January 14, 1946, Roman Catholic" and listed his blood type and personal identification number. He looked again at the tags in disbelief, but there was no mistaking it. The tags were those of his former teammate. Glenn Fish, the kid Roos had come to know so well after jogging alongside him on countless laps and sitting next to him on the bench for the entire 1962 season, now lay dead at his feet.

Roos went numb. It was surreal. On a hot tarmac half a world away in a country he scarcely knew existed six year earlier, he and his old teammate were reunited. Roos recalled little else of what occurred that day except for saluting the flag-covered casket of his fallen comrade and teammate as it was loaded onto the huge cargo plane for return to the states.

In Washington, D.C., Ed Flaherty, then serving in the Army, received a call from his commanding officer. He was informed that he had been personally requested by the family of Glenn Fish to escort their son's body back to Great Falls, Montana.

After arriving in San Francisco and then driving over to Oakland, Flaherty spent an entire day in an intensive briefing session designed to prepare military escorts for the grimmer aspects of the job. When he was through, he retrieved the casket of his childhood friend and accompanied it to Great Falls, where it arrived three hours late after a delay in Salt Lake City.

The late arrival meant Fish's body was not present for the Rosary that had been held that evening in the small dimly lit chapel of O'Connor's Mortuary. By the time Flaherty arrived, only Fish's immediate family and a few other close friends were still present. They were in the front pew praying. Flaherty had the delicate task of informing Mr. and Mrs. Fish that the body of their dead son had arrived.

It was one of the hardest things Flaherty ever had to do. The grief was tremendous. Glenny, as he was known, was the "caboose" of the Fish family—the youngest of three children. His father, mother, and two older sisters were devastated. They would never again see his infectious grin or hear his easygoing laughter.

As he was about to leave, Flaherty was asked by the family whether he had viewed the body. He said that he hadn't. Fearing the military had misidentified their son, the family wanted confirmation that the body in the casket was really Glenny's. Tom O'Connor, the mortician, fearing it would only compound the family's grief, advised the family against it. But they demanded assurance. O'Connor told them the grim truth. Their son's hands were the only part of his body to escape serious injury.

Fish's oldest sister said she was confident she could recognize her brother's hands, so she volunteered for the job. Hesitantly, O'Connor escorted her to the casket. He draped an arm around her to comfort her as she reached for the hand. After a moment, she began to sob uncontrollably. She knew the cold stiff hand she held in her own was that of her baby brother.

The following morning broke clear and crisp. At any other

time, it would have reminded Fish's former teammates of football season. A flock of geese that was headed south flew overhead. The trees were just beginning to turn colors. Instead, the young men had much more serious matters on their minds as they attended the funeral of their former teammate.

Holy Family Parish, a medium-sized Catholic church with a red brick exterior and high stained glass windows, was located only a few blocks from the high school where Glenn Fish had also sung in the choir. The Mass was presided over by Father Harvey Livix. During the course of the service, he said the same prayer he had recited six years earlier to the 1962 Mustangs before their first game with Havre:

> *The Lord gives strength to the weary*
> *and increases the power of the weak.*
> *Even youths grow tired and weary,*
> *and young men stumble and fall;*
> *but those who hope in the Lord*
> *will renew their strength.*
> *They will soar on wings like eagles;*
> *they will run and not grow weary,*
> *they will walk and not be faint.*

At the cemetery, the casket was carried by six of his former Mustang teammates—Fred Zadich, Greg Mills, Bob Kunz, Bruce Campbell, Bob Bailey, and John O'Rourke—to its final resting spot. Father Livix said a final prayer. "Requiem aeternam dona eis, Domine: et lux perpetua luceat eis. Anima ejus requiescant in pace." *Eternal rest give unto him, O Lord; and let perpetual light shine upon him. May his soul rest in peace.*

The silence that followed the ancient prayer was pierced by the three volleys of the military gun salute. As the echoes of the shots evaporated into the big sky of Montana overhead, the honor guard removed the flag from the casket and folded it. Ed Flaherty accepted the flag and, with a military precision that hid his quivering emotions, presented it to Mrs. Fish. She wept softly behind the cloak of her black veil.

Fish's teammates and family then said their final good-byes as the last haunting notes of taps escaped from the bugler's horn. One of the players placed a small gold football pin he taken from his old letter jacket and placed it inside the casket. Glenn Fish would always be a member of the 1962 Great Falls Central Mustangs.

COACHING FOR LIFE TIP #11:
Character breeds success.

QUOTE TO REMEMBER:
"Character is the firm foundation upon which one must build to win respect."
—R. C. SAMUEL

KEY QUESTIONS TO ANSWER:
Do your words reflect your actions at all times?
Are you developing people of character?

Learning to Reinforce the Foundation

1. Throughout the final week, how did the coaches' reiterate the key themes of:

    a. goal setting

    b. expectations

    c. persistence

    d. discipline

    e. attention to detail

    f. responsibility

    g. hard work

    h. leadership

2. Discuss how the coaches own preparation helped reinforce their leadership principles?

CHAPTER 12

"There is no substitute

for victory."

GENERAL DOUGLAS MacARTHUR

EXECUTION

November 9, 1962

The morning broke clear and cool. *It is a perfect day for football,* thought Bill Mehrens as he reached for his morning paper. The headline in the sports section read: "Mustangs Meet Blue Ponies for State Title." A quick scan revealed no quotes that would provide any motivational ammunition to his opponents; his tone was confident but respectful. He downed a single piece of toast—the only solid food he would have the entire day—and a cup of coffee.

Next up was his weekly radio program. Mehrens departed for Gordon's Supper Club to broadcast "Coffee with the Coaches," a show dedicated to keeping the football-crazy fans of Great Falls up to speed on the trials and tribulations of the Mustangs. Unlike most weeks when Mehrens had to share the microphone with the head coach of the larger public high school in Great Falls, today he was the lone guest. Great Falls High School, the city's public high school, had captured the Class AA championship the previous Saturday evening.

Following an ad for Eddy's Good Bread...*Just like bread from a country kitchen oven in airtight plastic*...the host and Coach Mehrens got down to the business at hand. The listening audience hung on Mehrens' every word. How did he plan to stop "the Gold Dust Twins"?

"Berry and Flaherty," came the response. "They will bird-dog them the entire game." In less public moments, Mehrens' younger assistant coach drove the point home by telling the two players that, if necessary, he even expected them to follow Havre's stars into the bathroom to watch them tend to their natural bodily functions. Mehrens never cared for McMahon's saltier language, but he did admit the crude analogy sufficiently covered what he wanted his linebackers to do.

"Did Havre's sophisticated aerial game give you cause for concern?" queried the host, a local sportscaster.

"Yes" was Mehrens simple and honest response. He did not elaborate.

"Who's on the injury list?"

Mehrens mentioned Vogt Richtscheid, Bob Kunz, and Bruce Campbell, but said nothing about Berry and Flaherty, who had more serious injuries.

After the radio program, Mehrens and McMahon headed to school. Late morning and early afternoon passed slowly for the pair, who were shown no favor by Father Reitz and were expected to take care of their regular teaching responsibilities. The day's only concession was that each class was shortened by 10 minutes in order to accommodate the pep rally at the end of the day. In between classes, Mehrens popped a steady supply of antacid tablets to calm his nervous stomach.

At 2:30, the entire student body gathered in the school gymnasium. Cheer Queen, Patty O'Loughlin, kicked things off by leading the convocation in the school fight song. Next, Father Reitz stepped to the microphone and offered a short benediction. Mehrens followed and, standing in front of a banner that read "Beat Havre, Win State!" talked about the challenges the Blue Ponies posed and suggested to the students that they could give his team a decided advantage with their cheering. The captains, sporting their letter sweaters, concluded the rally by thanking the student body for their support and promising to give everything they had to bring home the state championship title.

Confident that they had done everything in their power for the time being, Mehrens and McMahon returned home and busied themselves around the house with odd jobs. Mehrens tinkered on a sink. McMahon fidgeted under the hood of his blue 1961 blue Pontiac Tempest station wagon. They were just burning off nervous energy. At four o'clock the pair began getting dressed.

Although it would not have been noticeable to the casual observer, both men, in an uncharacteristic display of confidence, chose to wear their oldest suits. It was an indication that they felt the prospects for victory were such that they did not want to risk ruining their best suits in a post-game celebration.

Across town, Gary Wolf lay on his bed with his eyes closed and visualized the first offensive series. His mathematical mind rattled through a series of new adjustments Mehrens had instituted that week in the offense. Down the street, Ed Flaherty consumed a steak, a potato, and a cup of hot tea. Afterward, in an attempt to keep his adrenaline level in check, he retired to his room to listen to recordings of Perry Como and Enoch Light and the Light Brigade. He mentally reviewed his goals for the game. Wally Berry, always the most relaxed of the captains, visited with his girlfriend and then went home to catch a catnap.

Once dressed, Mehrens and McMahon returned to the school.

The three co-captains arrived shortly thereafter and walked down the dimly lit and unpopulated hallway to Mehrens' classroom. The coaches went over each of the captain's responsibilities one last time. As they did, the other team members began to arrive. By five o'clock, everyone was in their seat.

For the next hour, Mehrens diagramed plays and outlined his defensive schemes to thwart Havre's sophisticated aerial attack. He was moving so fast that small chunks of chalk were flying off the blackboard. He went through a half carton of chalk. By the end of the session, each player in the room was aware of his responsibilities in no uncertain terms. As a team, they had every confidence that their coaches had done everything in their power to prepare them for victory.

Outside the sky was turning into a brilliant hue of blue, red, and purple. The players knew it was almost time to get dressed. Mehrens wrapped up the chalk talk by reminding everyone that Havre was still the defending state champion, and in spite of the Mustangs' victory earlier in the season over the Blue Ponies and the "Power Ratings" that forecast the Mustangs as a one touchdown favorite in the game, Havre still had two excellent running backs and the state's most effective passing game. "They're a good team," he concluded, "but we're better."

Quietly, the players flowed out of the classroom and walked downstairs to the locker room. The only sound was the soft thumping of their leather soles striking the shiny linoleum floors. Once inside the locker room, the players approached a small space known as "the cage," where the student managers, Chuck Boyle and Pat Penberthy, distributed a clean game jersey, pants, jock strap, and a pair of fresh socks to each player. They accepted the materials with the reverence of a person receiving First Communion.

As he did before every home game, McMahon took an old "78" record out of its dust cover, placed it on a turntable, and flicked on the switch. It was a compilation of college fight songs and started with "On Wisconsin." This was followed by the University of Michigan, Notre Dame, and various other college fight songs. With each successive verse, the blood coursed a little faster in the players' veins and the adrenaline levels crept up.

As the music bounced off the gray steel lockers and echoed around the room, the players transferred the knee and hip pads from their practice pants into their game pants with the earnestness of medieval knights preparing for battle. No one spoke. Shoulder pad straps were cinched a little tighter, belts were ratcheted in an extra quarter inch, and socks were taped to prevent slippage. Once all the equipment was appropriately secured, the final vestment was donned. With the help of a teammate, the clean, tight game jersey was put on, pulled taut, and tucked in.

After they were dressed, the healthy players laid quietly on the wooden benches that lined the locker room, while those nursing injuries were taped, bandaged, and otherwise meticulously administered to by the coaches. Forty years later, Mehrens recalled using "all the tape in Montana" to patch his team together. Berry was still suffering the effects of a massive contusion on his back. Flaherty's ankle was just a quick twist from a break. Bob Kunz, Vogt Richtscheid, and Bruce Campbell were all in significant amounts of pain and in need of extra taping. As he taped up Berry, Mehrens reminded him to watch for the key on defense and said, "Don't give Havre any quarter. Let your actions on the field do your talking for you."

Mehrens allowed McMahon to work on Flaherty because his young assistant typically downplayed any serious injury and encouraged the player to "fight through the pain." This evening was no different. In typical fashion, McMahon reminded Flaherty and the others that their injuries were a long way from their hearts.

By 6:45, the entire team was taped and dressed. As was their custom, the players then made a short pilgrimage to the school chapel. After making the sign of the cross and kneeling in the pews, each boy bowed his head and prayed. Some thanked the Lord for providing the opportunity to play in the championship game. Some prayed for their health. Others prayed to do their best or for a chance to get into the game. All prayed for the team's success.

After communicating their hopes, desires, concerns, and fears to God, the team congregated in the school gymnasium. Signs from the day's earlier pep rally were still plastered on the wall and stray remnants of the cheerleaders' pom-poms lay scattered across the floor.

Recognizing it was still a full hour before the game, Mehrens attempted to lower the adrenaline level and focused his players on their responsibilities. He reiterated the theme that he had stated at their very first session two and a half months earlier. *"If all of you do the ordinary things extraordinarily well tonight, the outcome will be...extraordinary."*

When he was done, the players filed off from the wooden bleachers, holding their cleats—to protect the gymnasium floor—and exited the school in their stocking feet. As they stepped out into the cool, dark autumn night, the smell of burning leaves hung in the air. The players crossed the large blacktop parking lot and loaded into the yellow school bus that waited to take them to the stadium.

As the bus turned the corner on 25th Street to make its way to the stadium, a cheer erupted from the crowd. Many players were startled to see what looked like the whole city of Great Falls out in front of the school to greet them. Pom-poms of Carolina blue and gold waved in the air as the cheerleaders led the crowd in a cheer. Small children held balloons, and students and adults alike held aloft signs urging the Mustangs to victory. The band blared the school fight song. Outside Ursuline Academy, which was next to the school and was home to a number of nuns, Mother Mary James, Mother Maryrose, Mother Mary Angela, and others waved their encouragement.

Turning west onto Second Avenue, even more fans, including many of the members of the Roundtable, joined the entourage. Normally the seven block trip from the school to Memorial Stadium would have taken three minutes. Tonight it took a full 15 minutes as the bus crept down the avenue lined with maple, cottonwood, and birch trees. Residents stood outside their small, well manicured houses and waved.

Inside the bus, Mehrens went over last minute details with his quarterback, Gary Wolf. "Remember, if you see an opportunity, I expect you to take it. You're an extension of me out there." Wolf needed no reminding.

McMahon gathered "his" line and went over each player's assignments for the umpteenth time. Each player gave him his undivided attention. "Do you think Havre's line coach has prepared his guys as well as I have prepared you?" he asked. McMahon didn't wait for a response. He then answered for them, "Heck, no!"

They knew he was right. "Now I expect you to go out there tonight and prove me right." He ended with a simple reminder. "Focus on the fundamentals...fire out, stay low, and hold your blocks. It's not complicated."

Shortly before arriving at the stadium, the coaches stopped coaching and let the players savor the moment. A few stared out the window; most, however, just looked ahead—lost in their own thoughts. The dream that had begun a year earlier was now less than a half hour away.

As the bus pulled into the stadium lot, the players put on their cleats. The laces were pulled taut, and the shoestrings were double-knotted. This was the championship game, and nobody wanted to miss a single play over something as foolish as having an untied shoe. As they unloaded, the aluminum tips of their cleats clicked purposefully against the steel steps of the bus. It was the only sound that filled the air.

The coaches gathered the team together once more. "Go in as

357

a team," commanded Mehrens. The players needed no reminder. Together, the 37 Mustangs jogged through the north gate of Memorial Stadium—a classic-looking high school stadium with a brick façade—and onto the field. The floodlights high above the stadium drenched the field. The Blue Ponies were already on the field warming up, and more than a thousand fans from Havre were crammed into the visitors' section.

The captains took charge and assembled the team for calisthenics. Berry, Wolf, and Flaherty stood atop the three neat rows and called out the drills. Jumping jacks were first. The players, unlike that first practice two and a half months earlier, snapped in unison and barked out in a perfectly sequenced cadence the number as each evolution was completed. It was a picture of military precision.

Mehrens, meanwhile, searched out Ralph Frank, the Havre coach. Weighing 290 pounds and standing 6'2", he was easy to spot. The two coaches approached each other at midfield. With a sly smirk on his face, Frank extended his right hand to greet Mehrens and with his left presented the canister containing the film from the GFC-Glasgow game. "Take it easy on us and don't run up the score," said Frank as the two finished shaking hands.

Unwilling to be lulled into a state of overconfidence, Mehrens responded, "Yeah...sure." His team had been guilty of that sin once this season, and he was not about to let it happen again. Frank, however, was not kidding. Based on his scouting, he knew that the Mustangs had continued to steadily improve over the course of the season and was concerned about his team's ability to compete.

Following calisthenics, Mehrens took the quarterbacks and running backs, and McMahon organized the linemen. As each group ran through a set series of plays, the two men's different coaching styles were on full display. Mehrens calmly paced behind his backfield and offered words of encouragement. He occasionally clapped his hands and said, "Good job" or "That's it." McMahon, on the other hand, was his polar opposite. He was in the face of his linemen, barking at them, slapping their helmets, and exhorting them to a higher level.

The two groups eventually merged and together ran through a select series of plays at half speed. The only benefit of the drill was to burn nervous energy. Next, the coaches ordered the punting and kicking teams to go through their paces.

At 7:50 p.m., the two coaches looked at each other. Their team was ready. Mehrens ordered his Mustangs into the small warming room at the far south end of the field. Father Livix followed the team in. Mehrens turned to him and said, "Father."

The priest bowed his head, and everyone followed suit. "This reading is from the book of Romans, chapter 12, verse 4: *Just as each of us has one body with many members, and these members do not all have the same function, so in Jesus Christ we who are many form one body, and each belongs to all the others. We have different gifts, according to the grace given us.*" Livix paused and then added, "Lord, we ask that tonight You give each of us the strength to employ the skills You have so graciously bestowed on us. We ask further that You remind us that what we are doing tonight is not for our own individual glory but rather for our teammates, our school, and our community. We humbly ask for Your blessing in this endeavor. Amen."

The referee poked his head through the steel door just as Livix was finishing up. He informed Mehrens that he needed his captains for the coin toss. Livix used the opportunity to excuse himself. Flaherty, Wolf, and Berry followed behind him but not before receiving two words of advice from their head coach: "Call heads."

With the eyes of everyone in the stadium now upon them, the Mustang captains walked three abreast toward midfield to greet their lone counterpart, Lowell Gorseth, the Havre captain. The referee asked Flaherty to call it. "Heads," he replied, parroting his coach's advice.

Heads it was. Berry informed the referee that Great Falls would elect to receive the ball first. Havre, with its strong passing game, chose to play with its back to the wind in the first quarter. The captains then faced their respective directions, and the referee signaled to the crowd that the home team would be receiving the ball first. A roar went up from the largely partisan crowd. Knowing Mehrens would be anxious to start his pregame speech, the captains hustled back to the locker room at a double pace.

It was now 7:55. Mehrens stood before his team for what seemed a full minute. The long dramatic pause had its desired effect. He had every player's complete attention. Standing in a semicircle, Mehrens turned his head and his clear brown eyes swept across the faces of his young players. He made eye contact with every one. Then, in his deep authoritative voice he said, "This is it...the championship game. This is what we have been aiming for all season long. For some of you, it began last November when we went to Havre and watched them win the championship. Remember that feeling?" he asked. "Remember how the community reacted?" The six boys who were in attendance at last year's championship game nodded their heads.

"On the car ride back, you convinced yourself that you wanted to do that for Great Falls Central. You convinced yourselves we could win a championship. And from that moment on you committed yourself to that goal. It is now within reach. Forty eight minutes of hard nosed Mustang football and you're there. The championship is yours! You're prepared. You know your assignments inside and out, and you know how to execute them.

"No one is going to outwork you," he continued. "Remember all the long hours you put in during those hot summer evenings in June and July?" He looked at Jerry Kuntz who had practically slept with a football to cure himself of his "fumbleitis." "Remember the hours you spent lifting weights and studying the playbook...all the sacrifices you have made?" This time his gaze fell upon Gary Wolf and John O'Rourke. "Remember the 60- and 100-yard wind sprints in the August heat?" Billy Sprinkle nodded. "Remember the grueling practices the week after the Glasgow game in September?" Byron Weber returned his stare. "Remember how *all* of you contributed to our five victories in October?

"You're in top condition, and you know the consequences of not playing to your potential. If you work hard for the next 48 minutes, good things will happen. We've beat Havre once, and we'll do it again...provided we don't beat ourselves.

"Coach McMahon and I have every confidence that that won't happen. Everything is about to come together," he continued, catching Berry's eye, "but you have to give this game everything you have. You must seize this moment.

"I know some of you—many of you—are hurt." He looked at Ed Flaherty. "Play through it. The pain you feel now is nothing compared to the pain you'll feel over the course of a lifetime if you don't give this game everything you have. A lifetime," Mehrens reiterated, letting the phrase hang in the air so that the enormity of the game's significance could sink into the minds of the 37 teenage boys who surrounded him.

Their head coach then leaned in for the closer. "This is a game you will never forget. There are hundreds of thousands of high school football players all across this country. Few get the opportunity to play for the state championship. Fewer still have the privilege—the honor—of calling themselves champions. Don't let this opportunity slip away. For most of you seniors, this is it. This is your last game, period. You will never again put on the pads after tonight. You need to ask yourself this: How do I want to end my football career?

"Forty years from now you will still remember this game. You'll tell your children about it. Don't carry a loss with you. Make the most of this opportunity. Coach McMahon and I know you are champions," he said softly in a vain attempt to keep his emotions in check. His voice started to crack, and tears welled up in his eyes. It was clear that both coaches had come to believe this team was something special, something unique. The players sensed their coaches' feelings and absorbed their confidence in them.

Recovering, Mehrens' voice stiffened and with his volume rising, he concluded, "Now, let's go out there and prove to everyone else that you are the champions that Coach McMahon and I already know you are!"

November 9, 1962, 8:00 p.m.

The 37 members of the 1962 Great Falls Central Mustangs stormed out of the locker room. Ed Flaherty, followed closely behind by Gary Wolf and Wally Berry, took the lead and blasted through a six-foot paper ring held abreast by two cheerleaders. It read "Win State." The Mustang faithful went wild as each player ran through the hoop. Over 95 percent of the student body was in attendance.

On their respective sidelines, the teams gathered for the national anthem. Three local honor guards marched purposefully toward midfield. When they arrived at their destination, they positioned the U.S. and Montana state flags accordingly. From the west came a slight breeze. It was just strong enough to ripple the flag. The Great Falls Central Band struck up the Star-Spangled Banner. In the stands, the men took off their hats and on the field the Great Falls Central Mustangs stood rigidly at attention and placed their right hands solemnly over their hearts. In their left arms they held their freshly painted blue and gold helmets in a manner precisely prescribed by Mehrens. No one deviated from the pattern.

When the last notes of the national anthem evaporated up into the brisk Montana air, Mehrens gathered his team in a circle. Everyone put his right arm toward the center for the last pregame ritual, the Hail Mary. With 37 pairs of hands resting on top of one another, Mehrens started the prayer.

Hail Mary,
full of grace,
the Lord is with thee;
blessed art thou among women,
and blessed is the fruit of thy womb, Jesus.
Holy Mary, Mother of God,
pray for us sinners,
now and at the hour of our death. Amen.

All the preparation, including praying, was over. The kickoff receiving team sprinted onto the field. McMahon yelled after them, "No one is to let up until the whistle blows!" No one needed any reminding.

The Blue Ponies kicked off. Jerry Kuntz ably fielded the ball and returned it to the 36-yard line. After getting one last bit of advice from Mehrens, Gary Wolf trotted out to the field and joined his team. Ed Flaherty had already gathered up the other players in a tight huddle. Wolf called out the play once, and Flaherty departed to take up his position over the ball. Wolf repeated the play a second time, and, in unison, the team clapped and sprinted from the huddle up to the line of scrimmage. The Mustangs' zealousness seemed to catch Havre off guard. The defense was still shifting around as Wolf crouched behind Flaherty.

Just as McMahon had instructed them, every lineman's feet were shoulders-width apart and their left elbow was resting on their left leg. On Wolf's command, they snapped their right arm down. As they did, no one took his eyes off the player in front of them. *Let 'em know you're coming.*

Wolf hit Havre with a quick count, and the line surged forward as though it were one solid, connected unit. Wally Berry crashed through the middle for a six-yard gain. The next 12 plays were nearly identical. The Blue Pony defense had no response to the Mustangs' grind-it-out ground game. On the fourteenth play of the drive, Jerry Kuntz punched the ball across the goal line for the first score of the game. Mike Walsh drilled the extra point and, after eating up the first nine minutes of the first quarter, the Mustangs led 7–0.

Havre also tried to establish its ground game on its first series, but the Mustang line, behind the steady, workmanlike play of Dick Kuntz, Bob Murray, Greg Mills, and George Leffler, clogged the middle. After gaining no yards on three consecutive plays, the Blue Ponies were forced to punt.

The Mustangs took over at the start of the second quarter right where they had left off. Two short runs left them with a third-and-one on the 23-yard line. Wolf called for the 90 Belly Series—a play they had practiced hundreds of times that season. Wolf executed a perfect fake to Berry and then handed off to Kuntz. On the line, Byron Weber demolished the defensive end, and Flaherty sealed off two inside linebackers. Once past the line of scrimmage, Kuntz had nothing but open space in front of him. He galloped, untouched, 77 yards for the second score of the game.

Already down 14–0, Havre went to the air on its next possession. Billy Sprinkle, as instructed earlier in the week by Mehrens, keyed in on Harry Lippy, Havre's best receiver. The Blue Ponies tried a simple down-and-out route, but Sprinkle had it read all the way and stepped in front of the pass for the Mustangs' first interception of the game.

Central kept the ball on the ground, but as they approached the Blue Ponies' 25-yard line, Weber noticed that the defensive end had shifted to his inside shoulder in an attempt to stop the run and that Glenn Havskjold, Havre's speedy defensive back, had moved up to the line of scrimmage also in an attempt to stop the run. He recalled his one-on-one film session with Mehrens and returned to the huddle. "The 93 Pass is open, Gary."

Wolf, whose confidence in his teammates had grown

considerably over the course of the season, looked at Weber and said, "Are you sure?"

"I'm positive. I'll be open. Just hit me."

Wolf called the play, and it worked just as Mehrens said it would. Unchecked at the line, Weber broke inside and then angled back toward the sideline. Once past Havskjold, there was no one within 10 yards of Weber, and Wolf delivered a perfect strike. Weber lumbered toward the end zone. He was caught from behind by Havskjold at the one-yard line, but his momentum carried him across the goal line for the game's third score and the first—and only—touchdown of Weber's career. After Mike Walsh missed his first extra point since the opening game of the year, the score was 20–0.

More desperate than before, everyone in the stadium knew the Blue Ponies were going to have to go to the air. On third down, Berry noticed that the halfback was a half step deeper than usual. He called out a signal to Flaherty, who had already picked up on the key. Both players knew it was going to a screen pass to the flat. They just didn't know to which side. The play went left, and Berry broke in. The Havre quarterback floated his pass over the rush of Central's defensive line. He never saw Berry, who snatched the ball and streaked down the sideline for the fourth Mustang touchdown of the game.

As the Mustangs prepared for the extra point, Mehrens called over Mike Walsh. "I want you to quarterback this play," he said. Due to Walsh's heart murmur, it was the first time Mehrens had allowed him to play the position. He also called over Pete Rice, who had unsuccessfully but valiantly battled Byron Weber for the starting left end position all year, and told him to get in the game. Together, the two junior substitutes executed a perfect down-and-out pass pattern and scored the extra point.

At halftime, the Mustangs went into the locker room with a 27–0 lead. Neither the coaches nor the players showed any emotion. "You're halfway there," said Mehrens, "but this game is a long way from being over, and we can't afford to let up. Havre isn't going to take this lying down. We need to prepare ourselves for a battle in the second half." Mehrens and McMahon both continued to coach as if they were engaged in a zero-zero tie. "They're going to be forced to throw. Flaherty, Berry, Sprinkle, Kuntz, Wolf...remember your keys. We already have two interceptions, but if everyone keeps doing his job, we should be able to get some more. I don't want any mental mistakes—keep concentrating." Mehrens sent his team back out for the second half. "Keep working hard and good things will continue to happen."

The Blue Ponies received the opening kickoff and quickly knocked off two first downs—their first of the game. In the huddle, Flaherty called the Mustangs together. "Let's buckle down!" Bruce Campbell also chimed in. "This drive stops here!"

The next play was a sweep around Campbell's end. The lanky end forced the Havre runner out wide toward the sideline. George Leffler pursued from the inside, and from his position at linebacker, Flaherty made a beeline for him. Just as the Havre runner approached the sideline, he turned upfield but was met by Leffler and Flaherty. The two Mustangs lowered their shoulders and administered two punishing blows. The force of the two hits drove the Havre player straight back into the line judge. The game was temporarily delayed as the official was escorted off the field. He was later taken to the hospital and diagnosed with a broken collarbone.

The play convinced Ralph Frank to return to the air. He had made a number of adjustments at halftime, but, unfortunately, he didn't tell his halfback to lineup any differently for the screen pass. Berry again spotted the upcoming play. The only difference in the outcome was the length he returned the interception for a touchdown. Berry's second interception netted him a 60-yard touchdown and his second defensive score. Walsh's fourth extra point made the score 34–0.

On its next possession, Havre was finally able to move the ball and was within two yards of its first score when Flaherty stepped in front of an errant pass in the end zone and notched the Mustangs' fourth interception.

By the end of the third quarter, the outcome was no longer in doubt, and Mehrens began to substitute freely. Seniors Dale Roos, Bob Bailey, Glenn Fish, Fred Zadich, and Greg Steckler entered the game. They were followed by juniors Dave Nash, Jim Neufeld, Barry Newmack, Bob Kuntz, Joe Gilsoul, Gene Ouellette, and Pete Rice. In the final minutes, sophomores Tom Strizich and Clark Kochivar also got into the game.

As the final seconds ticked off on their 34–6 victory, the players basked in the sights and sounds of 5,000 Great Falls Central fans cheering their voices raw. Winning the championship was just as those six players had envisioned it would be a year earlier when Mehrens told them that their dream was possible.

After the game was over, the three Mustang captains collected the state championship trophy in a ceremony on the field. The team then returned to the locker room and doused Mehrens and McMahon in a cold shower. The coaches' suits were drenched, but they didn't care. They had prepared themselves for every aspect of the game, including the post-game celebratory cold shower.

A student photographer snapped a picture of Ed Flaherty in the school gymnasium hoisting the trophy over his head as the rest of the team celebrated. The clock in the background read 10:10. Fittingly, it was one year—almost to the minute—of the conversation where Mehrens he told Flaherty that if he focused on something more than himself the ultimate reward would also be greater.

A local reporter caught up with the still soaking Mehrens after the celebration and asked him about the victory. Mehrens praised every player by name and noted each boy's contributions. He concluded his remarks by saying, "They're just the greatest bunch of kids ever." Had the reporter thought to ask any of the players what they thought of their coaches, the response would have been reciprocated. To those 37 players, Mehrens and McMahon were the "greatest coaches ever."

November 24, 1962

The Mustangs' end of the year football banquet took place at the Rainbow Hotel in downtown Great Falls. Spirits were still running high from the team's dominating performance in the championship game, and much of the evening's early conversation focused on what would happen if the Mustangs squared off against the Great Falls Bisons—the city's public high school and Montana Class AA champions. The consensus opinion among the partisan crowd was that it would be no contest—the Mustangs were the better team.

Father Livix, the event organizer, convened the dinner with a prayer. He began by reciting a passage from the Book of Jeremiah: *"'I know the plans I have for you,' declares the Lord. 'Plans to prosper you and not to harm you, plans to give you hope and a future.'"* He followed with grace. A toast was then offered to the 1962 Mustangs before the capacity crowd of 400 dove into their roasted turkey and potatoes.

After dinner as the crowd was polishing off its peach cobbler, Livix introduced the evening's keynote speaker, Dr. Michael Pecarovich. He was a former professional baseball player and the former head football coach at Gonzaga University. He was also one of the country's most sought after motivational speakers.

Pecarovich stepped to the microphone and proceeded to regale the audience with anecdotes and stories. He peppered his talk with pearls of wisdom for player, coach, parent, and fan alike. As he neared the end of his talk, he said, "Knute Rockne once said, 'Four years of football are calculated to breed in the average man more of the ingredients of success in life than almost any academic course he takes.' Rockne was absolutely right. But he also said this:

368

'All football comes from Stagg.'" Amos Alonzo Stagg was then college football's all-time winningest coach.

"But of all the things Stagg did for football, and he did a lot—like introduce the huddle, the backfield shift, the fake punt, and the man-in-motion—there are three things I most respect about him. First, he said this: 'I never had a player I did not love.' I really like that quote, because, as a former coach myself, I know it is true." Pecarovich paused and dropped his voice a notch. "Now, I know you're not going to hear your coaches tell you they love you. In fact, if John McMahon did, I'm sure all of you players would choke on your food." The audience, now very familiar with McMahon's aggressive coaching style, burst out in laughter. Pecarovich waited until it died down before continuing. "But I know it's true, and someday you players will, too.

"The reason I know this is because of something else Coach Stagg once said. At the end of a season, he was once asked if he considered the season to be successful. Stagg looked at his questioner and in all seriousness replied, 'I won't know for the next 15 or 20 years.' Amos Alonzo Stagg said that because he understood that he wasn't just preparing his players for a season of football, he was preparing them for life. And his idea of success wasn't just to make them champions for a year; it was to prepare them to be champions in life.

"But the final and most important thing Stagg said was this: 'You must love your boys to get the most out of them. Love has dominated my coaching career as I am sure it has, and always will, that of many other coaches and teachers.'" There was a pause and then Pecarovich added, "Bill Mehrens and John McMahon are proud bearers of this wonderful tradition."

Pecarovich's words hung over the ballroom, and as a good public speaker, he then brought everything together in his closing remarks by weaving Livix's prayer at the beginning of the evening into his talk. "I believe, as was said in this evening's benediction, the Lord does have great plans for you. He does have plans to give you hope and a future.

"I know this because I have had the opportunity to speak with your coaches and Father Reitz and Father Livix at my dinner table tonight, and I know that over the course of this season they have given you the foundation to carry out those plans. It is now up to you to build upon that foundation and make something of the rest of your lives."

October 26, 2002

The hour was now very late at Borrie's Supper Club. Every player had told his story. Even Gary Wolf, the old quarterback, decided to speak. He began by saying, "You asked a lot of us in those days." He then added somewhat reflectively, "You don't see enough of that today; but as a former teacher, I can tell you that the best teachers are those who, after they have done their job, know they can let go. You taught us how to succeed on our own." He then paused and said, "You were great coaches...but even better teachers."

Flaherty turned to Coach Mehrens and extended the microphone. Mehrens rose to speak but found he was too overcome with emotion. Eventually, Mehrens composed himself. "I have never been to a reunion before," he said hesitantly, "and I had no idea what to expect. But I must confess I was reluctant to come here tonight because I have always thought of the championship as *your* accomplishment." He then looked around the room and said in a somewhat embarrassed tone, "I don't have any prepared remarks, and after hearing all of your stories, I don't know how I can possibly equal what has already been said."

But then, as he had done so many times before in the small, cramped confines of the warming hut at far end of Memorial Stadium, where he gave his teams so many memorable pregame and halftime pep talks, Mehrens' back grew straighter, and he cleared his voice. He radiated confidence. To those in the room, it was as though they had been transported back 40 years in time.

"I can't begin to tell you how proud I am of all of you," he said as his voice gained strength. And as each player caught a glimpse of their coach's moist eyes, they knew he meant it. Although they were now far removed from their high school playing days, it still deeply moved each man to hear their coach say he was proud of them. Mehrens, like McMahon, still had a way of making a little praise go a long way.

"I have always thought of you as 'my boys,' and it fills my heart to see what all of you have accomplished and gone on to do with your lives. As coaches, I think John and I knew we were preparing you in some small way for life, but it is difficult to put in words what it means when, all these years later, you see that 'your boys' really have succeeded in life. It is humbling," said Mehrens, choking back tears, "to think we played some small role in your success." A single tear escaped from his eye and rolled down his weathered cheek. "I just wish that Father Arbanas and Father Livix and the others—who were also responsible for your growth—could have been here tonight.

"I really did—and still do—love all of you. Both John and I would have done anything humanly possibly for you, but," he said, reverting to the old coach in him, "it had to be done with strict discipline." Recalling that strict discipline, smiles cracked among the faces of the players. "That is what ultimately leads to success," continued Mehrens. "I guess you'd call it 'tough love' today." He scanned the faces of his former players and added with a smile, "It is satisfying to know that it works so well." There were a few more smiles and laughs. "Of course, as a grandfather now, I have to admit I have softened a bit over the years. I'm afraid most of you wouldn't even recognize me when I'm with my grandkids." There were more smiles.

"Early in my coaching career, during a summer coaching

clinic, a then-famous coach, whose name escapes me now, made the comment: 'It is a privilege to coach another man's son.' I have always been impressed with the statement...because it's so true. Only a person who has coached can understand the special relationship and bond that occurs between a coach and his players. I have two wonderful daughters, whom I love dearly, but a coach always wants the opportunity to coach his own son. Because I never had that opportunity, I treasured my time with you. You were my sons.

"It is a privilege to coach another man's son," he repeated. "Think about it," he said softly. "How many men get the opportunity to spend two or three hours a day with their sons during the most formative period of their lives? It is sad...but not many. Well, John and I had the privilege of coaching all of you."

"So now it is *I* who must thank *you*. In so many ways, you are the sons I never had...and you will never know how much that season meant to me or how much I still cherish every hour I spent with you." Mehrens bowed his head and pinched the bridge of his nose in an attempt to hold back the tears. The memories of the 1962 season flooded back upon him. "On behalf of both John and myself, I want to thank you for the privilege of giving us the opportunity to coach such a fine group of young men. It's no surprise you have turned out the way you did—John and I always knew this team was full of winners."

Mehrens then looked directly at Billy Sprinkle, whose own father died his freshman year of high school and for whom Mehrens had become a second father. "I know most of your parents are now gone, but I know they would share my pride in seeing what all of you have become. As I look around this room, I can vividly recall the contributions each of you made to winning the state championship. You were—and still are—a very special group."

Mehrens had to stop yet again to compose himself. "You can't imagine what a great experience it has been for me and John to see all of you again," he said, wiping away the tears. "We're so proud of all of your successes and are humbled to think that we played some small role in preparing you for future success. Even though you are now in your 50s, I will always think of you as 'my boys,' and I will always love you. Thank you." Mehrens then handed the microphone back to Ed Flaherty and sat down.

The true magic of the 1962 season was now apparent in a way that it had never been before. Flaherty, like everyone else in the room, was speechless. He did the only thing he could. He raised his glass to Bill Mehrens and John McMahon and said, "To being coached for life."

The other players raised their glasses and responded, "Coached for life."

WEEK TWELVE GAME PLAN:
Execution

COACHING FOR LIFE TIP #12:
People will perform how they practice.

QUOTE TO REMEMBER:
*"A great coach will make his players see what
they can be rather than what they are."*
—ARA PARASHEGHIAN

KEY QUESTIONS TO ANSWER:
Do your daily actions reflect and reinforce
at all times what you are hoping the members of
your organization will become, and what you
hope your organization will achieve?

Learning to Execute

1. What techniques did the coaches use to focus their players' minds on the task at hand?

2. What elements of the game did the coaches encourage their players to focus on?

3. How did they reinforce the concept of teamwork?

4. What role did the players' responsibility to their school and community play in Mehrens' final remarks to the team?

5. How did he bring his remarks back to the importance of goal setting and instill confidence?

6. Which player did Mehrens choose to highlight at the end-of-the-season banquet? Why?

7. When could Mehrens and McMahon expect to find out whether they had achieved all of their own goals for the season?

8. What was the single most important element of their success?

EPILOGUE

"Success is peace of mind

which is the direct result of

self-satisfaction in knowing

that you did your best to become

the best you are

capable of becoming."

—JOHN WOODEN

Michael Pecarovich's concluding remarks at the end of the season football banquet were remarkably prescient. In fact, it could be said they deviated in only two minor ways. First, whereas Coach Stagg said he would not know whether a season was truly successful for 15 or 20 years, it took Mehrens and McMahon a full 40 years to appreciate the full depth of all they had achieved during those precious 77 days in the summer and fall of 1962. Second, Bill Mehrens did, in fact, come around to tell his players in no uncertain terms that he loved them. And although John McMahon didn't utter any such words at that singular fortieth reunion, much as Pecarovich predicted, the players had come to understand that his love was implicit in everything he did that season.

And that, in the end, is what separates the good coaches from the great coaches. It is not merely a coach's understanding of the fundamentals of the game, nor is it their will to win. The success they achieve on the field of play, or even their ability to coach, isn't what ultimately determines their success. It is their ability to love.

Amos Alonzo Stagg was right. The best coaches love their players.

Frank Leahy, who played under Knute Rockne for three years at Notre Dame, most likely learned this lesson from him, and it was why he helped John Gagliardi land his first college coaching position in 1949. Gagliardi, in turn, knew it and conveyed it to Bill Mehrens (along with the thousands of other players he has touched during his 60 years of coaching). And Mehrens passed it on to every player he ever coached—including the 37 members of the 1962 Great Falls Central Mustangs.

True to their heritage, the 1962 Mustangs have kept up the tradition. Ed Flaherty continues to pass on the lessons of love he learned from Mehrens and McMahon to family, employees, and strangers alike. Two of his children are now coaches. Hundreds of his employees—past and present—have borne witness to how the principles of goal setting lead to success and how ethics and values can only be communicated through action—such as his willingness to make a commitment to something greater than oneself by providing scores of scholarships to economically disadvantaged children and helping the less fortunate in Guatemala.

John O'Rourke, the former 135-pound backup quarterback, and Jerry Kuntz are now both coaches themselves and continue to set high expectations and demand excellence from all their players. Byron Weber, as a teacher; Billy Sprinkle, as the executive director of the Montana High School Athletic Association; and Dick Kuntz, as a school superintendent, are also continuing the legacy of love by encouraging the next generation of students to work hard, never quit, and follow their passions.

Every other member of the 1962 team—in ways big and

small—is doing the same. Whether it be Dave Nash's work to fund a camp for the Boy Scouts of Montana or Greg Steckler's (Brian Elliot) ability to touch the souls of millions with his music, the lessons of that season, like a small pebble being tossed into the ocean, continue to ripple out in an ever widening circle.

The Duke of Wellington once said that "the Battle of Waterloo was won on the playing fields of Eton." It was his way of saying that the discipline and ethos instilled through organized sport sowed the seeds of his country's later success.

The same can be said of America's grade school, high school, and college practice fields. But the lessons and values today's coaches instill in this country's youth go well beyond paving the way for just battlefield success. For, quite literally, they are the ones who weave into the fabric of the American spirit the principles and characteristics upon which this country's success is founded: high expectations, goal setting, hard work, persistence, pride, character, and teamwork.

Coaching will forever be a noble calling, and those lucky enough to earn the title of "coach" must always remember that they have been entrusted with a sacred mission, and at the heart of that mission is a single, simple philosophy: *love*.

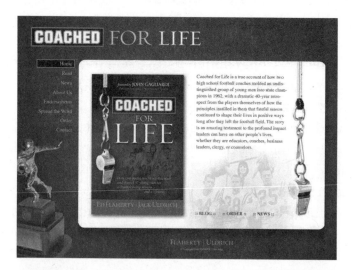

www.coachedforlife.com

- Share your own personal experiences gleaned from a mentor, leader, coach, teacher, or parent.
- Enroll your book club for group discounts.
- Discuss the book with others.
- Find online book reviews.
- Receive our e-mail newsletter.
- Nominate a coach, teacher, mentor, leader, or parent for monthly *Coached for Life* selection.
- See or hear online radio and video.
- Read Jack Uldrich's blogs.
- Link to social networks.
- View our monthly *Coached for Life* newsletter for the selection of the outstanding mentor, leader, coach, teacher, or parent of the month.
- Purchase additional copies of *Coached for Life*.
- Learn about our Optimist Club Scholarship Program for outstanding high school seniors.

Nominate Your *Coached for Life* Person for the Leader of the Month Award

We've all been touched by a special person in our lives. Share your inspirational stories with us of how they made a difference in your life, whether they were a:

- Coach
- Teacher
- Business leader
- Mentor
- Parent

E-mail us your personal story via our web site at **www.coachedforlife.com**.

Every month we'll select the BEST story. The winner will receive an autographed copy of *Coached for Life*, which they can present to the *Coached for Life* person whom they wrote about.

Inspire and lead others to greatness through these extraordinary stories.

Also, check out the new stories posted each month on our web site, **www.coachedforlife.com**.

Spread the Word

Coached for Life had been described as "the best-selling book *Tuesdays With Morrie* on steroids." It is a great story of ordinary people doing extraordinary things. Here's how you can inspire friends, colleagues, coworkers, neighbors, and relatives, especially during these difficult economic times.

- *Coached for Life* is the perfect inspiration gift for any teacher, coach, or business leader.

- Use *Coached for Life* in your book club.

- Pass the book around the office and discuss how its principles of leadership, motivation, and positive results apply to your team, organization, school, or business.

- Counselors will love the motivational stories that chronicle the triumph of the human spirit.

- *Coached for Life* brings a spiritual dimension that clergy and church members will want to pass along to others.

- Anyone who loves sports and team play will love the life-altering and life-fulfilling experiences found in *Coached for Life*.

- Get involved with selling *Coached for Life* to earn extra money.

The Perfect Fund-Raising Product for Schools, Clubs, and Organizations

Coached for Life is the perfect fund-raising product for schools, clubs, and organizations. It is a "G"-rated book that is a keepsake. Far better than candy, fruit, or cookies, it is FOOD FOR THE SOUL!

Credit can be arranged for your fund-raising programs, too!

Need Extra Money?
Become an Affiliated Reseller of *Coached for Life*. Earn commissions of 20–40% per book. See our web site at **www.coachedforlife.com**.

Coached for Life **Discount Pricing**
Use *Coached for Life* for Fund-Raising or Purchase in Quantity for Groups

# of Copies	Your Price	Suggested Retail	Discount
1	$19.95	$19.95	0
10	$19.50	$19.95	$.45
25	$18.45	$19.95	$1.50
50	$16.95	$19.95	$3.00
100	$15.95	$19.95	$4.00
250	$14.95	$19.95	$5.00
500	$11.95	$19.95	$8.00

Greater than 500, call for a quote.

Other Leadership Books by Jack Uldrich

Into the Unknown: *Leadership Lessons from Lewis & Clark's Daring Westward Expedition*

Tells the inspirational story of Lewis & Clark's amazing Journey of Discovery and explains what today's businesses can still learn from these courageous explorers' trek into the unknown.

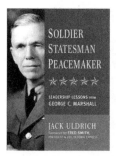

Soldier, Statesman, Peacemaker: *Leadership Lessons From George C. Marshall*

Explores the leadership principles of the man Winston Churchill called "The Last Great American," and whom Harry Truman, at the end of World War II, hailed as the "great one of the age."

Jump the Curve: *50 Essential Strategies to Help Companies Deal with Emerging Technologies*

Explores how exponential trends in information technology, biotechnology, robotics, manufacturing, material science, and nanotechnology are all converging at this unique moment in history, and lays out 50 specific strategies that executives, businesses, and industries can use to navigate and survive in this era of unparalleled change.

Book Jack Uldrich to Speak at Your Next Event

Jack Uldrich is a compelling, entertaining, and motivating keynote speaker and is available to speak on *Coached for Life* or any of his other leadership books. He can be contacted through Angela Schlep of the Executive Speakers Bureau at 1-800-754-9404 or angela@executivespeakers.com.

To purchase additional copies of *Coached for Life*,
go to our web site, **www.coachedforlife.com**.